HOUSING AND RACE IN
INDUSTRIAL SOCIETY

HOUSING AND RACE IN INDUSTRIAL SOCIETY

CIVIL RIGHTS AND URBAN POLICY IN BRITAIN AND THE UNITED STATES

DAVID H. McKAY

CROOM HELM   LONDON

ROWMAN AND LITTLEFIELD
Totowa, New Jersey

037682

Croom Helm Ltd,
2-10 St John's Road, London SW11

ISBN 0-85664-485-4

First published in the United States 1977
by ROWMAN AND LITTLEFIELD, Totowa, N.J.

Library of Congress Cataloging in Publication Data

McKay, David H
    Housing and race in industrial society.

    Includes bibliographical references.
    1. Discrimination in housing — Great Britain.
2. Discrimination in housing — United States. 3. Housing
policy — Great Britain. 4. Housing policy — United
States. I. Title
HD7333.A3M157   301-5'4'0941   76-57238
ISBN 0-87471-946-1

Printed in Great Britain by Biddles Ltd, Guildford, Surrey

CONTENTS

TABLES

ACKNOWLEDGEMENTS

The research for this book originated in a year spent at the University of Wisconsin, Madison, during 1970/71. At that time I was searching for a PhD thesis topic, and I can thank Murray Edelman, Matthew Holden, and especially Michael Kagay and Donald McCrone, for helping me find a topic and for providing intellectual and social succour during what was, I believe, Madison's 'coldest winter in living memory'. My thesis was eventually entitled 'Race and Housing in the United States : A Study of Federal Power and the 1968 Civil Rights Act', and during the three years following my visit to Madison, I was fortunate to receive advice and help from Anthony Barker, Peter Eisinger, Hugh Heclo, Larry Johnston, Anthony King, John Lewis, David Robertson, Jack Walker and Harold Wolman. I must also thank the British SSRC, the University of Wisconsin and the American Council of Learned Societies for providing financial support for two visits to the US.

What was originally an interest in public policy gradually grew during these years into an interest in comparative urbanism and social policy, and it was a natural step for me to develop the thesis into a comparative study of race and housing in Britain and the United States — especially given my perception that some important and disturbing parallels existed between the two countries. During this last phase of the research I owe thanks to Andrew Cox, Cecil Fudge, Valerie Karn, Richard Simeon, Adrian Sinfield, Peter Townsend, Robin Ward, and in particular to David Smith and Political and Economic Planning who provided valuable comments on draft chapters and permission to reproduce several tables from his recent surveys of racial disadvantage in Britain. I must also thank the numerous individuals on both sides of the Atlantic who subjected themselves to interview during the course of the research. Finally, thanks to June Palmer for exceptional secretarial help, and above all to my wife, Lynne McKay, for helping and encouraging me in every way possible over the years.

David McKay
October 1976

1 INTRODUCTION

This book is concerned with the relationship between race and housing in two advanced industrial societies, and particularly with comparing the ways in which governments have administered laws designed to reduce racial disadvantage and discrimination in housing. As the study is centrally involved in analysing governments' attempts to reduce inequality in society, it is very much a part of the response to the call for more 'relevant' research which emanated from American political scientists during the late 1960s and early 1970s. Vietnam and domestic racial conflict had, so the argument ran, exposed academic political science as a sterile scientistic discipline whose main paradigms supported existing power relations in society, rather than challenged them by generating work relevant to the pressing problems of the day.[1] In the public policy area, these arguments stressed the academic preoccupation with policy process, and noted the failure to study policy 'impact' or 'who gets what' as a result of the formulation and implementation of policy.[2]

On reflection, these pleas appear rather extraordinary for their assumption that American political science was in some sense discovering something new by realising the importance of policy 'impact'. After all, who gets what and the problems of equality and inequality in society are *the* central questions of social science, and sociologists and economists have long been concerned with linking patterns of inequality to class, status and power relations. Yet it can be argued that the analysis of policy implementation *by political scientists* does offer something new, because, uniquely among the social sciences, the central concern of political science is the working of government. More than any other discipline, therefore, political science is equipped to relate the way in which administrative and judicial processes of implementation interact with other factors to produce a particular distribution of resources in society. Given the volume of legislation, judicial decisions and administrative actions which increasingly flood modern industrial societies with promises of re-ordered priorities and redistributed resources, it is clearly important to trace the extent to which such promises are fulfilled. Only by studying the detail of the implementation process and attempting to assess the effects of a particular decision or item of legislation can we judge its importance and draw conclusions on its relationship to the distribution of political power and the nature of social change.

The Study of Civil Rights Laws

If any category of law qualifies for such detailed analysis, then surely civil rights legislation does. For civil rights laws imply or even explicitly promise that the state will take measures to correct the socially and economically subordinate position of minority groups. They raise, therefore, important questions about the capacity of modern governments to redistribute resources in the direction of population groups whose unequal position derives from specifically racial as well as from economic influences. In the United States, the civil rights laws of the 1960s were heralded by white liberals and blacks alike as a breakthrough in race relations. They represented what seemed at the time to be the culmination of the long struggle for racial equality in the United States. In particular, the omnibus 1964 Civil Rights Act and the 1965 Voting Rights Act promised not only the guarantee of legal equality for racial minorities, but also 'affirmative action' by governments to eliminate broad patterns or practices of discrimination. Hence, via complaint procedures, litigation and administrative action, blacks and other minorities would be provided with redress, and ultimately, so the rhetoric of the law implied, their subordinate position would be removed.

However, no sooner were these Acts passed, than America's Northern cities exploded into racial violence, and as the 1960s wore on so it became obvious that racial minorities had not progressed towards that state of equality with whites which the new laws seemed to have promised. Disillusionment in both the minority communities and among white commentators spread rapidly, so that by 1968, when the last civil rights law outlawing racial discrimination in housing was passed, the Kerner Commission on Civil Disorders was able to conclude that 'our nation is moving toward two societies, one black, one white — separate and unequal'.[3]

Given these events, it is not surprising that civil rights laws and their enforcement came into disrepute. By the early 1970s it was not uncommon for basic texts on American government to talk of the 'symbolic' role played by civil rights laws, or to claim that they were designed to placate an increasingly vocal black community with token gestures of legal equality.[4] Scholarship was diverted away from the study of civil rights law and towards other matters, in particular, in the race relations area, to the measurement of racial attitudes and to analyses of power within the black community and how, in the face of white racism, blacks could mobilise their limited resources to improve their position.[5]

Britain legislated against racial discrimination at almost the same time as the United States, and although Britain experienced nothing equivalent to the American racial troubles of the 1960s, disillusionment with the 1965 and 1968 Race Relations Acts soon developed. Most commentators based their critiques on the increasingly obvious fact that, as in the US, the social and economic position of blacks seemed not to have improved since the enactment of the laws. British civil rights laws were in many ways similar to the US variety, and indeed were partly modelled on the American example. Given this fact and the apparently not dissimilar experience with these laws during the same historical period, it is not surprising that commentators in both countries have reacted to civil rights legislation in similar fashion. In general, British and American critiques have been divided between those who generally dismiss the laws as at best irrelevant and at worst a deliberate attempt by white élites to manipulate actually or potentially rebellious blacks into political quiescence,[6] and those who believe the legislation has failed not because it is *ipso facto* doomed to failure, but because it has been inadequately formulated and/or implemented.[7] Yet the claims of neither group are based on a comprehensive knowledge of the enforcement of civil rights laws in their total social, political and economic environment. The radicals, eager to construct theories explaining the discrepancy between promise and performance, concentrate their energies not on the enforcement of the law *per se* (indeed they sometimes ignore the law altogether), but on linking the alleged existence of an élite consensus or of institutionalised racism to the subordinate position of non-whites. The liberals, on the other hand, concentrate on the details of the administrative process or on the nature of discrimination, in isolation from structural political and economic forces.

There is no doubt that the details both of the law and the manner in which it is enforced are of great importance. It is also the case that the nature of some civil rights laws renders them ineffective no matter how well they are enforced. They may, for example, contain few sanctions, have limited coverage or fail completely to identify the main sources of discrimination and disadvantage. A major objective of this study is to discover whether civil rights laws can lead to important changes, either, as the idealists of the 1960s expected, in the immediate social and economic position of minorities, or in minorities' long-term prospects and in the way in which élites and masses perceive the issue of race and racial discrimination in society. There will be a particular focus on the way in which the laws are enforced, and whether they provide not only redress against individual acts of discrimination, but also the correction of the effects of past discrimination and the elimination of what can be called racial disadvantage — inequalities deriving from practices which may or may not be racially motivated, but which are deeply rooted in established institutional practices. However, only by studying the implementation process in detail and the way it relates to the broader environment can these changes be traced. While broad patterns of activity can and will be discerned, many of them deriving from identifiable configurations of political power and structural economic change, this study dismisses the contention that civil rights laws are a manipulative device employed by élites to assure the political quiescence and economic subordination of blacks. As Anthony Richmond has pointed out, the choice in social science is not between those theories based on order and those based on conflict, but 'between those theories that are compatible with the empirical evidence and those that are not'.[8] In the area under discussion, little theory has, in fact, been generated. This is possibly explained by the generally dismissive attitude of scholars towards laws in which they once had so much faith. More generally, social scientists have had great difficulty accommodating racial inequality and conflict within those now predominantly influential theories of social science based on class stratification and conflict.[9]

The one attempt by a political scientist to construct a theory of the white institutional response to black migration to British and American cities falters precisely because the facts fail to fit. In his book *Black Men, White Cities,* Ira Katznelson claims that in both countries there has been a conscious attempt by white élites to depoliticise the race issue through the creation of 'buffer institutions' (mainly community relations agencies) whose function has been not to improve race relations and reduce discrimination, but instead to isolate black demands and thereby reinforce institutionalised racism.[10] Some of the facts fit; there has been an attempt to depoliticise the race issue (of which more later), and community relations agencies may well serve a 'buffer' function, but the white response to black migration also (perhaps primarily) includes the enactment of civil rights legislation, which Katznelson virtually ignores. Moreover, the failure of community relations and civil rights efforts may well have had effects quite incompatible with Katznelson's analysis. As Brier and Axford have pointed out:

> Why, after all, should political élites seek to remove race from the
> political arena, with the professed intention of defusing potentially
> conflictual situations, and at the same time set up buffer
> institutions which, if Katznelson and others are correct, function in
> such a way as to frustrate black demands and drive them to form
> political organisations outside the ambit of normal politics?

As Philip Mason, a former director of the Institute of Race
Relations objects, 'the government of the day, the Civil Service and
Parliament. . .[has been found] frequently insensitive, often
complacent and pompous, often reluctant to make any change,
sometimes legally pedantic, but never cynically determined on this
kind of policy. On the contrary. . .it has always been taken for
granted. . .that it was against the interests of this country that there
should be a section of society which is easily identified, which is
discriminated against and which is alienated from government and
the majority.'[11]

The present study does not, it should hastily be added, offer an
alternative theory, at least not in the generally accepted use of the term
theory. However, it does employ a simple explanatory framework which
assumes, along with E.E. Schattschneider, that 'new policies create new
politics',[12] and that only by studying the detail of the policy process
can we discover the nature of these politics, and find out whether or
not they have produced any significant changes in society.

Civil Rights and Housing

The framework employed is in part determined by the fact that the
provision of *housing* and its relationship to race is the central focus.
Until very recently, studies of housing and civil rights have, if anything,
been even scarcer than civil rights studies generally. In the United
States this probably relates to the waning academic interest in civil
rights which came a very few years after the passage of the first
federal 'open housing' law in 1968. In Britain, some detailed studies
have been undertaken, but few have specifically addressed the
relationship between civil rights law and housing opportunity.[13] This
absence of research is surprising, for residential location is critical in
determining not only immediate neighbourhood environment, but also
access to employment and education. As R.E. Park noted, 'social
relations are frequently and. . .inevitably correlated with spatial

relations',[14] and as far as racial minorities are concerned, residential location has been critical in determining their subordinate position in society. Hence, in the United States the problems of minorities are most obviously and immediately associated with the ghetto, and in both Britain and America, the high degree of residential concentration of non-whites in decayed inner city areas is intimately related to patterns of racial inequality.

Why minorities live in those neighbourhoods which offer the least in terms of opportunity, is a complex and difficult question and one which will be referred to in detail in later chapters. Certainly, employment opportunity, choice, and in particular poverty, play some part. However, urban sociologists in both countries have shown that these factors explain but a fraction of racial concentration, and easily the most important explanations are those based on specifically racial factors.[15] In particular, overt racial discrimination in the housing market, together with the operation of institutional rules and procedures which although they may not be racially motivated result in racial disadvantage, have reduced the housing choices and therefore the residential and social mobility of minorities. Generally speaking, civil rights laws are designed to combat such discrimination, although the extent to which they specifically address different types of discrimination varies from law to law. Clearly, in order to assess the independent effects of such laws, it is necessary to understand how the implementation of civil rights policy interacts both with the broader social and economic environment of the city, and also with other relevant public policies, in particular housing and general urban policies. In sum, the following stages of analysis need to be undertaken:

i. Putting the study in perspective by explaining the nature of residential change, the extent of inequality in housing among minorities, and the identification of those factors, including the extent and nature of racial discrimination and disadvantage responsible for these inequalities.

ii. Outlining the government response to discrimination and inequality by analysing the development, content, and the administrative and judicial implementation of civil rights laws, and then relating these processes to other relevant policies such as housing and urban deprivation programmes.

iii. Analysing the effects or impacts of policy in the two countries by establishing any changes in housing opportunity attributable to the law.

iv. Explaining *why* policy implementation has taken the shape it has by identifying the constraints and limitations imposed on the law by patterns of political and economic power, and by the role played by institutional and ideological factors.

Given the complexity of the subject areas covered, it is not possible to provide precise answers to these questions. But because, as Kenneth Dolbeare has put it, 'linkage between policy components and particular consequences is very hard to demonstrate evidentially',[16] scholars should not be deterred from studying broad, complex areas. This is particularly true when, as is the case with the present study, a single researcher can draw on the abundance of related research conducted by others, and when it is possible through the careful use of language and intellectual judgement, to come to general but important conclusions on the consequences of public policy.

The Comparative Focus

At all stages, but particularly with respect to explaining the effects of the law, the comparison of policy in the two countries will be a central focus. Perhaps surprisingly, this makes the present enterprise a pioneering exercise, for with the exception of Katznelson's work, there is no substantive comparative study of race and public policy in Britain and America. Indeed, comparison has generally been rare in the race relations areas. As Pierre Van den Berghe noted in 1967:

Much of the literature on race relations during the last three decades has dealt with the United States and has been written by scholars who lacked comparative experience. . .For every hundred published racial attitude studies done in the United States, we could perhaps find five to ten in all the rest of the world. This lack of comparative approach has led, among other things, to an implicit or explicit overgeneralization of American findings.[17]

This criticism is of particular relevance in the present context, for there are regular warnings that British cities are 'ghettoising' and will soon display all the pathologies of America's cities. Yet, in the absence of careful comparative analysis, such predictions should be recognised as purely speculative in nature. Indeed, a major justification for detailed cross-national comparison in social science is the increasingly common tendency among academics and commentators generally to overgeneralise from the experience of one country, especially if the subject under consideration concerns social or political conflict. As the first genuinely comparative analysis of the relationship between public policy and the spatial concentration of minorities in Britain and America, this study hopes, therefore, to provide some evidence confirming or disputing currently popular theories about the future of Britain's cities and their black populations.

Cross-national comparison of public policy can only sensibly be undertaken when broad similarities exist between the countries under examination. As Chapter 2 will show in some detail, such similarities do exist in the race and housing area in Britain and America. In both countries, racial minorities have been used as immigrant or migrant cheap labour, and their arrival in urban areas was a largely unplanned market phenomenon. In addition, the recent British pattern of urban change and its relationship to minority residential settlement resembles, although is by no means identical to, the American experience. Finally, Britain and the United States share a common legal and political tradition, and each had adopted a similar approach to the problem of racial discrimination and how it should be removed.

But while parallels are sufficient to allow sensible comparison, there are also important, sometimes dramatic differences between the two countries, and a major aim is to show how contrasting institutional, ideological and economic arrangements have produced sometimes quite different responses to policies which in design and content are very similar in both countries.

Neither the analysis of policy implementation in one country nor the comparison of policy could be attempted without extensive use of the considerable volume of research which has been undertaken in the many subject areas which this study touches on. Indeed, much of the analysis of the pattern of minority settlement and the nature of discrimination will be in the form of summarising the research findings of others. These findings provide an essential backcloth without which the major objectives of the study could not be achieved. All too often in the social sciences, subject compartmentalisation prevents this sort of interdisciplinary exercise. Without it, however, there is no way in which the full effects and significance of particular public policy measures can be identified.

The Chapters to Come

Chapter 2 will place the study in context by identifying similarities and differences between Britain and America in the following areas : the size and nature of minority populations, race as a political issue, the extent of racial discrimination and disadvantage, patterns of urban development and minority settlement, and the role of the state in housing and race relations. Chapters 3 to 6 will, in turn, look at civil rights policy as it affects private sector housing in the two countries, and publicly subsidised housing. Division of the housing market in this way is a slightly false dichotomy, for the British private sector is greatly influenced by public sector policies, and some of the American federal housing programmes are only quasi-public in nature. However, in both countries, the pattern of minority settlement that has emerged has done so primarily within the private sector, and the impetus to British and American anti-discrimination law owes much to the belief that racial discrimination is primarily a problem deriving from individual discriminatory acts in the private sector. For these reasons Chapters 3 and 4, in addition to analysing the enforcement of the law in the private sector, will identify the pattern of minority settlement in the two countries and trace the development of civil rights law. The public sector chapters will be more concerned with the development of urban policy, and, naturally, the extent of racial discrimination and disadvantage in public sector housing. Chapter 7 has three main objectives. First to summarise the extent to which civil rights laws have produced changes; second to identify, on a comparative basis, the main institutional, ideological, economic and political constraints on effective civil rights law enforcement, and finally, to discuss the implications that each country's experience has for the other. This last exercise comes close to what many public policy studies call 'policy recommendations', a phrase which implies that academics have a role to play in advising policy makers. Giving advice to those in power has its dangers, not least because, whether wittingly or not, the academic's analysis can be used to support the interests and values of dominant élites. In research on race and racial problems the main dangers are a tendency to offer only those solutions supportive of public order and the avoidance of political conflict, and to assume that the integration or assimilation of minorities into society should be the primary policy objective. This study considers neither of these objectives *necessarily* desirable, although it does not pretend to be value free. Indeed, it makes the expressed normative judgement that the unequal treatment of individuals on grounds of race is irreconcilable with any conception of the just or fair society, and that governments should be vigilant in removing racial inequalities. Policies designed to achieve this objective may result in 'integration' or a reduction in political conflict, but equally, a truly effective civil rights policy may be incompatible with these conditions, or with other policy objectives, such as the provision of economic equality.

Chapters 3 to 6 and the final chapter will point to such incompatibilities and will provide both those in power and the general public with indications as to the limitations of civil rights laws. In other words, this study hopes to follow C. Wright Mills' advice that, as social scientists, our overriding aim should be: 'to remain independent, to do one's own work, to select one's own problems, but to direct this work *at* kings as well as *to* publics.'[18]

Notes

1. See in particular, Kenneth M. Dolbeare, 'Public Policy Analysis and the Coming Struggle for the Soul of the Postbehavioural Revolution', in Philip Green and Sanford Levinson (eds), *Power and Community: Dissenting Essays in Political Science* (New York: Vintage, 1970), pp.85-111; David Easton, 'The New Revolution in Political Science', American Political Science Review, Vol.63 (December 1969), pp.1051-61.
2. Austin Ranney, 'The Study of Policy Content: A Framework for Choice', in Austin Ranney (ed.), *Political Science and Public Policy* (Chicago: Markham, 1960), pp.3-22; John G. Grumm, 'The Analysis of Policy Impact', *The Handbook of Political Science, Vol.6, Policies and Policy Making* (Reading, Mass. : Addison Wesley, 1975), pp.439-73.
3. *Report of the National Advisory Commission on Civil Disorders* (Washington, D.C.: US Government Printing Office, 1968), p.1.
4. See for example, Kenneth M. Dolbeare and Murray J. Edelmen, *American Politics : Policies, Power and Change* (Lexington, Mass. : Heath, 2nd edn., 1974), pp.296-7.
5. Typical of this trend is the work of Michael Lipsky, 'Protest as a Political Resource', in Kenneth M. Dolbeare (ed.) *Power and Change in the United States* (New York: Wiley, 1969), pp.161-78; see also Peter Bachrach and Morton Baratz, *Power and Poverty* (New York : Oxford University Press, 1970); J. David Greenstone and Paul E. Peterson, *Race and Authority in Urban Politics* (New York: Russell Sage Foundation, 1973).
6. For generally 'radical' perspectives, see the journal *Race and Class*; also, Ira Katznelson, *Black Men, White Cities* (London and New York : Oxford University Press, 1973); M. Parenti, 'Assimilation and Counter Assimilation: From Civil Rights to Black Radicalism', in Philip Green and Sanford Levinson, op.cit., pp.173-94.
7. This is the implied or explicit position of most of those who have conducted detailed studies of civil rights laws. See Duane Lockard, *Toward Equal Opportunity* (New York : Macmillan, 1968); E.J.B. Rose and Associates, *Colour and Citizenship* (London : Oxford University Press, 1969); W.W. Daniel, *Racial Discrimination in England* (Harmondsworth, Middx : Penguin, 1968).

8. Anthony H. Richmond, *Migration and Race Relations in an English City* (London: Oxford University Press, 1973), p.13.
9. For discussions of this problem, see the essays by John Rex and David Lockwood in Sam Zubaida (ed.), *Race and Racialism* (London: Tavistock Publications, 1970).
10. Ibid., Chapters 11 and 12.
11. Alan Brier and Barrie Axford, 'The Theme of Race in British Social and Political Research', in Ivor Crewe (ed.), *British Political Sociology Yearbook, Volume 2, The Politics of Race* (London: Croom Helm, 1975), p.11.
12. Quoted in Hugh Heclo, *Modern Social Politics in Britain and Sweden* (New Haven: Yale University Press, 1975), p.5.
13. Although housing and civil rights have been covered by more general studies. See Rose, op.cit., Chapters 12 and 17; Anthony Lester and Geoffrey Bindman, *Race and Law* (Harmondsworth, Middx. : Penguin, 1972), Chapter 6. Additionally, several studies of the relationship between race and housing which do not cover the question of civil rights have been completed. See, in particular, John Rex and Robert Moore, *Race, Community, and Conflict* (London : Oxford University Press, 1967).
14. Quoted in O.D. Duncan and S. Iieberson, 'Ethnic Segregation and Assimilation', in Ceri Peach (ed.), *Urban Social Segregation* (New York: Longman, 1975), p.96.
15. See Ceri Peach, Stuart Winchester, Robert Woods, 'The Distribution of Coloured Immigrants in Britain', in Gary Gappert and Harold M. Rose (eds.), *The Social Economy of Cities,* Vol.9 Sage Urban Affairs Annual Reviews (Beverly Hills : Sage, 1975); Karl E. Taeuber and Alma F. Taeuber, *Negroes in Cities* (New York : Atheneum, 1969), Chapters 3 and 4; John F. Kain and John M. Quigley, *Housing Markets and Racial Discrimination* (New York and London : Columbia University Press, 1975), Chapter 3.
16. K.M. Dolbeare, 'The Impacts of Public Policy', in the *Political Science Annual 1974* (Indianapolis: Bobbs-Merrill, 1974), p.119.
17. Quoted in Katznelson, op.cit., p.15.
18 C. Wright Mills, *The Sociological Imagination* (Fair Lawn, N.J. : Oxford University Press), p.181.

2 THE COMPARATIVE POLICY CONTEXT

The aim of this chapter is to provide an essential background to later chapters by noting those similarities and differences between the two countries which are relevant to the race and housing policy area. As Chapter 1 emphasised, it is assumed that there are sufficient similarities to justify comparison. In this respect, the study concurs with Douglas Ashford's comment following a study of British and American local government:

> a final comparative lesson can be drawn from this analysis. Though structural and institutional differences may be great, there is no reason to assume that they prevent comparison. Indeed they may in fact operate within the political system in very similar ways.[1]

The Minority Populations

In 1972, the black (negro) population of the United States was 23.4 million or 11 per cent of the total. In addition, some 9.2 million Americans were, according to the census 'of Spanish origin', that is they had Spanish surnames. Most of the latter are Chicano (of Mexican origin) or Puerto Rican. In 1970, another 2.6 million were classified as 'other races' (mainly native Indian Americans, Japanese and Chinese).[2] In general, problems of segregation and discrimination have been associated with the black rather than other minority populations. Blacks are the largest and one of the longest established groups, they have been the most vocal in protest at their condition, and have been at the centre of the political and social conflicts concerning race in the US. Also, compared with the second largest group, the Chicanos, they are highly urbanised, and as the focus of racial conflict has shifted to the cities so it has shifted to urban blacks. This is not to deny that other minority groups have experienced racial discrimination or been involved in racial conflict. On the contrary, in many areas their experience has been worse than that of the blacks. As an urban phenomenon, however, discrimination and segregation has affected many more blacks than other minorities, and for this reason this study will focus primarily on the black population — although there will be reference to other groups when relevant.

Probably more has been written about American blacks than about

any minority group on earth,[3] so there is little need for a detailed
summary of their cultural and social history. It is important, however,
to note that while blacks do have a distinctive culture, they are very
much a product of American society. Their language, religion, and
political and social institutions derive in large part from the United
States — even if these do not always conform to the norms of white
middle-class America.

Britain's minority population is very much smaller than America's
both absolutely and relatively, accounting for at most 2.5 per cent
(about 1.39 million) of the total population.[4] More than a small
element of controversy and debate has surrounded exactly how many
blacks are resident in Britain. In part, controversy has been
politically inspired; by exaggerating the number of non-whites some
observers have played on people's fears of a 'black invasion'. The
question of numbers is, however, problematical from a purely technical
point of view. Until 1971, the census did not distinguish racial
minorities, and even the 1971 census failed to ask questions of an
explicitly racial nature. Instead, a new category, the euphemistic 'Both
Parents Born New Commonwealth' (BPBNC) was created. As the New
Commonwealth is predominantly non-white (as opposed to the white
'Old Commonwealth' — Canada, Australia, New Zealand), and as the
vast majority of non-whites have arrived in Britain since 1950, this
category does contain most of Britain's black population.[5] Together
with data on country of birth, it is possible to build up a fairly precise
picture of this population as shown in Table 2.1. Note that of the
763,130 adults in the BPBNC category a mere 1.8 per cent were born
in the UK, thus demonstrating just how recent has been the arrival of
most blacks. Table 2.1 also shows that Britain's minority
population is composed of three main groups: Asians (mainly Indians
and Pakistanis) comprising 53.6 per cent of the total, West Indians and
others from Central and South America comprising 32.1 per cent, and
Africans (which includes African Asians) who
comprise 11.7 per cent. A second and obvious contrast with the
American situation, then, is that the British non-white population is
essentially an *immigrant* population recently arrived from Third World
countries some of whose cultures, religions and language differ
dramatically from those of Britain. Britain's minority population is also
highly heterogeneous, comprising (among others) Christian West
Indians, Moslem Pakistanis, Hindu Indians and black Africans and
African Asians of many religions. These differences within Britain's
black population will later be shown to be of great importance.

Table 2.1: 1971 Census: Adults Belonging to Minority Groups by
Country of Birth, UK

All adults aged 15+ with both parents born in the New Commonwealth

	No.	%
Born in UK	14,015	1.8
Visitors to UK	8,480	1.1
Birthplace not stated	2,905	0.4
Born outside UK	737,730	96.7
Total	763,130	100.0

Adults born outside UK with both parents born in the New Commonwealth

Country of Birth	No.	%	
Kenya	27,485	3.7)	
Nigeria	20,470	2.8)	11.7
Other Africa	38,100	5.2)	
West Indies	187,780	25.4)	
Other America	49,200	6.7)	32.1
India	206,675	28.0)	
Pakistan (including Bangladesh)	101,570	13.8)	53.6
Other Asia	86,860	11.8)	
Europe	13,885	1.9	
Total New Commonwealth	732,025	99.3	
Outside New Commonwealth	5,705	0.8	
Total	737,730	100.1	

Source: Adapted from David Smith, *The Facts of Racial Disadvantage* (London:
PEP, 1976), Appendix, Table C1

In terms of numbers and cultural links with the white populations, it
would appear that the non-white populations of Britain and the US have
little in common. In other respects, however, strong parallels exist.

British blacks are immigrants mainly from poor rural environments
and American urban blacks are largely first and second generation
migrants from the rural South. From 1940, after some initial movement
of blacks from the South to the Northern industrial cities during and
immediately after World War One, a great internal migration occurred,
so that by 1970 47 per cent of America's black population lived in the
Northern and Western cities, compared with just 23 per cent in 1940.

During the last fifteen years the urbanisation of the black population has continued with Southern blacks migrating to Southern cities. In addition, the Chicano population, once almost exclusively rural, is urbanising rapidly.

The forces at work explaining the British and American migrations are not dissimilar. Rural poverty combined with a high demand for less skilled labour in growing and affluent metropolitan centres is present in both cases. Racial minorities have come to constitute a 'replacement' labour force filling the less pleasant and lower paid jobs vacated by whites.[6] Being migrants in low status jobs puts British and American non-whites in a near colonial situation where they are not only poor but also alien. As John Rex has noted

> The colonial immigrant or his children are cut off from privately or publicly controlled gateways to privilege, and then find that their disadvantages as colonials are further increased because their position as new poor serves to confirm suspicions of their inadequacy.[7]

Admittedly, the colonial analogy applies most obviously and directly to the UK where the minority population has migrated from ex-colonies, although it is striking how America's urban blacks appear caught in a much more intensive cycle of class and ethnic disadvantage than that experienced by white migrants and immigrants in the US.[8] By most measures their social and economic status is substantially inferior to that of whites, and this also applies to Britain's minority population.

In 1971, 30.9 per cent of the US black population were below the official low income level (a measure which is widely accepted as excluding many poor people),[9] compared with 12.5 per cent for the population as a whole. Exactly comparable figures for the UK are not available, but there is no doubt that the minority population is poorer than the white. Figures from the Political and Economic Planning (PEP) surveys of 1974 show that in 1974, the median gross earnings of minority men in Britain were £36.70 a week compared with £40.20 for white men. Non-whites in both countries also tend to be employed in the less skilled jobs. So, according to PEP figures, only 8 per cent of West Indian and Pakistani males and 20 per cent of Indian males are white-collar workers, compared with 40 per cent of white males. In 1971, 29 per cent of black Americans were in this category compared with 50 per cent of whites. Moreover, 32 per cent of British West Indians and 58 per cent of Pakistanis are unskilled manual workers,

while only 18 per cent of whites are unskilled. In the US, 40 per cent
of the black population are unskilled compared with 20 per cent among
whites.

This catalogue of racial inequality can be applied to other areas.
American blacks are poorly educated in relation to whites. In 1972
only 24.9 per cent had completed high school and 11.6 per cent had
attended college, compared with 36.4 per cent and 24 per cent
respectively for whites. Among the British minority population, Asian
men do not quite fit into the pattern, however, their educational
attainment being as good or better than that of whites — in 1974
44 per cent had completed full-time education after the age of 17 and
12 per cent had higher educational qualifications. The comparable
figures for West Indian men and white men under 44 were 16 per cent
and 1 per cent and 22 per cent and 13 per cent respectively.[10]

Another area where there appears to be a divergence between the
two countries is unemployment. Among American blacks unemployment
has consistently approached twice that of whites in recent years, but
the level of unemployment among Britain's blacks has been (with the
notable exception of young West Indians) similar to that of the
general population.[11] Like American blacks, however, British minorities
are more vulnerable to fluctuations in the general employment situation.
Hence, during the 1974/5 recession, unemployment among American
blacks reached 12.8 per cent compared with 6.4 per cent for whites,[12]
and by August 1975 when unemployment was rising rapidly in Britain,
non-whites accounted for 3.5 per cent of the total implying a
disproportionately high rate of unemployment.

Finally, the housing conditions of non-whites are equally bad in
relation to white housing in both countries. In 1970, 16.5 per cent of
American blacks lived in sub standard housing (according to the very
limited official criterion this means housing lacking all or some
plumbing facilities). Just 4 per cent of whites lived in sub standard
housing. PEP survey data on the housing conditions of British
minorities are extensive and will be expanded on later, but by all
measures including one comparable to the American plumbing
criterion, non-white housing comes off very badly indeed. Thirty-three
per cent of West Indians and 57 per cent of Pakistanis/Bangladeshis do
not have exclusive use of bath, hot water and inside WC, while only
17.9 per cent of the general population are in this category.

All the above figures are, of course, averages. A large minority of
American blacks and certain sections of Britain's non-white (especially
African Asian) population have a good standard of living and are not

notably disadvantaged in relation to whites. In the US at least, there are signs that the middle-class black population is increasing in size.[13] None the less, the general pattern of lasting inequality among American blacks is striking, and there are no signs that the disadvantaged position of Britain's black population is anything but a permanent condition.

The Politics of Race

Perhaps obviously in the light of these inequalities, the political power of racial minorities in Britain and America is strictly limited. Whether measured in terms of the number of black incumbents in elective or non-elective positions of power, their electoral strength, or their lobbying and bargaining power, racial minorities are weak in relation to their numbers.[14] This is, however, particularly true of Britain where the minority communities are both much smaller than in the US and less well integrated into conventional politics. American blacks, in contrast, now have limited power both within their own communities and in the broader political context. Perhaps most importantly, racial debate and controversy in the United States now centres on the question of providing blacks with social and economic opportunity. The more extreme brand of racist politics is now isolated, even in the South, and the main concern of conservatives is to halt the 'affirmative action' programmes which via bussing and (as will be shown) integrated housing attempt to correct the disadvantaged position of non-whites. These issues, together with attempts by blacks to assert their electoral strength, make up the politics of race in the US.

Until a few years ago, it was common to claim that race was not an important political issue in Britain, but recent evidence suggests that in both local and national electoral politics, race has been of critical significance in particular contexts.[15] Right-wing racist political parties have been growing in strength, especially in local politics,[16] and successive surveys have shown that the electorate feel very strongly about racial issues. In dramatic contrast to the United States, however, strong feelings focus on the question of immigration and immigration controls, rather than on the provision of equal opportunity.[17] This focus together with immigration laws which specifically discriminate against British blacks living abroad, makes the politics of race in Britain potentially much more sinister than in the US, for the central issue is 'how can we keep them out?' or even 'how can we send them back?' These are not the views of isolated extremists, but of large sections of the population, and it is official Conservative Party policy to advocate a limited form of voluntary repatriation. Immigrants and immigration are seen by such people as threats to employment, the 'British culture' and to overworked social services — even though there is no evidence that any of these have been adversely affected by the black population. Immigrants or blacks, therefore, have in the eyes of many become synonymous with all that is wrong with contemporary Britain, a fact which has made good race relations and the job of reducing inequality that much more difficult.

A major reason for this unfortunate pattern is undoubtedly Britain's very limited experience with people of different races and cultures. American society has, of course, been constructed on the immigration of diverse peoples, and even if this experience has not always been successful, cultural and racial variety is probably more accepted in the US than in Britain. Public and private attitudes may, therefore, appear more racist in British culture where 'blackness' is often treated as an alien abnormality. One interesting guide to British attitudes is the language of the media which contains constant racist references (such as, when commenting on a black athlete, talking about the 'natural movement of the coloured boy'), and newspapers, radio and television frequently portray blacks in an unattractive, often criminal, light.[18]

While both countries have what might be called 'racial politics', the main political parties have worked hard to dissociate themselves from anything but a liberal position, and all are at least officially committed to implementing civil rights laws. Indeed some commentators have argued that the search for consensus among political élites on the race issue has had deleterious effects on the position of minorities by diverting public attention from their plight.[19] However, as will be argued in later chapters, in the civil rights policy area there are important differences between the main parties in both countries, even if these have not been sufficient to label the policy of any one party racist.

Finally, it would be quite wrong to leave the impression that Britain is more racist than the United States or that racial discrimination is more widespread in Britain. There are, of course, enormous problems involved in cross-national comparisons of attitudes and political culture, and America's history of racial violence and repression, together with the continuing problems of inequality among her large minority populations, means that the nature and scale of racial conflict is quite different from Britain's much more recent and relatively small scale racial problem. The main point being made is, rather, that the context

within which British racial politics occur is different. It is not one of
deep rooted historical conflict between the races, but is instead
characterised by an unfamiliarity with racial minorities, and a marked
tendency to think of blacks as synonymous with immigrants who are
considered a major cause of contemporary social problems.

The Nature of Discrimination

In spite of these very different contexts, the nature of racial
discrimination is not dissimilar in the two countries. For as Michael
Banton has emphasised, while it must be acknowledged that racism
and racial discrimination are complex psychological, sociological,
geographical and historical phenomena which are likely to vary quite
dramatically from society to society, they can play similar economic
and political functions in different societies.[20]

In the UK substantial evidence exists showing that discrimination
(especially in housing and employment) is pervasive,[21] and a large
volume of research in the US comes to similar conclusions for that
country.[22] Race relations theories suggest that racially distinct
minorities are almost invariably discriminated against when they are
used as cheap unskilled labour in industrial societies. The extent and
nature of discrimination will vary from country to country, but will
exist in all given the common presence of social and cultural differences
and the perceived economic competition between racial groups which
are at the roots of most discriminatory acts.[23]

Most research on racial discrimination in Britain and the US refers
to individual instances of discrimination — deliberate and conscious
acts of unequal treatment based on race or colour distinctions.
Individual acts of discrimination are usually easy to identify. Through
'testing' — the use of white and non-white testers applying for the same
job or house — the extent of discrimination can be fairly accurately
measured.[24] But during the last fifteen years, researchers and
governments in Britain and America have increasingly accepted that the
disadvantaged position of non-whites may also result from 'structural
discrimination' or racial disadvantage. Racial disadvantage derives from
the values and practices of societies' institutions, which may not
discriminate in any conscious way against non-whites, but whose
effects are discriminatory. Hence, in the US the policy practised by
many suburban local governments of excluding low income housing
may, because in some cities most poor people are also black, have the
effect of excluding blacks — even if this is not the motivation. In the
UK, public housing allocations based on length of residence in an area

may similarly discriminate against recently arrived blacks — even if such policies are not racial in design. In many cases (as with low income housing site selection in America) racial disadvantage touches upon the complex and delicate relationship between race and class, and as we shall see, attempts to challenge it can have far reaching consequences both for race relations and for the level of political conflict in society.

Racial discrimination and racial disadvantage then, exist in both countries. The extent and nature of discrimination depends on a variety of factors including the degree of cultural and class differences between groups and on the extent of *contact* between groups. Quite of their own volition, minorities may prefer to live among their own kind, in which case contact with other groups and the potential for discrimination will be lower. Yet the history of minorities in industrial societies suggests that voluntary separation is rare, especially when the minorities are in a subordinate economic and political position.[25] The question of contact and the nature of discrimination and disadvantage can only be understood in the context of the position of minorities in urban society. Let us look then, at the pattern of minority settlement in the two countries.

Residential Location and Urban Development

David Harvey has noted that:

> what is remarkable is not that urbanism is so different [in capitalist societies] but that it is so similar in all the metropolitan centres of the world in spite of significant differences in social policy, cultural tradition, administrative and political arrangements, institutions and laws and so on. The conditions in the economic basis of capitalist society together with its associated technology put an unmistakeable stamp upon the qualitative attributes of urbanism in all economically advanced capitalist nations.[26]

This is certainly broadly true of the pattern of minority settlement in Britain and the United States, although there are also important differences. Later chapters will look at this pattern and its relationship to discrimination and other factors in some detail, but for now it will be useful to draw some broad comparisons.

As is well known, the predominant feature of non-white residence in American cities is racial segregation. In the North, East, South and West, in large cities and small, in suburbs and industrial areas, segregation is the norm. Karl Taeuber's now familiar index of segregation in US cities confirms this point. Based on a comparison between the actual distribution of the races in a city and the hypothetical distribution which would prevail were there no forces making for segregation, the Taeuber index is a good pointer to the extent of segregation. Hence, if a city was 50 per cent white and 50 per cent black, in the absence of segregation this distribution would prevail in each and every of the city's neighbourhood blocks and the segregation index would be zero. An index of 100 would be obtained were all black families living in black residential blocks and all white families living in white blocks. A segregation index of 90 would signify that 90 per cent of that city's black population would have to be redistributed to white areas before the city could be labelled completely unsegregated.[27]

As Table 2.2 shows, the indices for 109 of the country's largest cities have been high for many years.

Table 2.2: Mean Indices of Residential Segregation between Whites and Non-whites, by Region, 109 Cities, US 1940 to 1970*

Year	Mean Indices of Residential Segregation			
	South	N.E.	N. Central	West
1940	84.9	83.2	88.4	82.7
1950	88.5	83.6	89.9	83.0
1960	90.8	78.9	88.4	76.4
1970	88.0	74.3	82.6	67.9
No. of cities	45	25	29	10

* These figures apply to white/non-white segregation, the figures for white/black segregation are generally higher

Source: Annemette Sorensen, Karl Taeuber and Leslie J. Hollingsworth, Jr., *Indices of Racial Residential Segregation for 109 Cities in the United States, 1940 to 1970* (Madison, Wisconsin: Institute for Research on Poverty, Reprint Series No 154, 1975), Table 3

All areas of the United States experienced a relative decline in segregation during the decade 1960-70, following a smaller decline in the 1950s and an increase during the 1940s. In Western areas the decrease was considerable (particularly in San Francisco, as a breakdown of these data shows), but in the South it was very slight. However, the most striking feature of the 1970 indices is the continuing high level of racial segregation. Moreover, recent years' decreases are probably attributable to a higher level of residential mobility and an easier housing market which have encouraged the emergence of an increasing number of transitional, temporarily integrated neighbourhoods, rather than being caused by the permanent erosion of discrimination and the other forces making for segregation.[28]

These figures apply to individual cities rather than to metropolitan areas, and although data in the form of segregation indices are not available on a metropolitan wide basis, Table 2.3 does show how nearly all of the very rapid increase in the urban black population since 1950 has been concentrated in central city areas. The ghettoes of the 1970s, therefore, are primarily central city based, and they are much more extensive than ever before.

Table 2.3: Central City and Suburban Population by Race, US 1950-1970

	(In thousands except per cent)		
	1950	1960	1970
Central city white population	46,791	49,440	48,796
Central city black population	6,608	9,950	13,097
Black population as a % of white	14.2%	20.1%	26.8%
Suburban white population	38,308	55,741	71,628
Suburban black population	2,242	2,760	3,689
Black population as a % of white	5.8%	4.9%	5.1%

Adapted from *Statistical Abstract of the US,* American Almanac Edition, 1972
(New York: Grosset and Dunlap, 1971), Section 1, Table 14, p.16

Britain's black population is almost exclusively urban and is heavily concentrated in the four largest industrial regions: London and the South East, the Midlands, the North West and Yorkshire. In general the Africans and West Indians have moved to London and the South East (according to PEP survey figures about 66 per cent of West Indians live in this region), while the Asian population is more evenly distributed between the four regions. The black population is also concentrated within the main conurbations of these regions. This is shown by Table 2.4 which looks at the distribution of non-whites at the more detailed level of census Enumeration Districts (EDs) each of which consists of about 500 individuals. We can see that a majority of blacks live in those EDs of more than 10 per cent non-white population, and that one quarter live in neighbourhoods where residence is in excess

Table 2.4: Distribution of the Immigrant Population of England and Wales across Census Enumeration Districts, 1971[29]

EDs with immigrant concentrations	% of total population contained in these EDs	% of immigrants contained in these EDs	% of population who are immigrants
30% or more	0.5	10.8	37.2
20% or more	1.6	25.6	28.6
15% or more	2.8	37.5	23.7
10% or more	4.8	50.5	19.1
7.5% or more	7.5	58.7	16.2
5% or more	9.1	67.4	13.4
2.5% or more	15.1	79.4	9.5

Note: The table is based on PEPs sample of 1,500 EDs in England and Wales. The data about these EDs are from the 1971 census.

Source: David Smith, *The Facts of Racial Disadvantage,* Table B4

of 20 per cent black. American observers might consider this evidence of dispersal rather than concentration, and compared with the extent of segregation in the US, the degree of concentration is low. Certainly the terms 'segregation' and 'ghetto' are largely inapplicable in the British context. On the other hand, the tendency towards concentration is obvious. In some towns and cities within conurbations the percentage of blacks exceeds 10 per cent, so in spite of the fact that, overall, blacks are comparatively few in number, their spatial concentration can make them *appear* more visible and numerous. Moreover, a recent attempt to apply the Taeubers' index to Britain did produce figures ranging from 34 for West Indians in Coventry to 69 for Asians in Birmingham, so the beginnings of segregation have clearly developed in the United Kingdom.[30]

But what is the significance of concentration? Migrants and immigrants do, after all, tend to move to those areas which offer some sort of security or refuge in a strange and sometimes hostile environment — neighbourhoods where family and friends have already settled and where jobs and housing are available. While this is true, it is also the case that in both countries non-whites have moved to the most decayed and depressed areas of the inner city.

In the United States the facts of inner city decay and the

concentration of minorities in the inner city are indisputable and require little further documentation. Both phenomena are related to the political economy and social dynamics of urban growth in the US. Put very briefly, the marginal costs of investment in the inner city areas have been increasing rapidly relative to the suburbs. Therefore, during the periods of rapid economic and urban growth of the last thirty years, manufacturing industry has gradually been moving out taking with it the younger white skilled workers and their families. A complex mixture of factors have prevented blacks and other minorities from following, the most important of which are housing discrimination and poverty. As a result, they have been left with the jobs available in the remaining (and much less dynamic) inner city manufacturing industries and with less skilled work in the service sector — a sector which has expanded rapidly in many cities. The consequent income disparities between suburbs and inner cities have led to fiscal imbalance, with inner city local governments forced to rely on declining property tax revenues (which in the US make up 85 per cent of all local government revenue) to finance educational, welfare and other municipal services, which, because the population is poor and the physical stock of the city is old and deteriorating, are increasingly costly. Hence the familiar cycle of deprivation experienced by non-whites. Discrimination and poverty prevent them from leaving the ghetto for better jobs, and while they remain in the ghetto, poor schools, housing and employment opportunities, together with generally inferior municipal services and soaring crime rates further intensify their disadvantaged position.[31] Even those ghetto dwellers who have middle-class incomes and life-styles suffer, for they too are exposed to inferior services and an unsafe environment.

It should be added that while this pattern applies with some force to many (especially the larger) cities in the US, there are considerable regional and intra-conurbation variations. In particular, the Southern and Western cities whose capital stock is newer suffer less from fiscal polarisation — although they too have ghetto areas. Also, it would be misleading to characterise the large urban conurbations into which most non-whites have recently moved, as depressed. All large metropolitan areas of the US have a degree of affluence; the most depressed regions are those of Appalachia and the South and these are rural. Conurbations like those around Chicago and New York are generally dynamic and growing. Only in the inner city and in a few poor suburbs are unemployment, poor housing conditions, inferior municipal services and high crime levels the norm.

In Britain, the situation is much less clear cut. Department of

Environment indicators of urban deprivation based mainly on housing conditions and unemployment levels do show quite clearly that many inner city areas are suffering, or are beginning to experience, decay and stagnation.[32] Certainly British cities can, like American cities, be divided into ecological zones, and the older inner city zones have been losing manufacturing industry at a fairly rapid rate. But the extent and intensity of contrast between inner city and suburb is not as great as in the US. Instead, the main contrasts tend to be regional in nature with Clydeside, Merseyside and the North East being the most severely affected.[33] Several reasons can be identified to explain this distinctive pattern. British urban growth and suburbanisation has been less dramatic than America's, therefore inner city decline has not been as acute. Also, the much more intrusive role played by government in Britain's unitary political system has affected market forces by directing growth to depressed areas and by raising inner city investment, especially in housing. This particular contrast can be overestimated, however, for many regional cities remain depressed, and the other major aim of Britain's post-war planning policy, which was to direct growth *away* from inner areas and towards new towns, may have had deleterious effects on inner city industrial investment.

Another contrast is that some of Britain's most deprived urban areas, in particular, Glasgow, Belfast and the Tyneside conurbations, have few blacks among their populations. Most blacks have settled in the relatively affluent London and Midlands areas, although they have also moved to the textile towns of West Yorkshire and to parts of Lancashire which can hardly be described as affluent. In all cases however, job opportunities, especially in areas where a 'replacement' population was needed, have determined the pattern of settlement, and unemployment has traditionally been highest in Scotland, Northern Ireland and the North East.

Yet perhaps the contrast with the US is not as great as has been implied. Most Southern migrants moved to the economically wealthy metropolises of the North such as Chicago, Detroit and New York, rather than to relatively depressed cities like Pittsburgh. Moreover, as in the US, British non-whites living in generally affluent conurbations are concentrated in areas of urban deprivation in the inner city. Department of the Environment analysis of census data shows that in those EDs where the proportion of people of New Commonwealth origin is greater or equal to the 10 per cent 'cut-off' value of 8.8 per cent (i.e. the 10 per cent of *all* British urban EDs which have a black population of 8.8 per cent or more) there also exists a high incidence of urban deprivation. Table 2.5 shows the overlap between this 10 per cent cut-off value for EDs, and 10 per cent cut-off values for some major urban deprivation indicators.

Table 2.5: Comparison of mean 10% Cut-off Values of Selected Urban Deprivation Indicators, Great Britain Urban EDs, 1971

Indicator	GB Mean	10% cut-off value	Mean Values in the EDs in the Following Overlaps					
			1	1 + 2	1 + 3	1 + 4	1 + 5	1,2,3, 4 & 5
1 % of population of New Commonwealth Origin	3.6	8.8	21.6	25.3	28.2	23.5	24.3	29.7
2 % of households who share or lack hot water	9.7	28.0	25.2	40.6	32.8	30.6	33.8	41.8
3 % of households living in shared dwellings	4.8	13.4	20.8	32.2	29.0	40.1	16.8	51.2
4 % living at density > 1.5 person per room	2.3	6.2	6.2	8.8	11.5	7.6	9.7	12.6
5 % of economically active males seeking work or sick	5.8	11.7	7.1	8.7	9.0	7.0	16.3	9.0

Note: Data are for urban EDs only (87,570 of a total of 120,000 EDs in Great Britain)

Source: Department of the Environment, *Areas With a High Proportion of the Population of New Commonwealth Origin*, Census Indicators of Urban Deprivation, Working Note No. 8, DOE, 1975, adapted from Table 3

Apart from the considerably higher than average levels of deprivation in those EDs with a high proportion of New Commonwealth immigrants (especially in housing), there also exists a high incidence of deprivation in those EDs with a high percentage of non-whites and which overlap with one or several combinations of other indicators of deprivation. Of course, because an ED has a relatively high black population and is deprived does not mean to say that it is the black population within the ED which is deprived — although the already quoted PEP data would tend to confirm that for many indicators this is so. While these data are by no means comprehensive, they do confirm the oft quoted claim that Britain's black population live in areas of urban deprivation — even if they constitute only a minority of the population within these districts (in Table 2.5, the *average* non-white population at the 10 per cent cut-off level is 21.6 per cent).

In conclusion, in both countries inner city decay is evident and in both countries the non-white populations tend to be concentrated in decaying areas. This said, in Britain both racial residential concentration and inner city/suburban economic differences are much less extreme than in the US.

The Role of Government

By now it should be obvious that any study of public policy towards race and housing must involve government at several levels. Naturally, race relations law and its implementation is one level. But merely to study the administrative and judicial machinery of the law would explain little. As important, is analysis of how governments have influenced the pattern of discrimination and racial concentration. Urban land use and public and other subsidised housing policies are relevant in this context. Also critical is the extent to which governments *can* act or are *obliged* to act. These questions lead into discussions of governmental structure and political culture. How then do the US and the UK differ along these dimensions?

(a) *Race Relations Law*

With a written constitution and Bill of Rights, the US has a long tradition of formal constitutional protection of individual rights. Ratified in 1866 and 1868 the 13th and 14th Amendments, by abolishing slavery and guaranteeing the 'equal protection of the laws' to all citizens, provided the first civil rights to America's black population. However, the 14th Amendment, together with many civil rights laws passed by Congress in the Reconstruction period, fell into disuse until the rise of the civil rights movement in the post-war period. Perhaps the climax (and also the end) of this movement was the 1968 Civil Rights Act which bans discrimination in 80 per cent of the US housing stock. Passed in the wake of the assassination of Martin Luther King, the 1968 Act was the last major federal civil rights law, most other areas (public facilities, employment, education, voting) having been covered by the 1964 and 1965 Civil Rights Acts. Soon after the new 'open housing' Act was passed, the Supreme Court, resurrecting an 1866 Act, declared all discrimination in housing unconstitutional.[34]

Beginning with New York State in 1945, states and localities legislated extensively in the open housing area during the 1950s and 1960s, but few state laws have the authority and force of federal law, so the 1968 Act was potentially of great significance.

The Act sets up a complaint procedure run by the Department of Housing and Urban Development (HUD) but HUD's powers do not include the right to initiate complaints or to issue injunctions. However, the agency can subpoena witnesses, and can attempt to resolve complaints via 'conciliation, conference and persuasion'. The Attorney General (Department of Justice) can initiate investigations and the courts are given injunctive powers both with respect to cases brought by the government and with respect to cases filed by private individuals. In both instances, the award of damages and court orders (which can transfer the disputed property to the plaintiff) are sanctioned. The Act says little about the public sector, although HUD is required 'to administer its programmes and policies in a manner affirmatively to further the purposes of the law', and other laws and regulations have required a policy of non-discrimination in government programmes. Generally speaking, the 1968 Act is weak in enforcement provisions — especially when compared with some of the stronger state laws.

The historical antecedents of Britain's 1968 Race Relations Act are, not surprisingly, dramatically different. Britain first legislated to protect racial minorities in 1965 following increasing evidence of racial discrimination. The 1965 Race Relations Act did not specifically cover housing, but it was soon followed by the 1968 legislation which did. Both laws were passed as a result of the work of a powerful lobby of legal experts and concerned politicians and community leaders who were articulate in persuading the government that British civil rights legislation should be modelled on American laws.[35] In consequence, there exists a remarkable degree of similarity between British and American anti-discrimination legislation, a common legal tradition making the transposition possible. This fact alone is perhaps sufficient reason to compare the two countries' experience in race and housing.

The 1968 Race Relations Act covers most housing and assigns the running of a complaint procedure to an administrative agency, the Race Relations Board. The Board can, like its American counterpart, attempt to conciliate cases which come to its attention, but it also has limited powers to initiate complaints. However, it cannot subpoena witnesses and evidence, and the Attorney General can only act when the Board's conciliation process has broken down. Injunctive powers of the courts are limited to those cases where there is evidence that the discriminator will continue to discriminate, and even then the injunction can only take the form of an order not to discriminate. Actual redress in the form of the complainant or plaintiff receiving the disputed property is unavailable. Also, the 1968 Act makes little reference to what governments should do to discourage discrimination (and segregation) in their own programmes. In both countries, racial discrimination is a civil rather than a criminal offence.

In their emphasis on conciliation and persuasion, the two laws reflect the Anglo-American legal tradition and its concern with equity. Also, there is at least the implication in both laws that administrative complaint procedures and court action will be sufficient to combat discrimination. Neither law makes extensive reference to the social and economic forces at work in producing discrimination and segregation. Instead, the problem is seen almost exclusively in terms of individual instances of discrimination.

To be fair, a new Race Relations Bill going through Parliament in 1976 does recognise some of the structural roots of discriminatory practices, and suggests quite sweeping changes in the law, including easier recourse to the courts for aggrieved parties, and the creation of a new body, the Commission for Racial Equality, which will have much wider powers to investigate discrimination. The government is also encouraging local authorities to allocate more and better public housing to blacks. If passed, however, this new legislation will, if anything, bring the British law nearer to American practice — especially in those states like New York and Pennsylvania which have the most effective civil rights laws.[36]

(b) *Housing, Urban Land Use and the Role of the State*

Table 2.6 shows that in the provision of housing, government is much more important in the UK than in the US. State intervention in the social policy area to provide basic needs on a universalistic basis is well established in Britain, whereas American social policy provision is much more selective and based on the assumption that the state will intervene only when the private sector completely fails to provide a service. Because of the relative success of the American private housing market (in terms of number and quality of units built, if not in reducing some of the gross inequalities within the market) most American governments have not considered housing a social service, and as a result, America's small public housing sector has been reserved for the near destitute and the non-productive — often poor black families. There are other federal subsidised housing programmes, many of which

Table 2.6: Tenure Status of Households in the US and UK, 1972

	% of Households	
	US	UK
Owner Occupier	62	51
Private Rental	36	18
Public Rental	1.5	31

Source: Reprinted by permission of the publisher, from Harold L. Wolman, *Housing and Housing Policy in the US and UK* (Lexington, Mass.: Lexington Books, D.C. Heath and Company, 1975), Table 1-1

have been used to house poorer blacks and other minorities, but they are nowhere near as large as Britain's public housing programme, a fact reflected by the 1 per cent of public expenditure devoted to housing in the US in 1970, compared with 5.8 per cent in the UK.[37] However, in both countries the strikingly large owner occupied sectors operate within similar markets. Houses are bought and sold through real estate agents, and the provision of mortgage finance is largely via private banking or specialised housing finance institutions. As will later be shown the style and pattern of discrimination in these private sectors is also similar.

The much more extensive and intrusive role played by government in the UK also relates to urban land use policies and political structure. With respect to the former, the British government, while by no means controlling market forces, does have at its disposal comprehensive planning legislation which can be used to direct growth along particular lines. In contrast, American land use policies are very much geared to the needs of the private sector. Local governments have the primary responsibility in this area, but they hardly *plan* land use; instead they serve the particularistic interests of local property markets. American local governments are also administratively and politically near autonomous. Add to this a staggering degree of local government fragmentation (for example, the New York and Chicago conurbations each have more than 1,000 distinct governments) and we have the stereotype of American local government: vast numbers of near autonomous governmental units each pursuing its own distinct policies free of federal and state control. But local autonomy is not absolute. Increasing economic dependence on the federal and state governments has limited local freedom of action, and in some instances has also increased the federal government's ability to influence local policies.

In Britain, the system is different not only in the extent to which government is active, but also in the extent to which central government controls. But the stereotype of British central government dominating pliant local authorities is also partly false — especially in the area of public housing where local authorities have considerable discretion.

Jealously guarded local autonomy in America is closely linked to income and class residential segregation. White middle-class communities resist any attempt by higher authorities to introduce low income housing into their midst, and when, as is often the case, low income housing is a synonym for black housing, the political confrontations can be intense. Indeed, two observers of the American scene have claimed that 'the racial integration of the nation's residential patterns, most particularly through the location of low income housing in suburbia and the deep rooted community conflict it has generated, is the most crucial domestic urban issue facing America in the 1970s'.[38]

As a policy issue, race and housing is politicised in the US in part because of the juxtaposition of starkly contrasting class and race social groups in urban areas, but also because it is not generally accepted that government (and especially the federal government) should play a major role either in providing a social service or in influencing the priorities and directions which individuals and the market set out for society. This contrasts with the British situation, where racial segregation and consciousness of a racial problem are much less intense, and where government's role as provider and social engineer is much more widely, but not universally accepted. Therefore in theory at least, the ability of the state to change existing patterns of behaviour and practice in an area such as race and housing is much greater in Britain than in America.

This said, during the main periods of immigration, British governments did not, either in their public housing policies or their urban policies generally, greatly affect the pattern of racial residential living. At least until 1968 the private property and employment markets determined this. In this respect, the British experience has not been greatly different from the American. Since 1968, however, policies have been adopted on both sides of the Atlantic to change the prevailing pattern. The next four chapters will examine these policies as they have applied to racial discrimination and disadvantage in the private and public housing sectors.

Notes

1. Douglas Ashford, 'Parties and Participation in British Local Government and Some American Parallels', *Urban Affairs Quarterly*, Vol.11, No.1 (Sept. 1975), p.79.
2. Unless otherwise stated, all social statistics on the US are taken from various editions of the annual *Statistical Abstract of the US,* American Almanac Edition (New York: Grosset and Dunlap).
3. Gunnar Myrdal, *An American Dilemma* (New York: Harper and Row, 1944) remains one of the best and most comprehensive accounts of black history, culture and politics.
4. All the social statistics on the British minority population derive from two sources: the 1971 census as interpreted by Gillian Lomas, *The Coloured Population of Great Britain* (London: Runnymede Trust, 1974) and by David Smith, *The Facts of Racial Disadvantage* (London: PEP, 1976), and the PEP surveys, the results of which are analysed in *The Facts of Racial Disadvantage*.
5. Nomenclature is a delicate question in race relations in both countries. 'Coloured' has been widely used as a description of Britain's non-white population. However, 'coloured' has unfortunate colonial connotations, and can be considered pejorative. Throughout this book, Britain's non-whites will be referred to as 'black' or 'minority'. Black is not strictly accurate, in the sense that it is usually applied to people of African origin. However, it is simple, clear and probably the label most acceptable to the minority communities.
6. For a discussion of the 'replacement' status of blacks, see Ceri Peach, 'West Indians as a Replacement Population in England and Wales', *Social and Economic Studies,* Vol.16, No.3 (1967), pp.289-94.
7. John Rex, 'Racialism and the Urban Crisis' in Leo Kuper (ed.), *Race, Science and Society* (London: George Allen and Unwin, 1975), p.270.
8. For explanations of the relationship between race and poverty in the US see John F. Kain (ed.), *Race and Poverty: The Economics of Discrimination* (Englewood Cliffs, N.J.: Prentice Hall, 1969).
9. See S.M. Miller and Pamela A. Roby, *The Future of Inequality* (New York: Basic Books, 1970), Chapter 1 and sources cited.
10. The apparently very good educational qualifications of Asian men has to be balanced by the large number of Asian men with very poor educational qualifications (17 per cent have *no* formal education compared with 3 per cent and 0 per cent for West Indians and whites), and the generally low level of educational attainment among Asian women. See David Smith, op.cit., Table B.22.
11. Although this is a recent (and possibly temporary) phenomenon. In February 1963 the level of unemployment among non-whites was four times that of the general population, David Smith, ibid., p.60.
12. In December 1974, reported in *Newsweek,* 20 January 1975, p.38.
13. Hence, between 1966 and 1971 the percentage of black white-collar workers in firms of 100 employees or more increased from 2.5 to 4.6 per cent. A similar trend occurred in the higher grades of government service, Charles S. Bullock III, 'Expanding Black Economic Rights', in Harrell R. Rodgers, Jr. (ed.), *Racism and Inequality* (San Francisco: Freeman, 1975), Table 4 and Fig.1, pp.93-9.
14. There have been dramatic increases in the number of black office holders in the US in recent years, but most of these have been in lower grade posts, see H.V. Savitch, 'The Politics of Deprivation and Response', in Rodgers, ibid., Table 2, pp.22-3. In Britain, blacks are grossly underrepresénted in official positions, there being *no* black MPs or top civil servants.

15. See Daniel Lawrence, 'Race, Elections and Politics', in Ivor Crewe (ed.), *British Political Sociology Yearbook,* Vol.2. *The Politics of Race* (London: Croom Helm, 1975), pp.55-82, and sources cited: Donley Studlar, 'British Public Opinion, Colour Issues and Enoch Powell: A Longitudinal Analysis', *British Journal of Political Science,* Vol.·4, Part 3 (1974), pp.372-81.

16. In the May 1976 local elections the National Front fielded 176 candidates and 80 of these polled more than 10 per cent of the vote, and in a July 1976 local by-election in Deptford, South London, the two main racist parties, the National Front and the National Party together polled 44 per cent, compared with 43 per cent for the successful Labour candidate, *Sunday Times,* 4 July 1976, p.6.

17. David Butler and Donald Stokes, *Political Change in Britain* (London: Macmillan, 1969), pp.349-54; Donley Studlar, op.cit.

18. See, *Race in the Provincial Press,* Centre for Contemporary Cultural Studies, University of Birmingham, 1976.

19. See in particular, Ira Katznelson's *White Men, Black Cities* (London : Oxford University Press, 1973).

20. Michael Banton, *Race Relations* (New York: Basic Books, 1967), Chapters 7 and 8.

21. See Simon Abbot (ed.), *The Prevention of Racial Discrimination in Britain* (London: Oxford University Press, 1971), pp.97-229. Elizabeth Burney, *Housing on Trial* (London: Oxford University Press, 1967); Nicholas Deakin, *Colour, Citizenship and British Society* (London: Panther, 1970), pp.317-35; Neil McIntosh and David Smith, *The Extent of Racial Discrimination* (London: PEP, 1967); David Smith, *The Facts of Racial Disadvantage,* David Smith and Anne Whalley, *Racial Minorities and Public Housing* (London: PEP, 1975).

22. The documented evidence supporting this is overwhelming, but see in particular, the various publications of the US Commission on Civil Rights, and Louis L. Knowles and Kenneth Prewitt, *Institutional Racism in America* (Englewood Cliffs, N.J.: Prentice Hall, 1967).

23. See John Rex, *Race, Colonialism and the City* (London: Routledge and Kegan Paul, 1974), Part III and sources cited.

24. This method has been used by PEP in the UK. In the US testing is widely used to produce evidence of discrimination in civil rights litigation.

25. See John Rex, op.cit., also Michael Banton, op.cit., Chapters 14 and 15.

26. David Harvey, *Social Justice and the City* (London: Edward Arnold, 1975), p.278.

27. Karl F. Taeuber and Alma F. Taeuber, *Negroes in Cities* (Chicago: Aldine, 1965), pp.28-31.

28. Even in geographically integrated neighbourhoods, social life remains segregated. See Harvey Molotch, 'Integration in a Transition Community', in Scott Greer and Ann Lennarson Greer (eds), *Neighbourhood and Ghetto* (New York: Basic Books, 1974), pp.204-9.

29. ˙Immigrants' refers to those born in India, Pakistan, Bangladesh and 'New Commonwealth' America. Africans are excluded from this table.

30. Ceri Peach, Stuart Winchester and Robert Woods, 'The Distribution of Coloured Immigrants in Britain', in Gary Gappert and Harold M. Rose (eds), *The Social Economy of Cities* (Beverly Hills: Sage, 1975), Table 7, p.409.

31. The literature on this general subject is enormous, but on the specific problem of fiscal disparity and its relationship to race and deprivation, see Kevin R. Cox, *Conflict, Power and Politics in the City: A Geographic View* (New York: McGraw Hill, 1973), and James O'Connor, *The Fiscal Crisis of the State* (New York: St Martin's Press, 1973), Chapter 5.

32. Department of the Environment, *Census Indicators of Urban Deprivation,* Working Note No.6, (London: DOE, 1975).
33. Ibid., Appendix D.
34 *Jones v. Mayer* 392 U.S. 409 (1968).
35. See Anthony Lester and Geoffrey Bindman, *Race and Law* (Harmondsworth, Middx.: Penguin, 1972), Chapter 3.
36. See Duane Lockard, *Toward Equal Opportunity* (New York: Macmillan, 1968) for a good review of state anti-discrimination laws.
37. Harold Wolman, *Housing and Housing Policy in the US and UK* (Lexington, Mass.: Lexington Books, 1975), p.19.
38. Charles M. Haar and Demetrius S. Iatridis, *Housing the Poor in Suburbia* (Cambridge, Mass.: Ballinger, 1974), p.1.

3 CIVIL RIGHTS AND PRIVATE SECTOR HOUSING IN THE US

That residential racial segregation is a major characteristic of American cities has already been established. Studies have also established that only a small part of this segregation can be explained by factors other than racial discrimination. Claims that segregation is essentially class or income based or that it is a result of free choice have been discredited.[1] So, high, middle and low income blacks and other minorities tend to be confined to central city ghetto areas, and many low income whites live in the suburbs. Indeed, analysis of 1970 data on eleven of the largest SMSAs has shown that in six of them more low income whites lived in the suburbs than lived in the central city, and in all eleven SMSAs the percentage of *high* income blacks living in the suburbs was lower than the percentage of *low* income whites living in suburban rings.[2]

Neither is this pattern a result of minority groups exercising a free choice. While acknowledging the problems involved in interpreting survey data, it is possible to build up a general picture at least of black preferences. Table 3.1 shows how blacks increasingly prefer integrated

Table 3.1: Black Attitudes towards Residential Integration, 1963-1969

Q. In living in a neighbourhood, if you could find the housing you want and like, would you rather live in a neighbourhood with Negro families, or in a neighbourhood that had both whites and Negroes?

Total Sample	1963 %	1966 %	1969 %
Negroes	20	17	16
Whites and Negroes	64	68	74
Not Sure	16	15	10

Source: *Newsweek* Polls of 1963, 1966 and 1969, cited in Peter Goldman, *Report From Black America* (New York: Clarion Books, 1971), p.269

neighbourhoods to the ghetto. Further surveys have shown that middle and high income blacks (who constitute about 35 per cent of the total) are more desirous of integration than are low income blacks.[3] However, the picture is more complex than these findings imply. Aberbach and Walker's Detroit surveys demonstrate that more blacks are interested in more and better housing where they already live than in integrated housing.[4] Given that the former alternative is rarely available, it is logical for blacks to claim in other contexts that they favour integration. It would seem, therefore, that blacks are primarily interested in better housing and see integration as a means to better housing.

Ghetto housing is inferior to non-ghetto housing not only in terms of quality, but also in terms of housing or neighbourhood environment. The disadvantage suffered by blacks of all social classes is, therefore, considerable. To understand why this is so it is necessary to discuss the nature of the American housing market and the role played by racial discrimination in that market.

Racial Segregation and the American Housing Market

The most influential 'model' of the US housing market is based on the 'filtering' concept. Filtering assumes that as housing units are vacated by upwardly mobile families, so their houses lose status, decline in value and filter down to lower income families. Constant building at the upper end of the housing market gradually increases the housing stock, and via the filtering process the housing of all social classes improves.[5] Filtering assumes a free and open housing market and steadily increasing incomes, and a superficial look at many American metropolitan areas provides some evidence that filtering does work to some extent. Families do gradually improve their housing conditions as their incomes rise, and neighbourhoods rise and decline in status as they are occupied and then vacated by different social groups. Filtering also assumes the constant *growth* of metropolitan areas, and puts great premium on new building. Perhaps for this reason it is strongly supported by real estate interests. Until recently the federal government also supported the filtering reasoning, for via federal tax laws the subsidies going to middle and high income owner occupiers have encouraged the growth of the high income housing sector.[6] Filtering also dispenses with the need for any public sector subsidised low income housing — a fact which no doubt has helped its popularity among the real estate industry and among conservative politicians.

In spite of the fact that studies have shown that in some circumstances filtering can improve housing opportunities for lower income families,[7] it clearly does not work in any total sense. This is because the housing market is often highly imperfect, and strictly non-economic factors often intervene to upset the filtering process. It is also because the incomes of all social classes do not constantly rise, and as important, property values do not always decline in value as they age and pass from higher to lower income families. As a result, low income families often cannot benefit from filtering unless they receive a housing subsidy. However, as Chapter 5 will show, until very recently housing subsidies have been few and far between in the US, so the housing opportunities of the lowest income groups have remained very limited. This is confirmed by evidence provided by the Douglas Commission on Urban Problems which showed that 'lower economic status groups' had not benefited from the general improvement in the US housing stock experienced during the 1950-70 period.[8] In fact, the housing status of the poorest one fifth of the population declined in relation to the top four-fifths during the period.[9] As blacks are much over-represented among the poor (they constitute 30 per cent of the 'officially' poor population, but only 11 per cent of the total population), they have suffered especially in terms of housing opportunity. But independently of economic forces, racial factors operate in a variety of ways which make nonsense of the free market in housing which filtering assumes.

Racial discrimination against middle and high income blacks prevents their gaining access to housing within their 'housing class' in the outer zones of conurbations. Instead they have to make do with units vacated by white families at the periphery of the ghetto and with housing situated in the middle-class areas of the ghetto. It is not uncommon, therefore, for the black families moving into ghetto-periphery property to be of higher income and occupational status than the white families moving out.[10] It is true, however, that some filtering occurs *within* the ghetto, with younger upwardly mobile black families moving from inner city apartments to single unit owner occupied housing within the more middle-class ghetto neighbourhoods. While such families may 'percolate' up within the ghetto, lower income black families have much less chance of occupying the units vacated by the middle class, because they cannot afford them. Low income white families also face this dilemma, but because they are participants in a much larger (white) housing market which even has some suburban low income housing opportunities, they have more choice and are less disadvantaged than poor blacks.

Low income blacks suffer from serious housing shortage, therefore, but often in the context of urban areas which, in terms of the number of units available in relation to the number of families in need of housing, display a housing surplus. Mismatch between demand and supply accounts for this apparent anomaly.

A surplus of inappropriately priced property partly explains the
abandonment phenomenon which plagues many American cities.
Faced with a low demand for their property, or with the wrong sort
of demand (low income families living in overcrowded conditions),
and unable to find finance to improve properties, many owners
abandon apartment buildings when the maintenance costs exceed
rental income. Forman points out that tax arrangements further
aggravate the position by encouraging owners to claim tax
depreciation allowances on their property during the first few years of
ownership and thus encouraging them to dispose of it as quickly as
possible.[11] In 1973 100,000 units were abandoned in the New York
metropolitan area, and an estimated 300,000 further units were
'approaching' abandonment.[12] Abandonment brings decay, blight and
high fire risks, as well as reducing the total housing stock in ghetto
areas. However, the rate of abandonment together with the extent of
low income housing shortage depends to a great extent on the social
economies of particular cities. Cities with a good employment base and
hence higher incomes are likely to be less affected by abandonment
than cities where employment is contracting and incomes falling.
Indeed, Nourse and Phares have shown that changing income levels are
the most important variables in the whole cycle of abandonment and
decay which affects many cities. As falling incomes spread in particular
localities so they produce 'waves' of decay, blight and abandonment
behind them. Race and age of city were found not to be as important
in explaining decay as falling incomes, but given the high incidence of
poverty among blacks, low income, high black residential density and
decay usually went together.[13]

Low income blacks suffer, therefore, both because they are poor
and black, and middle and high income blacks suffer serious racial
disadvantage in housing because their housing choices are severely
restricted by racial discrimination. Kain and Quigley in the most
sophisticated study of the effects of discrimination on the housing
market to date, found that in St Louis black renters paid 12-18 per
cent more for housing than did whites for comparable units, and black
owner occupiers paid 5-6 per cent more.[14] In addition, the much
smaller, tighter housing market within which blacks are confined means
that, when controlling for income, they have a much smaller chance
of becoming owner occupiers than have whites. In St Louis, Kain and
Quigley found just 32 per cent of blacks were home owners, when, had
these same people been exposed to the white housing market, this
figure would have been 41 per cent. Even bigger differentials were

found in some metropolitan areas.[15] Given the enormous subsidy
enjoyed by owner occupiers via federal income tax laws, and the
capital accumulation advantages of owner occupation, these differentials
add up to significant costs which have to be borne by black householders.
Kain and Quigley summarised their findings thus:

> Taken as a whole, the empirical findings presented in previous
> chapters on the differences in housing expenditures and type of
> housing consumption between comparable black and white
> households appear to be most consistent with the hypothesis that
> housing market discrimination seriously limits the residential
> location choices of black households and effectively restricts the
> supply of housing – particularly certain housing attributes or
> bundles – available to them. Our analysis indicates that these supply
> restrictions are reflected in the unavailability of units suitable for
> owner occupancy, in the dearth of high-quality dwelling units, and
> in the discriminatory mark-ups for both owner and renter
> occupied units in the ghetto.[16]

Discrimination affecting price and choice in housing is only one
dimension of the disadvantage suffered by blacks and other minorities.
Another relates to the way in which employment, educational and life
chances are affected by confinement to the ghetto. These are much less
easy to measure but that black areas have inferior schools, poor
employment opportunities and are unsafe is undisputed. It is also the
case that within the ghetto, the lower income neighbourhoods have
the least attractive environments in terms of all these factors.

The Nature of Discrimination

The process whereby neighbourhoods change from all white to all
black occupancy is a complex one, and can vary in detail quite
significantly from city to city, neighbourhood to neighbourhood and
even block to block. Urban sociologists have devoted much effort to
analysing the 'zone of transition' which appears during this process.[17]
However, in spite of variations between areas and disagreement over the
precise nature of transition, certain basic facts are clear. One is the
totality of change which normally occurs once a neighbourhood
reaches a certain percentage black occupancy. Once this 'tipping point'
(usually around 30 per cent), is reached, the transition to near total
black residency is swift.[18] Duncan and Duncan's 1957 study of racial
succession in Chicago summarised this process as:

1. *Penetration:* the stage of initial entry of negroes into an area occupied by whites.
2. *Invasion:* the movement in these areas of substantial numbers of negroes.
3. *Consolidation:* the continued increase in number and proportion of negroes until areas consist almost entirely of negro occupancy.
4. *Piling Up:* the continued increase in the negro population of these areas.[19]

This does not *always* happen when blacks move into a neighbourhood, but it is the usual pattern. Some doubt exists, however, as to whether Duncan and Duncan's fourth stage of development, 'piling up', now occurs with great frequency. Recent evidence suggests that the black central city population is stabilising and that ghetto expansion is spatial in nature rather than related to increasing population density. In particular, better off blacks moving between ghetto areas and into transitional neighbourhoods are a major source of spatial growth. No doubt this trend relates to the termination of black migration from the rural South, and to the higher incomes now being enjoyed by some sections of the black community.[20]

Some doubt also exists about the exact nature of white movement out. In some cases it seems to be related to the upward mobility of white communities. It is, in other words, part of a filtering process with families moving, not necessarily because blacks are moving in, but because the neighbourhood no longer supports the employment opportunities or provides the status expected of mobile young white families.[21] In other instances, whites move because they fear that once blacks have moved in, the neighbourhood's services and facilities — especially schools — will deteriorate.[22]

While accepting that the growth of the ghetto is a complex phenomenon which is not fully understood, we do know that racial discrimination plays a major role in the process. After all, a dual property market based on race exists and this results almost entirely from discrimination. Let us examine how discrimination operates both to extend and perpetuate the ghetto.

(a) *The Real Estate Industry*

With the exception of the tiny public housing sector, almost all owner occupied property transactions in the US and many rental sector transactions are handled by real estate brokers. These operate in much the same way as British estate agents: they are market intermediaries whose prime function is to provide the buyers and sellers of property with market information so as to expedite transactions. In this role the real estate industry has been instrumental in establishing and maintaining the dual property market. Rose Helper, in her study of the racial policies and practices of real estate brokers, interviewed a sample of Chicago area real estate brokers and discovered that it is the norm for real estate brokers deliberately to exclude blacks from white areas.[23] Their motives in doing so were mixed, but Helper concludes:

> The main cog in the exclusion practice of the respondents seems to be their ideology, centred on the belief that unrestricted selling or renting is *unethical*. Such selling or renting constitutes an unethical act because, according to their way of thinking, it runs counter to white people's wishes, hurts them financially and socially, and creates a dangerous situation for the family, especially the children.[24]

Whether whites are in fact opposed to integration is open to some doubt. As Table 3.2 shows, only 44 per cent of a 1970 national sample of whites expressed any opposition to a black neighbour. Note, however, that the question refers to a single family and one of similar socio-economic status to the respondent. Whites are probably much more wary of lower income families moving into their neighbourhoods, and given Nourse and Phares finding that it is the reduction of income

Table 3.2: White Attitudes towards Interracial Housing Contact, 1970

Q. If a Negro family with about the same income and education as you moved next door to you would you mind it a lot, a little, or not at all?

Mind a lot	Mind a little	Mind not at all	Already Negro Family Next door	Don't Know	Total
19%	25	49	4	3	100%

Source: Angus Campbell, *White Attitudes Toward Black People* (Ann Arbor, Michigan: ISR, University of Michigan, 1971), Table 1-1

levels in a particular area which is most responsible for the spread of decay and blight, these sentiments seem rational. Nourse and Phares also found that the spread of low income families could affect property values,[25] and it is on this subject that the real estate industry has been

most vocal. Indeed, it is the assumption that the introduction of
blacks into a white neighbourhood lowers property values that is at
the heart of the real estate industry's widely held view that whites are
opposed to integration. A substantial literature exists on the
relationship between property values and race and most scholars agree
that rather than prices falling on the entry of non-whites into a
neighbourhood, they tend to remain stable or even rise.[26] There is
evidence that some whites, panicked by the thought of black
neighbours, sell their homes cheaply, but these same houses soon
regain their value — whether the neighbourhood in question ultimately
remains white or becomes absorbed into the ghetto.[27] It may be, of
course, that whites fear blacks moving into their neighbourhoods
because they think of blacks as synonymous with low income status
people who are likely to downgrade neighbourhoods. As has been
suggested however, at least as far as owner occupied housing is
concerned, this is rarely the case; the expanding periphery of the
ghetto is usually occupied by middle income blacks.

The myth that declining property values are induced by racial
factors is strongly encouraged by the real estate industry. With the
market divided along racial lines agents have a strong financial stake
in maintaining the myth, for the more controlled the market the
greater is their chance of making excess or monopoly profits. More
accurately, each broker is in an oligopoly position. He controls his
geographical segment of the market and via exclusion agrees not to
trespass on adjacent brokers' territories. The dual market allows the
broker to subdivide the market further and to channel customers into
either a white area or a black area. This reduces consumer choice and
gives the broker, the supplier, greater control over demand.

It is difficult to find examples of brokers admitting that the
maintenance of the dual market is solely a device to serve their self
interests. Instead, as the quote from Helper indicates, segregation is
defended in terms of the broker serving the public interest, or at least
the interests of the 65.4 per cent of white household heads who in 1970
owned or were buying their own homes.[28] Appeals to public rather
than to special interests are common among professional and
quasi-professional groups who often claim that they are providing a
service to the community as a whole. An additional feature of
professional groups is the strength of their professional associations.
Olson has demonstrated that this strength is based on the selective
benefits which associations distribute to their relatively small number
of members.[29] As a result of such benefits, the National Association of

Real Estate Boards (NAREB) with 85,000 members organised in 1,500 local boards, has a tenacious grip on the real estate industry. NAREB accords status to what is not a particularly prestigious profession by allowing members to be referred to as 'Realtors'.[30] More important, NAREB controls some real estate services vital to the operations of individual members. As John Denton notes:

> NAREB influence is paramount in the real estate market. It has outright control of organisations dominating most of the real estate specialities such as appraising, management, consulting, industrial real estate etc. and it has close working relations with all the other large membership associations covering other real estate specialities.[31]

NAREB has also been influential in maintaining segregation. In 1924 Article 34 of NAREB's professional Code of Ethics instructed members: 'A Realtor should never be instrumental in introducing into a neighbourhood a character of property or occupancy, members of a race or nationality, or any individuals whose presence will clearly be detrimental to property values in that neighbourhood.'[32] When, in 1948, the Supreme Court struck down the practice of making racially restrictive covenants judicially enforceable, NAREB revised Article 34 (now Article 5) to read: 'A Realtor should not be instrumental in introducing into a neighbourhood a character of property or use which clearly will be detrimental to property values in that neighbourhood.'[33] This is a clear invitation to discriminate, as most brokers believe that the meaning of the Article remains unchanged, and most believe that the introduction of non-whites into a neighbourhood lowers property values.[34] As NAREB members handle 90 per cent of all real estate transactions in the US,[35] what Helper calls the real estate ideology — a segregationist free enterprise philosophy — is pervasive. On the legislative front NAREB has lobbied against all bills supporting federal control of the property market. In particular, public housing and open housing legislation have been strongly opposed by NAREB. Some evidence exists to suggest that NAREB was important in defeating the 1966 federal open housing bill.[36]

Real estate agents indulge in a multitude of practices to exclude blacks and other minorities from white areas. Those operating in the suburbs make sure that blacks are steered to areas of minority concentration — to ghetto or near ghetto areas and those suburbs which already have a high percentage of blacks. These have emerged for a variety of reasons and some have existed for many decades,[37] but there has been an increasing tendency for the suburban black population to be concentrated in these areas. Harold X. Connolly has noted, following study of the 1970 census data, that 'while this suburban black population growth [of the 1960s] succeeded in dispersing Negroes more widely throughout their SMSAs, it did not herald a decrease in racial separation'.[38]

The real estate industry's discriminatory techniques have been well documented.[39] Before the civil rights laws of the 1960s, blacks were simply refused service, or told no homes were available. More recently, more subtle devices have been employed. Applicants for housing are referred to the least desirable plot of an estate, or their applications are delayed or given low priority. In the main, discrimination of this sort involves owner occupied housing which is the main constituent of the suburban housing stock. Owner occupied housing also dominates in the changing or transitional neighbourhoods, but here real estate tactics are quite different.

As the ghetto is steadily moving outwards in most cities, areas adjacent to black neighbourhoods are constantly under threat of 'ghettoisation'. Real estate agents, exploiting both the high demand for housing in the black communities and the white population's fear of blacks, have systematically encouraged blacks to move to the transitional neighbourhoods, while encouraging whites to move to the suburbs. The initial introduction of a black family into a neighbourhood on the ghetto periphery has acquired the unattractive but apt label of 'blockbusting' — the practice of breaking the racial homogeneity of a residential block. Agents have directly caused this phenomenon by panicking nearby whites into selling their homes 'while they can'. White home owners, fearing the encroachment of the ghetto into their communities, have quickly sold their homes at below market rates to agents who have sold the same homes to blacks, reaping considerable profits in the process. 'Panic peddling' of this sort has been very effective. Robert Forman notes:

The basic message of the blockbuster is quite simple: the neighbourhood is becoming Negro, the homeowner should sell his house as soon as he can, and the longer he waits the worse off he will be. In actual practice it is not likely to be phrased this directly. A homeowner in New York City commented: 'In most cases more was hinted than actually spoken. But every word, every gesture, was designed to make us feel we were idiots if we didn't sell immediately.' There need not even be any reference to race but only to 'something

like this happening in the neighbourhood', 'what is happening in
the neighbourhood', or that the 'neighbourhood is changing',
phrases reported to have been used in respectively San Francisco,
Chicago, and the New York area.[40]

NAREB officially brands blockbusting unethical, and it is probably
the case that many of the most active panic pedlars are not NAREB
members.[41] None the less, NAREB directly encourages blockbusting
by restricting blacks' housing choice in white suburban and outer
central city areas. The expanding black population must move
somewhere and if it cannot move to the newer white areas, it must
expand at the ghetto periphery.

Other links between discrimination in the outer areas and
blockbusting in transitional areas exist. For instance, NAREB has
consistently prevented black brokers from joining NAREB and its
local boards.[42] The boards are vitally important to individual realtors
because generally it is the boards which operate multiple listing
services — lists of residential properties shared on a cooperative basis
between board members. Sharing of market information and the
subsequent division of the market between producers is a major
feature of oligopolistic enterprise, and as far as realtors are concerned,
such division is strictly confined to white brokers. To admit black
brokers would be to open the white market to blacks and therefore
reduce the monopoly element in the industry. For the black broker,
exclusion from the board and from the listing services severely
restricts his operations. Without full market information, the black
broker is largely unaware of what is going on in the 'white' market,
and when black customers ask him for houses in white areas he is
usually unable to help. Instead, the black broker plays a marginal
role in the property market; he is mainly confined to negotiating
property transactions within the ghetto. (Ironically, black brokers are
also organised in an association with the initials NAREB, which stands
for the National Association of Real Estate Brokers.)

White NAREB members sometimes operate both in suburban and
in ghetto and transitional areas, and are, therefore, able to practise the
full range of discriminatory tactics. For those brokers (both black and
white) working *exclusively* within the ghetto the question of
discrimination does not directly arise, for they are unable to offer
their exclusively non-white customers anything but ghetto properties.
Of course, not all white brokers discriminate in the ways described
above. Some local variations exist, both between and within cities, and

it is possible to find brokers who subscribe to an 'integrationist' philosophy. However, these are rare, and tend to operate in areas where, largely because minorities are few in number, a dual market has not developed.[43]

In some of the larger cities yet another real estate residential sector exists — the downtown high and upper middle income apartment market. Generally, segregation is the norm in this sector, but in some developments a degree of stable integration has been achieved. With residents having less permanent investment in the surrounding community, downtown apartment dwelling is often less racially restrictive than owner occupied housing. Also, high rents provide an economic barrier across which only a few non-whites can travel. Even in this market, however, racial restriction exists, for in order to prevent a project from achieving more than a certain proportion of even affluent blacks, realtors and developers sometimes apply racial quotas to their buildings. Clearly quotas discriminate, but whether or not they are illegal and against the interests of the minority groups is a delicate question, and one we will return to later.

(b) *The Mortgage Credit Industry*

In the past, corporate lending agencies have been as permeated with a segregationist ideology as have real estate brokers. Like brokers, lenders have an interest in defending property values and in maintaining the 'character' of particular neighbourhoods.[44] However, the fact that 42 per cent of all black household heads are owner occupiers[45] does demonstrate that while it may be more difficult for blacks to obtain mortgages, a large proportion none the less succeed. The rub comes when the location of the mortgaged property is examined. As Forman notes, 'the greater importance of lending agency policies and practices undoubtedly lies in their influence on *where* blacks can buy property rather than in their ability to keep them from buying property at all'.[46] With very few exceptions, mortgagors have granted credit to blacks only if the property concerned has been in a ghetto or transitional area. Eunice and George Greer note:

> In recent testimony before the Commissioners of the District of Columbia, the President of the Mortgage Bankers' Association of Metropolitan Washington stated bluntly that 'applications from minority groups are not generally considered in areas that are not recognised as being racially mixed'. A study of the Chicago Commission on Human Relations found that such a policy was

pursued by almost all lending sources in the City. Voluminous evidence from both social research surveys and testimony before legislative and executive bodies indicates that the same is true of most real estate boards in cities throughout the country.[47]

Racial discrimination is reinforced by economic discrimination, for properties in central city areas are less attractive credit risks for most mortgagors. Properties are older, property taxes and maintenance costs are higher and the general physical surroundings are inferior to those in the suburbs. Anyone buying in the central areas, therefore, is likely to be offered less favourable terms than the buyer of a new property in the suburbs. Indeed, within the ghetto, properties in more decayed or blighted areas may not be mortgageable at all. These 'redlined' areas — areas within which any finance is refused by a lending agency — further restrict the housing choices of blacks, and partly account for the very low rate of owner occupation among blacks in some cities. For example, in Chicago, a notoriously redlined city, only 18 per cent of blacks own their own homes.[48]

A final cautionary note should be added to this brief analysis of the racial practices of the real estate and mortgage lending industries. It is often assumed that racial discrimination has been the prime mover in developing and accelerating the economic and social decline of the American inner city. However, it is not at all obvious that this is so. As was emphasised in Chapter 2, the decline of inner cities relates in the main to more fundamental social and economic factors, in particular to cities' employment bases and income producing potential. This applies irrespective of race, as such cities as Glasgow and Pittsburgh demonstrate. It may be that the movement into cities of large numbers of poor blacks accelerates this movement, especially if it also induces 'flight' by economically productive whites. But we do not know to what extent this occurs, and it should also be remembered that racial discrimination confines *middle-class* blacks to the central cities. Other things being equal, these people would long ago have moved to the suburbs. It may be then, that as far as some neighbourhoods are concerned, discrimination has *prevented* rather than encouraged decline. We will return to this question, and the problems it raises for public policy later, but first we must consider what role governments have played in the growth and maintenance of the ghetto.

(c) *Local Governments*

The autonomy of small local communities, both urban and rural, is jealously guarded in the US. Frequently this means protecting the social and economic integrity of a community through the exercise of local democratic rights. Zoning ordinances, the most important of these, carefully define land use in particular localities. This can mean separating industrial or commercial development from residential development, but it can also mean defending the economic exclusivity of residential neighbourhoods. So, by defining minimum plot sizes for owner occupied housing, zoning laws can assure that a neighbourhood establishes a single class, homogeneous character. Multi-unit developments can be restricted to certain areas, assuring that apartment blocks do not intrude into owner occupied single family developments. There is no doubt that, used in this way, zoning laws may serve to improve some neighbourhoods, but they are also discriminatory in nature. In particular, low income groups, especially those confined to multi-unit developments, are excluded from the more attractive neighbourhoods.

In the more populist states, referenda have been employed to the same effect, and almost everywhere local executive power is used to 'defend' the community from low income development.[49] All these mechanisms are employed to resist low income housing developments; there is very little that local governments can do to prevent individual middle income black families from moving into a community.

Community response to incoming individual black families may manifest itself in other ways, however. Violence and intimidation directed against 'intruding' blacks is not uncommon in some areas. This is particularly so in white blue-collar suburbs and neighbourhoods adjacent to the ghetto. Typical of these are Warren, Michigan and Cicero, Illinois where white antagonism is based on a fear that carefully constructed ethnic communities will be destroyed by the encroaching ghettoes of Detroit and Chicago. The defensive techniques employed by individuals in these communities appear effective as is evidenced by the sudden and total termination of the ghetto in adjacent neighbourhoods. Why such communities as Cicero and Warren have successfully resisted the ghetto while other communities have failed is, however, a difficult question to answer. It may be related to the strength of ethnic ties and more generally to the social economies of particular areas. It may be, for example, that many of the areas which have resisted 'ghettoisation' have had stable employment bases, thus giving white populations good reason to stay.

(d) *The Federal Government*

As Chapter 5 will show in some detail, until the late 1960s the federal government played a passive role in relation to the private property market. The primary federal involvement was via the Federal Housing Administration (FHA) insurance guarantee programme which was designed to help middle income families obtain mortgages. Between 1935 and 1969 some 19 per cent of all owner occupied housing was financed with FHA help,[50] and further federal mortgage finance has been provided by a similar programme operated by the Veteran's Administration. Segregation was as acute in this housing as in other parts of the private sector. Indeed the FHA 'redlined' inner city areas in much the same fashion as did all market institutions. Other federal programmes such as Urban Renewal also operated to encourage the growth of racial separation. Since its inception in 1949 Urban Renewal has consistently resulted in the replacement of low income (and sometimes slum) housing by high income housing and commercial office block development.[51] Probably no racial motivation was present in this process, but the effects of the policy were to reduce the housing opportunities of the poor — who were often black. Local authorities receiving urban renewal money were not compelled to replace housing destroyed by renewal, so in cities with large black populations renewal reduced the supply of low income housing and aggravated the outward pressure at the ghetto periphery.

Even though some of these programmes have affected the private sector, they are more appropriately dealt with in the chapter on the public sector, largely because controversy has centred not on relations between public and private interests, but between different levels of government.

Private Sector Housing and Civil Rights 1945-68

The first official government measures against housing discrimination came not from federal but from state sources. In 1945 the New York state legislature outlawed racial discrimination in employment and established a State Commission Against Discrimination.[52] Ten years after this date, in 1955, housing discrimination was also outlawed by the state, and by 1958 thirteen states had established commissions to aid the enforcement of state open housing and other civil rights laws.[53] Most of the commissions relied on individual complaint procedures to enforce the law and the resolution of complaints was usually confined to 'conference, conciliation and persuasion' rather than recourse to legal sanctions. By 1972, thirty states had passed open housing laws and some 349 localities had adopted fair housing ordinances.[54] These laws vary in coverage and enforcement provisions but the processing of individual complaints remains the main approach of state and local civil rights agencies.

Having studied state and local civil rights commissions individually and collectively, scholars generally agree that they are only of limited value in combating discrimination. They have limited jurisdictions, are poorly financed and manned and generally have been confined to providing redress for those who have experienced individual acts of overt discrimination. Some agencies, notably those in New York State and Massachusetts, have stronger enforcement powers and have been relatively successful in combating some types of discrimination — mainly discrimination in the renting of apartments.[55]

The first federal attempt to combat housing discrimination was made in 1962 when President Kennedy signed an executive order banning discrimination in some federal programmes, and this prohibition was further extended by Title 6 of the 1964 Civil Rights Act. Discrimination in private housing, however, went untouched, and by 1966 it was the only area of social interaction not subject to broad federal civil rights protection. Why housing should have been the last area of discrimination subject to control could be related to the fact that it is more intrusive into individuals' lives than place of employment, education or public accommodation. Paul Sheatsley has produced a Guttman scale of Pro-integration Sentiments from an NORC survey conducted in December 1963. He found that only 44 per cent of white respondents gave pro-integration responses to a question on the right of whites to keep blacks out of their neighbourhoods, whereas 82 per cent, 77 per cent and 63 per cent of respondents gave pro-integration responses to (respectively) questions on integration in employment, public accommodations and education.[56]

Given these sentiments, a federal open housing bill was potentially more radical than other civil rights measures. The 88th Congress was preoccupied in 1964 with the omnibus 1964 Civil Rights Act, and the following year the 89th Congress concentrated on enacting the Voting Rights Act. The next logical step was to enact an open housing law, and on 12 January 1966 President Johnson promised such a law in his State of the Union Message. However, the Civil Rights Bill of that year which contained open housing measures was to come to grief in the Senate. In fact, Congress never warmed to open housing in the way it had to voting rights or equal educational opportunity. *Congressional Quarterly* has noted that Congressional voting on open housing in a 1965 amendment and in the 1966 legislation 'showed a decided cautiousness on the part of Congress in moving towards a policy of non-discrimination in housing'.[57]

Perhaps this was because open housing might have offended constituents (Northern as well as Southern) much more than had other civil rights measures. It may also have been because lobbying against the 1966 Bill came not only from sectional and ideological groups, but also from vested economic interests. In particular, NAREB mobilised all its resources against the measure, and some commentators have concluded that this lobbying effort was significant in defeating the Bill.[58] In addition, Senate Minority Leader Everett Dirksen (Democrat, Illinois) failed to muster the Republican forces behind the Northern Democrats — an exercise which was a necessary and oft-repeated strategy in the enacting of social reform legislation in the 89th Congress. The Bill itself prohibited all discrimination in housing and proposed establishing a Fair Housing Board, which, following investigation of complaints by HUD, would issue court enforced orders providing complainants with relief.[59]

Quite apart from Congressional attitudes and NAREB's lobbying activities, from about 1966 on, public opinion supporting the extension of civil rights to non-whites apparently began to wane. In 1966, a Louis Harris Poll showed that 75 per cent of whites thought that blacks were moving too fast. The corresponding figure for 1964 was 50 per cent.[60] The obvious inference here is that urban riots, beginning with Watts in 1965, accounted for this change. However, Angus Campbell notes that a majority (about 65 per cent) of whites thought blacks were pushing too fast *throughout the period,* and concludes: 'These attitudes did not develop during the 1964-68 period, they were present in 1964 and changed rather little during the years of urban violence.'[61]

Whatever the case, it would appear that after 1966 the ingredients necessary for the passage of an open housing bill were more difficult to bring together than before. Executive leadership, so necessary for the enactment of the 1964 and 1965 legislation, was being diverted from domestic policy and directed towards Vietnam. Congress was increasingly hostile to the President and to civil rights, and probably public opinion was too. Moreover, the civil rights movement had lost impetus by 1966, and although black leaders and groups lobbied hard for an open housing law, their efforts lacked the vigour of earlier periods. In this context, passage of the 1968 Civil Rights Act was in some respects surprising.

The 1968 Act derived from measures originally introduced into Congress in 1967, which provided for wide coverage but not for a separate Fair Housing Board to enforce the law. Instead, HUD alone was given this responsibility. However, acting on various civil rights measures separately, the House shelved the open housing provisions but passed one measure designed to provide civil rights workers with federal protection. When introduced into the Senate in February 1968, an open housing amendment, sponsored by Edward Brooke (Republican, Mass.) and Walter F. Mondale (Democrat, Minn.), was attached to the House passed measure (HR 2516). Following a narrowly defeated attempt to invoke cloture on debate, Senate Minority Leader Dirksen agreed to compromise and sponsor the passage of the Bill. Compromise weakened the Bill by exempting from coverage single family homes sold by their owners without the aid of a real estate broker, and by weakening HUD's enforcement powers. Finally, after cloture was invoked and major anti-riot amendments, sponsored by Strom Thurmond (Republican, S. Carolina) were added to the Bill, it was passed 71-20 on 11 March 1968. Given Dirksen's stand on open housing in 1966, his decision to support it in 1968 was surprising. It may be that his ability to mobilise the Republicans in the Senate and use this as a bargaining counter with Johnson when legislating on Administration bills had weakened by 1968.

Even more surprising was the House acceptance of the Senate version with a vote of 250-172 on 10 April 1968. Commentators at the time were convinced that the House would reject the bill.[62] The House was much more conservative than in 1968, in 1966 the Democrats had lost 47 seats, and many of these had been held by liberal Northerners. NAREB's lobbying efforts continued unabated, and Johnson preoccupied by Vietnam, was not providing the executive leadership characteristic of his 1964-6 period. However, just before the House voted on whether to send the Senate version to conference (to have done so would have weakened further or even have killed the bill) Martin Luther King was assassinated. The ensuing riots were widespread extending into Washington D.C. itself and may have been instrumental in persuading the House not to send the bill to conference (by a vote of 229 to 195) but instead to enact the legislation.

Title 8 of the Act declared that 'It is the policy of the United States to provide, within constitutional limitations, for fair housing throughout the United States.' Coverage extended to all property except: a) those multiple rental units which were owner occupied and the number of units to rent did not exceed more than four units; b) owner occupied housing which was sold privately without the aid of a real estate agent or broker (Section 803). The former exemption was to protect the so-called 'Mrs Murphy' — the elderly widow living on social security who rented out a few rooms in her own home, and the latter exemption allowed an owner occupier to sell privately to a friend or neighbour of the same race. With these two exemptions, the Act covered about 80 per cent of the US housing stock.

Responsibility for administering the law was assigned to HUD and much of the text of Title 8 was devoted to how HUD should run an administrative complaint procedure. But HUD was given very weak enforcement powers, being required to rely on 'conference, conciliation and persuasion' to reconcile discriminator and complainant. In this respect, Title 8 was weaker than some state and local laws, many of which had injunctive powers.

In addition, Title 8 provided for judicial enforcement by private persons who could file cases in district courts, and where a 'pattern of practice' of discrimination existed the Attorney General could file suits. In both instances, the courts could issue temporary injunctions and restraining orders to freeze the sale or rental of property during litigation. In the case of private judicial action, unspecified amounts of actual damages plus up to $1,000 in punitive damages plus costs could be awarded to plaintiffs.

In all three areas of enforcement — HUD's administrative complaint procedure, private litigation and enforcement by the Attorney General — the focus was on providing remedies in individual instances of discrimination. Most of Title 8, therefore, avoided the dilemma of defining what federal policy should be towards the integration or segregation of federal facilities and housing programmes, although, as will be shown later, it did make some very general references to the public sector.

Parallel with legislative action came judicial activity. Between the 1948 *Shelly v. Kramer*[63] decision (in which the Supreme Court overturned its 1917 *Buchanan v. Warley*[64] decision making racially restrictive covenants and ordinances judicially enforceable) and 1968, the Court passed down no significant decision in the open housing area. However, in June 1968, just two months after the passage of Title 8, in the *Jones v. Meyer* decision, the Court resurrected the 1866 Civil Rights Act which by declaring that 'all citizens of the United States shall have the same right, in every State and Territory, as is enjoyed by white citizens thereof to inherit, purchase, lease, sell, hold, and convey real and personal property' [65] extended open housing coverage to all housing. *Jones v. Meyer* was important in reinforcing the main message of Title 8 – that the federal government had responsibility for extending equal housing opportunities to all citizens. However, because it contained no specific enforcement provisions, the 1866 Act played mainly a supportive rather than a directing role in the various open housing programmes that were to follow.

Private Sector Housing and Civil Rights Since 1969

The substantive sections of the 1968 Act providing for administrative and judicial redress have been used almost exclusively to combat discrimination in the private sector. Analysis of private sector housing can, therefore, concentrate on the ways in which HUD's complaint procedure and judicial action have affected market behaviour. Official procedures have been used to a much lesser extent to counter discrimination in publicly subsidised housing, largely because such discrimination is built into programmes, or is a function of the values and actions of disparate governmental units. The procedures set up by the 1968 Act were not designed to deal with this type of discrimination, but to combat individual instances of discrimination as practised by . discrete actors in the open property market. Hence, the activities of real estate agents, apartment owners and managers and individual private citizens have been the main targets of federal legislation. What has been the experience of the official procedures?

(a) *HUD's Complaint Procedure*

During its first few years of operation, HUD's complaint procedure was, to say the least, the subject of some criticism, even of scorn. The reasons for this are not hard to identify, and are primarily related to the weak enforcement powers provided by the 1968 Act.[66] HUD cannot initiate investigation and it has no injunctive powers to order the release of a particular property or to impose financial penalties on discriminators. Instead, once an investigation has been received and deemed to fall within the Act, HUD investigates and then via 'conference, conciliation and persuasion' attempts to reconcile the differences of the disputing parties. Should conciliation break down, HUD can threaten judicial action. HUD can also subpoena witnesses and evidence, but respondents (those accused of discrimination) are under no compulsion to agree to conciliation. Therefore, only if the evidence against them is overwhelming and would stand up in court is a respondent likely to agree to conciliation. A successfully conciliated case might result in the respondent agreeing to release an apartment, or to provide some cash compensation.

These powers are weak, both because of the near total absence of compulsion involved, and because in eleven states and in several cities the law *does* provide injunctive powers to civil rights commissions along with a requirement that the case be resolved at public hearings.

An obvious requirement of any civil rights agency which depends on receiving complaints is that it publicise its procedures and is able to cope with the flow of incoming complaints. Until 1972, HUD failed badly on the publicity front, and as a result received remarkably few complaints. In 1969-70 2,004 complaints were received nationwide. Some perspective is thrown on this figure by Table 3.3 which shows that in relation to minority population, the Chicago office of HUD was attracting very many fewer complaints than many city civil rights agencies. HUD's publicity efforts were in fact minimal and although in 1972 they were stepped up through the introduction of a centralised telephone complaint centre in Washington, they have not reached that level likely to make HUD as important as some state and local agencies in this area.

Table 3.3: Housing Complaints Received per 100,000 Minority Population by Selected City Human Relations Commissions and by HUD in the City of Chicago

City	No. of Cases	Cases per 100,000 minority population
New York	405	19.5
Chicago	139	10.6
Philadelphia	227	26
Pittsburgh	62	35
Chicago (HUD)	60*	4.6

* 1970, all other agencies 1966

Source: Computed from figures provided by HUD

HUD's complaint procedure has generally been accorded low priority by Washington. Appropriations have been low and staffing inadequate. In addition, staff have interpreted their legislative brief very literally, placing great emphasis on principles of equity. Never have they assumed anything but that a 'difference of opinion' exists between complainant and respondent, and in order to ensure fairness all round, very high standards of evidence have had to be established before a complainant has agreed to concede anything tangible. Conciliation has also been extremely lengthy in most cases. In 1970 the average was about 2½ months. Given the nature of housing search by most people, where housing has to be provided quickly, this has meant that many complainants have simply given up and withdrawn their complaint before conciliation has been completed.

As a result of all these factors, very few complainants have benefited from HUD's complaint procedure. Only about 10 per cent of all cases have been successfully conciliated, and as Table 3.4 shows, between January 1969 and July 1970 just twenty-one complainants gained access to housing as a result of the complaint procedure.

Table 3.4: Relief for Complainants under Title 8, January 1969 — July 1970

Form of Relief	Jan. 69-June 69	July 69-Dec. 69	Jan. 70-July 70	Total
Housing: Immediate Occupancy	5	13	3	21
Priority in Application for Housing	1	2	3	6
Application Accepted	3	1	1	5
Rescind Eviction	2	2	0	4
Cash Award	0	4	18	22
Nothing	11	27	9	47
No. of Cases	22	49	34	105

Source: HUD, Office of the Assistant Secretary for Equal Opportunity, *Summary of Title 8 Issues* (undated, mimeo)

There is evidence that since 1972 HUD's complaint procedure has been improved,[67] but no amount of improvement can remove the limitations which are inherent in all administrative complaint procedures no matter how well constructed or efficiently managed they happen to be.

These limitations are a function of the nature of discrimination and the response to discrimination by the minority population. They operate in a number of ways:

i. Even with extensive publicity, the number of complaints received never truly reflects the extent of discrimination. Many are unaware of the existence of official remedies and only a minority of non-whites are prepared to complain. Most will not bother, might be reluctant to drag personal experience through official channels, they may be intimidated by the official nature of the process, or they might consider the experience humiliating.

ii. Middle income better educated blacks are likely to be grossly overrepresented among complainants. In his study of the Massachusetts Commission Against Discrimination, Leon Mayhew found that 91.5 per cent of all housing complaints came from this group.[68] Quite apart from the obvious fact that better educated people are more likely to have the confidence and skill to approach a civil rights commission, lower income blacks are much less likely to experience overt discrimination. Most are confined to the ghetto core and are unlikely to have the economic wherewithal to consider housing that is also available to whites.

iii. Most complaints concern rental rather than owner occupied property. An analysis of complaints filed with the Chicago office of HUD between 1969 and 1971 shows that only 18 per cent of complaints deriving from the central city concerned owner occupied housing, even though 35 per cent of the city's housing stock is owner occupied. Only a handful of complaints were received from Chicago suburban areas, and of these one third were rental in origin. The reasons for this pattern are again fairly obvious. Discrimination in rental property is usually much more blatant than is owner occupied housing. Many transactions are conducted over the telephone, and landlords and estate agents are less able to produce reasons for refusal which are not obviously discriminatory, such as mortgage potential which are often invoked in the owner occupied sector. Moreover, discrimination in the rental sector is likely to involve those apartment buildings already housing some whites and in many cities these tend to be middle or high income. Blacks applying for such accommodation are, therefore, likely to be among the better educated upwardly mobile and therefore much more likely to complain of discrimination.

iv. Administrative solutions rarely attract publicity and fail to establish precedents equivalent to those produced by court decisions. There is little evidence that, apart from discriminators dropping some of their more crass discriminatory techniques, they fundamentally change market behaviour.

For all these reasons, complaint procedures must remain only of limited value. Their existence is important because individuals should always have the right of redress, but they cannot totally remove discrimination.

(b) *The Role of the Courts*

Traditionally in the United States, much faith has been placed in judicial remedies for the redress of grievances, and under Title 8 and following the *Jones v. Meyer* decision, many individuals and civil rights groups have sought this remedy. Also, the federal government can take action on behalf of individuals should there be a 'pattern or practice' of discrimination.

Section 812 of the 1968 Civil Rights Act not only permits individuals to seek judicial redress, but also gives the courts the power to award damages and to grant injunctions. The latter is of major significance for, immediately after a case has been filed, it enables a federal judge to order a real estate agent or property manager to hold a property open until the case is settled, and then to grant the property to the plaintiffs should the case be settled in their favour.

Civil rights groups have used these provisions extensively, and gradually the courts have been building a body of law in this area. Analysis of the cases brought by one such group, the Leadership Council for Metropolitan Open Communities, which operates in the Chicago area, shows that in the 1969-72 period 131 cases were filed in District Court on behalf of aggrieved individuals.[69] Of these approximately 60 per cent resulted in findings favourable to the plaintiff, either through judgement, or more frequently via court orders requiring defendants to provide damages, provide a property or agree to cease discrimination. In one of these orders, damages of $5,000 were awarded against a real estate company which had refused to sell a house to a black in a Chicago suburb.[70] About half of these cases were suburban based, and a majority (60 per cent) involved rental property.

Professional testers were employed by the council in order to produce evidence. A typical scenario would begin with a complaint from a black who (say) had been refused a house in a white suburb. The council would then send its own employees posing as white family

interested in precisely the same house involved in the earlier rebuffal.
Should they be served by the same salesman and be treated favourably
in relation to the black applicants, then they would have a cast iron
case, and the real estate company would almost certainly agree to a
consent order granting the house and offering damages.

Although frowned on by some district judges, the practice of
'scenario testing' is well established in American law and has been an
invaluable asset to groups like the Leadership Council.[71] Moreover,
according to council lawyers, judges, having at first shown some
resistance to open housing cases, gradually came to accept that the
courts should play a leading role in the area. By 1973, therefore, the
amount of damages awarded and the severity of the orders imposed on
defendants had both increased. This said, most of those involved in
these cases, including some defendants, agree that judicial action
against individual discriminators was of only limited value in breaking
down the dual property market. There are several reasons for this.

i.   Most cases end with consent orders rather than judgements. With
     the parties agreeing to settle out of court, the publicity attracted by
     individual cases tends to be minimal, and settlements do not, of
     course, create judicial precedents.
ii. As with HUD's complaint procedure, only particular types of people
     are likely to resort to legal action. Most are middle or upper income
     blacks who have experienced discrimination in rental housing. The
     poor have been almost completely unaffected by the judicial process.
iii. Even when cases do end in judgements which are widely reported,
     the impact of individual cases tends to be at best local. This is partly
     because of the localised nature of the judicial system. Even in the
     case of Federal District Courts, local factors are vitally important.
     Scholars have noted the extent to which District Court
     decision-making is in fact a product of local and regional political
     culture.[72] What may be hailed as an important decision in once city,
     therefore, may have no impact elsewhere.[73] Federal appeal courts
     and the Supreme Court can, of course 'nationalise' the impact of
     cases, but the sort of cases involved in private sector discrimination
     rarely raise those constitutional issues which deserve attention by
     the highest courts. The same cannot be said, incidentally, for cases
     involving disputes over land use or the powers of local governments,
     which will be discussed in Chapter 5.
iv. The number of cases nowhere near reflects the extent of
     discrimination. Having brought 131 cases in the Chicago area in just

three years, the Leadership Council was aware that this was but a drop in the ocean. Moreover, real estate interests, although they may change their behaviour superficially or temporarily as a result of a court case, rarely change in any fundamental way. As was pointed out earlier, most benefit, or believe they benefit from the dual market, and a relatively small financial sanction ($5,000 is very little to many of the larger firms, and this sum was exceptional — the average damages awarded in Leadership Council cases was about $800), and a public chastisement is insufficient to change fundamental values and practices. In addition, non-discrimination orders require monitoring, and neither the courts or groups like the Leadership Council have the resources to engage in careful monitoring.

The monitoring of orders requiring affirmative action on the part of discriminators should be the responsibility of government agencies. However, neither HUD nor the Department of Justice have been particularly active in this area. Indeed, HUD, both in following up its own administrative procedures and in seeking judicial redress when conciliation has broken down, had, by 1974, hardly taken any action at all. No doubt this reflects the low status accorded HUD's complaint procedure by the federal government, and any dramatic change in HUD's behaviour will have to wait on a change in the political complexion of the national administration.

The Department of Justice, because the law requires it to bring cases where there is suspicion of a 'pattern or practice' of discrimination, is more centrally placed for judicial action, and during the three years following the passage of the Act it brought eighty-nine cases, all but one of which involved alleged systematic discrimination by real estate agents, developers or builders.[74] Justice was successful in obtaining a favourable settlement in about 75 per cent of these cases, largely because when faced with court orders which could 'freeze' properties until the case was over, most dependants agreed to comply with Justices' demands and settle out of court. Some of these demands have been far reaching. For example, in *US v. Life Realty,* Samuel J. Lefrak, the owners of 21,000 apartments in New York who had admitted to segregating their properties, agreed to pursue a policy of non-discrimination in the future, and to make good the past effects of their discrimination by keeping a special list of apartments available in 'white' buildings and giving existing black tenants first priority in renting the apartments. In addition, Lefrak were required to keep a time-punched log of all applications and transactions involving the apartments, containing data on race, family size and income of the tenants and applicants involved, and the reasons for the rejection of any application.[75]

However, in spite of occasional well publicised and apparently far reaching cases like Life Realty, the structural constraints which apply to private litigation also apply to Justices' cases. Litigation has helped a few middle income blacks, but has made little impact on the dual market. Like the Leadership Council, most cases have involved relatively clear cut acts of overt discrimination and have ended with consent orders whose effects have been predominantly local and/or temporary. In addition, Justices' resources have been limited by low appropriations and political control. The latter has worked mainly to prevent Justice bringing cases against local governments and will be discussed in Chapter 5, but a lack of resources has reduced the number of cases Justice has filed as well as restricting the type of case brought. Therefore, cases involving mortgage finance which are often complex and require great time and effort to expedite, have been rare. In addition, the monitoring of consent orders has been sporadic and frequently ineffective.[76]

It is clear that administrative and judicial attempts to eliminate racial discrimination in private sector housing have failed because the processing of individual cases and the application of individual sanctions have rarely involved challenges to the major structural forces at work in maintaining the dual property market. However, outside the confines of the 1968 Civil Rights Act and its administrative and judicial procedures, other activities have challenged the dual market, or at least the process whereby neighbourhoods change from white to black.

One concerns attempts by some cities to contain blockbusting or panic peddling by passing ordinances prohibiting real estate canvassing or otherwise restricting the activities of the real estate industry in transitional neighbourhoods. Several cities have passed such laws, and they may have been effective in some instances. However, the severity of restriction on real estate behaviour has varied from locality to locality, enforcement problems have been considerable, and in some cities, like Detroit, the existence of such statutes seems to have made very little difference.[77] One serious problem is that such laws rarely take account of the social economies of particular localities. It may be that transition from white to black occupancy, although facilitated by real estate activities, is not fundamentally caused by them. This is especially so if a neighbourhood is already losing economic and social status and 'white' flight is a reaction to this decline, rather than to the arrival of blacks. In such areas, anti-solicitation ordinances will be of little use. Given all these problems, it is not surprising that the few ordinances which have been passed have met with mixed success.[78] Of course, if they are effective they could halt ghetto expansion and therefore reduce the supply of housing available to blacks.

A second weapon that can be employed at the ghetto periphery or in already integrated neighbourhoods is the racial quota. The increasing use of quotas to ensure that participation or representation of minorities and the underprivileged has aroused fierce controversy in recent years largely because quotas violate the liberal principle 'that the individual and the individual's good are the test of a good society' as Nathan Glazer has put it.[79] Their use has not, however, been as extensive or as controversial in housing as in such areas as employment and political representation. It is important to stress that there are two types of quota: access or preferential quotas which fix a lower limit for the participation of minorities, and integration quotas which set an upper limit on minority participation. The former have been applied to delegate selection at conventions and also to the location of federally subsidised housing, and will be discussed in Chapter 5. Integration quotas have been employed by apartment owners and by HUD in some federally subsidised apartment developments. Data on how extensively they have been used are unavailable, but it is clear that they raise a variety of delicate issues. They certainly violate any assumption that the Constitution is 'colour blind' and their legality has yet to be firmly established.[80] As important, they are a further restriction on those unfortunate people who happen to tip the balance in an apartment block beyond the 30 per cent or whatever level has been established as an 'acceptable' racial mix. No doubt the debate on quotas will continue, but even if widely applied (which is extremely unlikely) they could not affect owner occupied housing, and as far as private developments are concerned they mostly affect middle and high income units — often those situated in already integrated cosmopolitan neighbourhoods such as Hyde Park in Chicago.

Conclusions

The most striking feature of federal attempts to eliminate racial discrimination in private sector housing is the extent to which policy has concentrated on providing individual remedies rather than on attempting to develop a strategic approach to the problem. Any strategic solution would have to involve not only more comprehensive remedies for individuals, but also an attack on those forces, not all of them a result of overt racial discrimination, responsible for the maintenance of the dual property market. Among these are the basic values and practices of the property industry which are fundamentally incompatible with the provision of equal opportunity in housing. It is evidence that these have not been effectively challenged that the judicial and administrative enforcement of the law in the private sector has aroused little political controversy. Apart from the lobbying involved in the original legislation, the real estate and mortgage credit industries have simply not found it necessary to organise an opposition to the implementation of civil rights law. Few have been affected by it, and those that have, have usually been able to satisfy HUD or the courts without conceding any meaningful change in behaviour.

The power of the property industry partly results from its independence. Government rarely impinges on market behaviour, and those government policies which do (such as tax laws) tend to have been approved and administered by politicians and officials sympathetic to the basic ethos of the free market. There is, it is true, some state and local regulation of brokerage business, and in some localities real estate brokers' licences can be revoked under anti-discrimination laws. However, this sanction is rarely applied, and the more scrupulous brokers can usually avoid the sort of overt discrimination which results in litigation or administrative action. The federal government impinges directly on the market hardly at all, so the sanctions available in combating discrimination are almost exclusively confined to those embodied in civil rights law. It is true that the federal government, through various housing and urban programmes, can affect resource allocation in urban areas and can therefore affect property market behaviour, but it usually does this through state and local governments. Chapter 5 will look at these processes and policies in some detail.

Another feature of the implementation process was the extent to which the potential population which the law (even if it was efficiently administered) could help, was confined to middle income non-whites. This is a function of the dual market and the way in which the spatial growth of the ghetto has confined housing contact between the black and white populations to the ghetto periphery and to higher income already integrated neighbourhoods. There are, admittedly, local variations, but this is the basic pattern, and it is one which civil rights legislation such as the 1968 Act can do very little about.

Again, governments including the federal government do not have sufficient power within the property market to supplement civil rights law with more drastic and coercive measures such as reinvigoration of the inner city or the 'dispersal' or lower income families into higher income neighbourhoods — although, as will be shown in Chapter 5, in public sector housing programmes some attempts along these lines have been tried.

Finally, although the implementation of civil rights law has brought little political controversy, the incumbency of a Republican Administration since 1969 has had important consequences for the detail of the administrative and judicial process. Accorded low priority by the Republicans, civil rights programmes have proved even more ineffective than they would have been anyway given a weak law and the structural constraints of the property market.

Notes

1. John F. Kain and John M. Quigley, *Housing Markets and Racial Discrimination: A Microeconomic Analysis* (New York: National Bureau of Economic Research, Urban and Regional Studies No. 3, University of Columbia Press, 1975), Chapter 3; Davis McEntire, *Residence and Race* (Berkeley and Los Angeles: University of California Press, 1960), Chapter 6; Anthony H. Pascal, *The Economics of Housing Discrimination* (Santa Monica: Rand Corporation, 1965); Karl F. Taeuber and Alma F. Taeuber *Negroes in Cities* (Chicago: Aldine, 1965), Chapters 3 and 4.
2. Kain and Quigley, op. cit., pp.58-61.
3. William Brink and Louis Harris, *Black and White* (New York: Simon and Schuster, 1967), p.232.
4. Joel D. Aberbach and Jack L. Walker, *Race in the City* (Boston: Little Brown, 1973), Table 2.16 (c), p.66.
5. For a comprehensive discussion of filtering, see William G. Grigsby, *Housing Markets and Public Policy* (Philadelphia: University of Philadelphia Press, 1967), Chapter III; also Alan Murie *et al., Housing Policy and the Housing System* (London: George Allen and Unwin, 1976), pp.69-81.
6. See Henry J. Aaron, *Shelter and Subsidies* (Washington D.C.: Brookings, 1972), Chapter 10.
7. Brian J.L. Berry, 'Short Term Housing Cycles in a Dualistic Metropolis', in Gary Gappert and Harold M. Rose (eds), *The Social Economy of Cities* (Beverley Hills: Sage Urban Affairs Annual Review No. 6, 1975), pp.165-82; J.B. Lansing *et al., New Homes and Poor People: A Study of Chains of Moves* (Ann Arbor: University of Michigan Press, 1969), Chapter 1.
8. See Robert E. Forman, 'Housing and Racial Segregation', in Harold R. Rodgers, Jr. (ed.), *Racism and Inequality* (San Francisco: Freeman, 1975), pp.38-45.
9. Quoted in Forman, ibid., pp.39-40.
10. See Taeuber and Taeuber, op.cit., Chapter 8.
11. Forman, op.cit., pp.50-1.
12. Ibid., p.52.
13. Hugh O. Nourse and Donald Phares, 'Socioeconomic Transition and Housing Values: A Comparative Analysis of Urban Neighbourhoods', in Gappert and Rose (eds), op.cit., pp.183-208.
14. Kain and Quigley, op.cit., p.295.

15. Ibid.
16. Ibid., p.297.
17. See in particular Otis D. Duncan and Beverly Duncan, *The Negro Population of Chicago* (Chicago: University of Chicago Press, 1957); R.J. Johnston, *Urban Residential Patterns* (New York: Bell, 1971); Harvey L. Molotch, *Managed Integration: Dilemmas of Doing Good in the City* (Berkeley and Los Angeles: University of California Press, 1972); C.W. Rapkin and W.G. Grigsby, *The Demand for Housing in Racially Mixed Areas* (Berkeley and Los Angeles: University of California Press, 1960); McEntire, op.cit.; Taeuber and Taeuber, op.cit.
18. McEntire, op.cit., pp.83-4; Taeuber and Taeuber, op.cit., p.100 *et seq.*
19. Duncan and Duncan, op.cit., p.101.
20. Black incomes have increased relative to white incomes in recent years. Hence, taking 1947 as a base year, white incomes increased by 1971 to 339 and black incomes to 416. However the gap between average white and black incomes remains great, *Statistical Abstract of the United States,* American Almanac Edition (New York: Grosset and Dunlap, 1973), Tables 531 and 535.
21. Harvey Molotch, 'Racial Change in a Stable Community', *American Journal of Sociology,* Vol.75 (1969), pp.226-38; E.P. Wolf, 'The Tipping Point in Racially Changing Neighbourhoods', *Journal of the American Institute of Planners,* Vol.29 (1963), pp.217-22.
22. Duncan and Duncan, op.cit.
23. Rose Helper, *Racial Policies and Practices of Real Estate Brokers* (Minneapolis: University of Minneapolis Press, 1969), pp.263-301.
24. Ibid., p.276.
25. Nourse and Phares, op.cit., p.203.
26. See particularly, Luigi Laurenti, *Property Values and Race* (Berkeley and Los Angeles: University of California Press, 1960); A.T. King and P. Mieskowski, 'Racial Discrimination, Segregation and the Price of Housing', *Journal of Political Economy,* May 1973, pp.590-606; R.K. Wilkinson and S. Gulliver, 'The Impact of Non-Whites on House Prices', *Race,* Vol.XIII, No.1 (1971), pp.21-36.
27. Robert E. Forman, *Black Ghettoes, White Ghettoes and Slums* (Englewood Cliffs, New Jersey: Prentice Hall, 1971), pp.56-9.
28. *Statistical Abstract of the U.S.,* American Almanac 1972 Edition (New York: Grosset and Dunlap, 1971), Section 27, Table 11.10.
29. Mancur Olson Jr., *The Logic of Collective Action* (New York: Schocken, 1968), pp.137-41.
30. NAREB's Code of Ethics proclaims: 'The term Realtor has come to connote competence, fair dealing and high integrity resulting from adherence to a lofty ideal of moral conduct in business relations. No inducement of profit and no instructions from clients can ever justify departure from this ideal, or from the injunctions of this code.' NAREB, *Code of Ethics,* Conclusions (as amended, 1962).
31. John H. Denton, *Apartheid American Style* (Berkeley, Cal.: Diablo Press, 1967), p.48.
32. NAREB, Code of Ethics Part III, 'Relations to Customers and the Public', Article 34 (1924), Quoted in McEntire, op.cit., p.235.
33. NAREB, Code of Ethics, Part I, 'Relations to the Public', Article 5 (1948).
34. Helper, op.cit., p.201.
35. *Wall Street Journal* (San Francisco edition), 4 February 1966, p.1, quoted in Denton, op.cit., p.54.
36. David McKay, *Title IV and the Real Estate Lobby: A Study in Pressure Politics,* unpublished M.A. dissertation, University of Essex, 1969.

37. See Reynolds Farley, "The Changing Distribution of Negroes Within Metropolitan Areas: The Emergence of the Black Suburbs", *American Journal of Sociology*, Vol. 75 (1969-1970), pp.512-29; Harold X. Connolly, 'Black Movement into the Suburbs', *Urban Affairs Quarterly*, Vol. 9, No. 1 (Sept. 1973), pp. 91-111.
38. Ibid., p.99.
39. See Denton, op. cit., Chapters I and II; James L. Hecht, *Because it is Right: Integration in Housing* (Boston: Little Brown, 1970), Chapter 1; Forman, op. cit., pp. 59-66; Helper, op. cit., pp. 277-301.
40. Forman, op. cit., p.85.
41. NAREB spokesmen claim that *none* of their members engage in panic peddling, interviews with NAREB officials, Chicago, April, 1971.
42. Denton, op. cit., pp. 50-51; Helper, op. cit., pp. 236-8.
43. Helper, ibid., Chapter V.
44. See Forman, op. cit., pp. 67-9; Denton, op. cit., pp. 59-61 and sources cited.
45. *Statistical Abstract*, Section 27, Table 1110.
46. Forman, op. cit., p.67.
47. Quoted in Denton, op.cit., pp. 59-60.
48. Kain and Quigley, op.cit., p.145. Redlining is only partly responsible for this very low figure; the nature of the housing stock is also critical. In Chicago, for example, much of the inner city consists of multi-family housing, so a high owner occupancy rate is not possible.
49. For a discussion of how local governments exclude low income housing by these means, see Charles M. Haar and Demetrius S. Iatridis, *Housing the Poor in Suburbia* (Cambridge, Mass.: Ballinger, 1974).
50. Henry J. Aaron, *Shelter and Subsidies* (Washington D.C. : Brookings, 1972), p.77.
51. Lawrence M. Friedman, *Government and Slum Housing* (Chicago: Rand McNally, 1960), Chapter IV.
52. McEntire, op. cit., p.278.
53. Ibid.
54. *Federal Government's Role in the Achievement of Equal Opportunity in Housing*, Hearings Before the Civil Rights Oversight Subcommittee of the Committee on the Judiciary, House of Representatives, 92 Cong. 1 & 2 Sess. (1971/2), Testimony of George Romney, p.449.
55. Duane Lockard, *Toward Equal Opportunity : A Study of State and Local Anti-Discrimination Laws* (New York : Macmillan, 1968), Chapters 4 and 6, Leon Mayhew, *Law and Equal Opportunity* (Cambridge, Mass.: Harvard University Press, 1968), Chapter 3; Joseph P. Witherspoon, *Administrative Implementation of Civil Rights* (Austin: Texas University Press, 1968), Chapter 4.
56. Paul B. Sheatsley, 'White Attitudes Towards the Negro', in John F. Kain, *Race and Poverty: The Economics of Discrimination* (Englewood Cliffs, N.J.: Prentice Hall, 1969), p. 133.
57. Congressional Quarterly, *Revolution in Civil Rights* (Washington D.C.: C.Q., 1968), p.79.
58. David Mckay, op.cit.; Congressional Quarterly, ibid., pp.76-7.
59. Congressional Quarterly, ibid., p.77.
60. Quoted in ibid., p.73.
61. Campbell, op.cit., p.139.
62. Congressional Quarterly, ibid.; on 28 February and 9 March the *New York Times* noted that the relatively conservative House of Representatives was unlikely to pass the ball.
63. 334 U.S. 1 (1948).
64. 245 U.S. 60 (1917).
65. 392 U.S. 409 (1968).

66. The following section is based on interviews with HUD officials in 1971 and 1972 and on the analysis of data provided by HUD.
67. In 1973 more than 2,500 complaints were received — a marked increase on previous years, but still low in relation to the extent of discrimination.
68. Leon Mayhew, op. cit., p. 157.
69. The following section is based on interviews with Leadership Council staff and real estate spokesmen conducted in 1971 and 1972.
70. *Brown v. Town and Country Sales,* No. 71 C 1063 (N.D. 911).
71. Cases endorsing the use of testers include *Evers v. Dwyer* 358 U.S. 202 (1958), which stated: 'It is well settled that, in cases involving racial discrimination, the motives of the victims are immaterial to the issue of whether or not the defendants violated the law.'
72. Kenneth M. Dolbeare, 'The Federal District Courts and Urban Public Policy', in Joel Grossman and Joseph Tanenhaus (eds), *Frontiers of Judicial Research* (New York: Wiley, 1969); Richard J. Richardson and Kenneth N. Vines, *The Politics of Federal Courts: Lower Courts in the US* (Boston: Little Brown, 1970), pp. 93-100. For a good account of how Southern judges responsible for desegregating educational facilities have been influenced by local political values and pressures, see Jack Peltason, *58 Lonely Men* (New York: Harcourt, Brace and World, 1961).
73. Very little research has been conducted into the impact of lower federal court decisions in the US, but it is common for observers to claim that a particular local decision is 'of great significance' or is 'pathbreaking'. Unless such cases are appealed to the Supreme Court, there is no way of knowing what these effects will be, however, and even research into the impact of Supreme Court decisions is in its infancy.
74. Analysis of the Department of Justice's administration of anti-discrimination law is based on interviews conducted in 1971 and 1972.
75. *U.S. v. Life Realty Inc.* No. 70C 964 (E.D.N.Y.).
76. An examination by the author of monitoring procedures in one case, *U.S. v. West Suburban Board of Realtors,* No. 69C 1460 (N.D. 911) showed that the defendants were willing to go to extremes to avoid Justice attorneys carefully examining their records — in spite of the prospect of contempt proceedings. Justice attorneys admitted that they simply did not have the time to monitor consent orders effectively.
77. For a discussion of these ordinances, see Forman in Rodgers, op.cit., pp.68-71.
78. Ibid., p. 70.
79. Nathan Glazer, 'Equal Opportunity Gone Wrong', *New Society,* 22 January 1976, pp. 151-3.
80. For a discussion of the legal position of quotas, see Bruce L. Ackerman, 'Integration for Subsidized Housing and the Question of Racial Occupancy Controls', *Stanford Law Review,* Vol. 26 (January 1974), pp. 245-309.

4 CIVIL RIGHTS AND PRIVATE SECTOR HOUSING IN THE UK

At first sight there are considerable similiarities between British and American private sector housing. In both countries owner occupied housing dominates the private market, and much of this consists of single family detached or (in Britain) semi-detached dwellings. In addition, most new private sector developments have been concentrated in suburban or semi-suburban areas, and in both countries young mobile families have left rented accommodation in the cities in increasing numbers to take up residence in these new locales.

It is possible, in fact, to discern a similar pattern of urban growth and decline in the two countries by comparing patterns of residential succession. Inner city decay and the emergence of transitional or twilight' areas consisting of housing at one time occupied by the middle classes or by 'respectable' working-class people, but which has now filtered down to racial minorities, transients and the economically non-productive, are major characteristics of urban change in both countries. While movements within the private sectors have facilitated these changes, the two sectors do display important differences especially with respect to residence and race.

A general difference concerns the quality and quantity of private rental housing. In 1972, only 18 per cent of all households in Britain rented privately compared with 36 per cent in the US.[1] The British private rental sector figure was as high as 61 per cent in 1947, the precipitous decline since that year being a result of government policies (some intended, others not) favouring owner-occupied and public sector housing.[2] In particular, rent control, changes in the law on security of tenure and the fact that private rental housing is the only housing which does not receive a subsidy of one sort or another, have gradually squeezed private rental housing until now it has come to represent the housing of the last resort for those in the most desperate need. With the exception of a small luxury market and some Housing Association rental housing Britain has no equivalent of the privately developed purpose built apartment buildings so abundant in the US. Britain's private rental housing is, therefore, uniformly old and run down, with many tenants living in multi-occupied Victorian and Edwardian houses in the inner city. Indeed, the 1971 National

House Condition Survey showed that 54 per cent of all houses 'unfit for human habitation' in England and Wales were in this sector. Of all private rental units 23 per cent were unfit compared with 1 per cent of council houses and 4 per cent of owner occupied units.[3]

Most of America's lowest quality housing also occurs in the inner city private rental sector, and there is a shortage of low income housing in many cities. However, the housing market generally is much 'looser' in the US, and in some areas housing is in obvious surplus. Housing standards, especially in urban areas, tend to be higher, and low income families are as likely to be living in reasonable housing which they cannot afford as they are to be exposed to low quality housing.[4] In contrast, housing shortage among lower income groups in parts of Britain is so acute that homelessness serious overcrowding and squatting have become serious urban problems, especially in London which displays the most chronic housing shortage in the country.

As far as race and housing are concerned, however, the major and obvious difference between the two countries is the extent and nature of racial concentration. Chapter 3 noted that notwithstanding the important variations in ghetto growth that exist between different cities, and even between different neighbourhoods in the same city, the fact of racial segregation in the US is incontrovertible. American blacks live in ghettoes. Individuals, institutions and governments have erected racial barriers around well defined areas, and much of the debate on race and housing in the US has centred on how these barriers can be broken down. The situation in Britain is quite different. Ghettoes as such do not exist. There are no neighbourhoods in any British city consisting entirely of blacks, and homogeneously black neighbourhood blocks or even streets are rare. It is not possible in the British context, therefore, to talk of racial discrimination 'maintaining the ghetto'. As will be shown, racial discrimination exists and is important, but it operates more in confining blacks to particular types of housing in integrated or 'transitional' neighbourhoods, than in imposing a pattern of segregated living on the black community.

However, in both countries the pattern of racial residential living that has developed has done so largely within the confines of private sector housing. Until recently, British and American governments have played an essentially passive role in this area, both in their housing programmes and in their urban policies generally. Chapters 5 and 6 will develop this point, and will document recent changes in government policies in some detail. Governments have *influenced* private sector housing patterns, however, either, as in USA, via the defensive tactics employed by local governments and through urban renewal legislation or, in Britain, through slum clearance and other policies affecting the inner city. Much of the American government activity has taken the form of political protection for private interests and communities, and has led to intense political conflicts between different levels of government. However, except in the case of housing subsidies (which will be examined in Chapter 5) government *programmes* in the USA have not been of critical importance in influencing the private sector. The same cannot be said of the United Kingdom where, as we shall see, slum clearance and other programmes have had significant effects on inner city private sector housing.

The Pattern of Minority Settlement in the UK

Chapter 2 showed how, in terms of housing conditions and residential location, British blacks are severely disadvantaged in relation to the white population. The pattern of settlement that has developed over the years is by now quite familiar. As a replacement population, blacks moved to those cities where the demand for their labour was high. However, being poor and strangers in an often hostile environment they gravitated to those parts of cities where housing of one sort or another was available, and this almost always meant the less attractive areas of the inner city. Chapter 2 also pointed to the high degree of spatial concentration among Britain's black population. One recent analysis of this concentration has applied Taeuber and Taeuber's index of dissimilarity or segregation which was developed for American cities[5] (see Table 2.2 Chapter 2). When applied to Britain, this index, which essentially shows what percentage of a group would have to be moved in order to establish the pattern of settlement which would prevail were there no segregation, produced the figures in Table 4.1 for the city of Coventry.

Clearly, blacks (generally those with New Commonwealth birthplaces) are more segregated than other migrants, and among blacks, Asians display the highest degree of segregation, although in all cases the extent of segregation is much lower than in the US. Peach *et al.*'s study revealed further important facts. One was that between 1961 and 1971 segregation among Asians generally increased, and in some cities (notably Birmingham) the increase was sharp (from

Table 4.1   Residential Segregation of Birthplace Groups in Coventry
on a Ward Basis — 1971

Birthplace	Index of Segregation
Wales	10.3
Scotland	7.8
Northern Ireland	11.9
Irish Republic	14.1
Old Commonwealth	13.5
New Commonwealth	51.9
Africa	52.4
America (West Indies)	34.3
Ceylon	43.1
India	58.9
Pakistan	69.9
Far East	29.0
Remainder	12.1

Source: Ceri Peach, Stuart Winchester and Robert Woods, 'The Distribution of
  Coloured Immigrants in Britain', in Gary Gappert and Harold M. Rose (eds),
  The Social Economy of Cities (Beverly Hills: Sage, Urban Affairs Annual
  Review, Vol. 9, 1975), Table 5, p. 404

54 to 69). However, to varying extents segregation among West Indians
declined.[6] Peach *et al.* offer no full explanation for this pattern, but it
seems certain that it is related to a quite high degree of voluntary
separation among Asians, and the very rapid increase in council
tenancies among West Indians between 1961 and 1971 (see Chapter
6, pp.158-9). Most council housing is not situated in the areas of
highest minority concentration, although most blacks have been
allocated council housing in inner city areas with moderate
concentrations of blacks.[7]

The central question when explaining racial or ethnic segregation,
and a critical question for the purposes of the present study, is the
extent to which it results from racial discrimination as opposed to
other factors such as poverty or self-imposed separation. Poverty,
it would appear, explains only a small part of segregation. Peach *et al.*
controlled for income in their study and found that in 1971 only
between 10 and 17 per cent of racial segregation in Birmingham,
Coventry and London is a result of low income'.[8] However, this study

also found a very high degree of segregation within different sections
of the black population, particularly between West Indians and
Asians, implying a strong element of voluntary separation
at least within ethnic groups.[9] Certainly some voluntary separation
exists, but as we shall see there is also considerable evidence that
black housing choices are circumscribed either directly by racial
discrimination, or by a combination of racial discrimination and
racial disadvantage.

One somewhat peculiar feature of blacks' housing is their pattern of
housing tenure. As Table 4.2 shows this pattern does not, at first
sight, seem at all compatible either with widespread discrimination
or low housing quality. Owner occupied housing is the
dramatically dominant tenure type among Asians, and among
West Indians the extent of owner occupation is the same as for the
white population. Given that generally owner occupied housing is of
much higher quality than rented housing this would lead a casual
observer to think that most blacks lived in good housing. Indeed,
the relatively small number of blacks in the worst category of
housing, privately rented accommodation, would tend to confirm
this impression.

Table 4.2 Tenure — West Indians, Asians and the General
Population, 1971

Heads of Household	West Indian %	Asian %	General Population %
Owner occupied	50	76	50
Rented from council	26	4	28
Privately rented	24	19	22
Not stated	1	1	

Source: 1971 Census — households in England and Wales, reproduced in David
    J. Smith, *The Facts of Racial Disadvantage* (London: PEP, Broadsheet
    No. 510), Table A62, p. 121

However, a closer look at the evidence reveals that the quality of
black housing, including owner occupied housing, is substantially lower
than the housing conditions prevailing among the general population.
David Smith's 1974 PEP surveys show this convincingly, as does the
1971 census. Table 4.3 deriving from the survey results reveals that in
terms of overcrowding, access to basic housing amenities

and the sharing of amenities, West Indians and Asians live in very poor housing indeed.

Table 4.3 Quality of Housing — Four Summary Comparisons
between Minorities and Whites, 1974

	West Indian	Asians	Whites/general population
Dwelling is shared	22%	30%	3.8%*
Average no. of persons per bedroom	1.83	1.66	1.25
Lower quartile amenity score	7.59	9.19	12.00
Not having exclusive use of bath, hot water and inside WC	41%	33%	17.9%

* General population figures from the 1971 Census (England and Wales)

Source: David J. Smith, *The Facts of Racial Disadvantage,* Table A71, p. 135

The PEP surveys further reveal that these poor housing conditions apply almost as much in the owner occupied sector as in the private rental sector. Moreover, the relatively small number of blacks in public housing also live in poor conditions compared with white council tenants.[10]

The very high incidence of owner occupation among Asians and the relatively high rate among West Indians is at least partly a function of limited supply. With the private rental sector constantly shrinking and consisting of almost uniformly inferior properties, it has often been rational for blacks to buy rather than to rent. In fact, in some of the northern towns where the purchase price of older properties has traditionally been low, house purchase has been comparatively easy, and has frequently been the only means whereby poorer families can obtain cheap housing. It is not surprising, therefore, that the highest rates of owner occupation are in the northern towns, and the lowest in London and the South East where property values are highest.[11]

In addition, high rates of owner occupation among blacks, and particularly among Asians, reflect a desire to be independent and to accumulate wealth in the community.[12] While this is no doubt true, there is also evidence that many Asian families are unaware of alternative housing supplies (particularly council housing), and among the 19 per cent of Asians in privately rented accommodation demand

for council housing is high.[13] Moreover, claims that blacks get great
satisfaction out of owner occupation are not entirely reconcilable with
survey evidence showing that they are a good deal less satisfied with
their housing than are white owner occupiers. The PEP survey shows,
for example, that 69 per cent of white men are satisfied with their
own homes but only 54 per cent of blacks.[14]

The supply of housing available to blacks is further limited by
local authority policies which in the past have made it very difficult
for them to gain access to council housing. Precisely why this is so
will be discussed in some detail in Chapter 6, but for now it is
important to note that these policies have helped create additional
pressures within the private sector and have reinforced the views
widely held among whites that blacks are a major cause of
housing shortage and housing deterioration.[15]

Finally, as in the US, there is evidence that blacks suffer from
price discrimination in housing. Research by Collard, Fenton and
Karn has shown that blacks can pay considerably more than
whites for private rental and owner occupied housing.[16] However,
research is very much in its infancy in this area and definitive claims
of widespread price discrimination must be treated with caution.

The Nature of Discrimination and Disadvantage

In some respects it is misleading to talk in terms of *the* pattern of
minority settlement in the UK, or *the* pattern of racial
discrimination because very considerable variations exist between and
within cities. This has been amply demonstrated by the many case
studies of racial residential change in British cities published over the
last thirty years.[17]

However, the seminal work in this field, Rex and Moore's study of
Sparkbrook in Birmingham, generates a more general theory by
claiming that the movement of large numbers of blacks into an
inner city area aggravated competition between different housing
'classes' and resulted in widespread discrimination aimed at denying
blacks access to housing, and at containing the spatial expansion of
black areas. So, denied access to council housing or housing within
higher status areas, blacks were obliged to resort to buying houses
which soon became multi-occupied and which gradually spread
throughout an area hitherto consisting of single-family occupied
houses inhabited by 'respectable' whites. Blacks, therefore, were
perceived by whites as the agents responsible for deterioration and
decay.[18] Rex and Moore's theoretical assumption that

economic conflict between housing classes inspires discrimination and ultimately racial conflict has been contested, as has the implication in the study that the empirical circumstances of Sparkbrook are a model for racial residential change in all areas of Britain.[19] In the most comprehensive and penetrating critique of Rex and Moore to date, Robin Ward has claimed that it is the threat to the status of a locality rather than to economic interest that produces conflict and discrimination. Moreover, Ward points to the important fact that the extent of pressure within the local housing market is largely determined by local structural economic factors, especially whether or not employment opportunities and populations are expanding or contracting.[20] The West Midlands, as an area (at least until recently) with a dynamic economy, has produced a much 'tighter' housing market than many northern towns. Competition for housing (whether it be inspired by economic or by status factors) has been correspondingly higher and this may have resulted in a higher level of racial conflict and discrimination than in more depressed areas.[21] Ward's propositions on the relationship between social economy and race relations rightly stress the important differences that exist between different cities. However, Ward also acknowledges that the *number* of blacks entering a particular area can aggravate race relations, largely because large numbers are likely to increase competition for limited housing resources.[22] Given that *most* blacks in Britain have moved to cities in numbers sufficient to produce quite high local concentrations, this would suggest that racial discrimination and conflict are likely to affect a majority of the black population. What form this discrimination takes no doubt does vary from area to area. Certainly, the implication in Rex and Moore that blacks being forced into lodging houses by white defensive tactics is a general feature of residential racial change in Britain, can hardly be reconciled with the fact that a majority (and an increasing majority) of blacks are owner occupiers, and a minority of these and of blacks generally live in multi-occupied dwellings. This is true in Birmingham and nationally.[23]

But while most scholars working in this field acknowledge that there remains considerable ignorance as to the precise nature of racial residential change, what can be said with certainty is that in those localities where blacks have settled in some numbers, discrimination in the property market has occurred This discrimination is not strictly analogous to housing discrimination in the United States, largely because there is no British equivalent to the American dual property market based on race and designed to maintain ghetto conditions. Within particular parts of the British market, however, some of the discriminatory practices so commonly found in the United States do exist and can be detected. In addition, certain practices and pressures in the private housing market have led to racial disadvantage. Let us look at these in some detail.

(a) *Private Landlords*

During the 1960s the most common cases of discrimination involved landlords discriminating against blacks in the private rental sector. Indeed, the 1967 PEP report on racial discrimination found that in a series of 'tested' personal applications, 75 per cent of all West Indian applicants experienced discrimination — usually by being dishonestly told that a room or flat had been let. The discrimination rate was lower for telephoned application, but still in excess of 60 per cent.[24] As Table 4.4 shows, belief in and experience of discrimination appears to have decreased since 1966-7. However, the extent of *contact* between minorities and private landlords has decreased sharply since 1966, partly because of the spread of owner occupation, and partly because increasing numbers of blacks rent from black landlords. However, among those exposed to the possibility of discrimination (i.e. those who have applied to rent from a white stranger), the experience of discrimination remains very high. The 1976 PEP report found that in this group 65 per cent of West Indian men and

Table 4.4 Discrimination by private landlords — belief and experience — 1974 and 1966-7

Men	West Indians		Pakistanis		Indians	
	1966-7	1974	1966-7	1974	1966-7	1974
	%	%	%	%	%	%
There are landlords who discriminate	88	74	44	35	55	47
Have personally experienced discrimination	39	21	15	6	19	8

Source: David J. Smith, *The Facts of Racial Disadvantage*, Table A83, p. 157

71 per cent of Pakistani men had personal experience of

discrimination.[25] Significantly this group tended to be more middle class than the black population generally.[26] So, as in the United States, those blacks who directly experience discrimination tend to be the more upwardly mobile who have direct contact with whites. We may not yet be able to talk of a dual property market in Britain, then, but the beginnings of one have appeared − at least in the private rental sector. By 1975 virtually no whites rented from a black landlord, and of those blacks renting from individuals rather than institutions (more than 80 per cent of the total) less than 15 per cent rented from a white landlord.[27] Self-imposed racial concentration and housing shortage may partly account for this pattern, but the extent of discrimination experienced by those who have had contact with white landlords is sufficient evidence that discrimination is in fact responsible for private rental housing being divided along racial lines.

(b) *Estate Agents and Accommodation Agencies*
Accommodation agencies are a peculiarly British phenomenon and are almost entirely a consequence of housing shortage and the decline in the private rental sector. As the sector has declined, so the relative demand for rented accommodation (especially among the poor and among young singles) has increased. Accommodation agencies have sprung up in response to this and purport to help bring landlord and tenant together by providing each with market information. Landlords, most of whom are small scale and often let out a part of their own homes, do not have the resources to find suitable tenants, and shortage assures a steady stream of sometimes desperate potential tenants to the agencies. Until the 1968 Race Relations Act, discrimination by agencies was ubiquitous and overt, with files and advertisements explicitly marked 'no coloureds' or 'whites only' a commonplace.[28] Since the Act such open racial discrimination has all but disappeared, but the nature of accommodation agency business, where agent and landlords can agree on certain procedures in private, leaves great scope for discrimination. Moreover, the agencies are not organised professionally, so self-regulation is impossible. However, while accommodation agency business remains significant within the private rental sector (especially in London), they are probably less important in providing housing for blacks than they used to be. The private rental sector is constantly shrinking, owner occupation among blacks has risen steadily and those remaining in private rental housing tend to apply for rooms or flats through friends or acquaintances.[29]

With owner occupation as high as it is in the black community, estate agents can play a central role in determining the quality and location of black housing. Certainly a majority of black households use estate agents as their source of house purchase information, and as British estate agents are almost entirely unregulated by government at any level they have considerable scope for the exercise of prejudice, preference and the pursuit of economic self-interest.[30] Unfortunately, however, of all the various parts of the British housing market, estate agents have been the least studied, and their practices are the least understood. The 1974 PEP report, *The Extent of Racial Discrimination,* did reveal that 29 per cent of West Indian applicants to estate agents were given inferior or different treatment in forty-two tested situations spread across six towns, and this was a drop from a figure of 64 per cent deriving from similar tests conducted in 1967.[31] Indeed, by 1968 the weight of evidence supporting claims of widespread discrimination by estate agents was considerable,[32] and PEP's finding that discrimination has sharply declined since 1968 apparently indicates a change in practices — possibly following the passage of the 1968 Race Relations Act. It may be, however, that the decline in detectable discriminatory practices is a result of an increasing racial division of the market. If certain agents concentrate on housing blacks in particular 'integrated' areas, while others exclude them from 'white' areas, then many blacks applying for houses in integrated inner city areas would be unaware of any discrimination. Some preliminary findings from research being conducted by the SSRC Unit on Ethnic Relations at Bristol University suggest that market specialisation along racial lines does exist, with inner city agents catering for blacks, and suburban agents and those operating in 'white' areas specifically excluding blacks.[33]

Moreover, the collusion and market sharing which is a general feature of brokerage practices in the US also exists in the UK,[34] and although there is no evidence that British estate agents have organised nationally to resist racial integration, they have done so at the local level. Certainly, they believe that the introduction of blacks into a neighbourhood lowers property values, and like their American counterparts they see their role as defending the middle-class public's interest in high property values.[35] Estate agents, therefore, act as social 'gatekeepers' reinforcing existing patterns of class and race segregation.[36] Working with other actors in the property business — surveyors, building societies, lawyers, bank managers — they endeavour to exclude from favour all those who they perceive as an undesirable influence on property values. This includes the poor and those like minorities and students, whose life-style is thought to be at odds with mainstream middle-class values.

(c) *Mortgage Credit*

Over the years a stereotype of black house purchasers has evolved which implies that most buyers, unable to obtain mortgages from building societies, have resorted to fringe banks and usurious money lenders to raise deposits and obtain mortgages on old properties.[37] No doubt money lenders and banks are important in providing finance, particularly for Asian buyers. However, as Table 4.5 shows, building societies (which are roughly equivalent to American Savings and Loan institutions) have been quite widely used by black house buyers, with local authority finance also being very important. By comparison, banks and private mortgages account for just 8 per cent of all West Indian buyers' finance and 21 per cent of Asians' finance. Table 4.5 applies only to those blacks with a mortgage. Among Asians some 23 per cent are outright owners — a high figure considering their income levels and the relatively short time they have been in the country. This may be due to difficulties in obtaining a mortgage, but it no doubt also reflects a high desire for outright ownership among Asians; by contrast the outright ownership figure for West Indians is just 4 per cent.[38]

The pattern of mortgage finance among blacks is distinctive and could result from a combination of racial discrimination and disadvantage. Blacks may simply be refused finance on racial grounds alone, they may be offered unfavourable terms such as excessive down payments and short repayment periods, or they may be discouraged from buying properties of a certain type or located in certain areas. There is some evidence that building societies have discriminated on grounds of race,[39] but we have little more than an impressionistic picture of their practices.[40] It does, in fact seem much more likely that racial minorities have experienced racial disadvantage rather than racial discrimination in this area. Remember that other types of discrimination, choice and poverty have helped to limit blacks' housing choice to older inner city properties. It is just such properties on which building societies have been reluctant to lend. They constitute a poor risk in terms of investors' savings, and the societies have steered well clear of them. Recent evidence collated by the magazine *Roof* suggests that many

Table 4.5 Source of Mortgage — Whites and Minorities Compared, 1974

Heads of households who are owner occupiers with mortgages	W. Indians %	Asians %	Whites %
Source of Mortgage			
Building Society	51	43	73
GLC	23)	8)	1)
Local Authority	16) 39	25) 33	12) 13
Insurance Company	1	2	9
Bank	2	15	4
Private Mortgage	6	6	1
Other Sources	1	2	2
Not Stated	—	—	—

Source: David J. Smith, *The Facts of Racial Disadvantage,* Table A68, p. 131

of the biggest societies have 'redlined' large areas of inner Birmingham, Leicester, Leeds, Huddersfield and London. In some instances *no* mortgage finance was available in these areas, irrespective of house or purchaser.[41] Building societies also prefer lenders to be small family units with one able breadwinner; to be, in other words, the safest possible investment risk. Blacks are much less likely to conform to this standard; many families have several breadwinners, and extended families sharing one unit are not uncommon.

Table 4.5 shows, however, that many blacks have received building society funds and many of the properties involved must have been older inner city types. Once again the problem of data arises. The truth is that we do not know the precise nature of building society lending policies. No doubt considerable local variations exist both between societies and with respect to property types and the credit worthiness of buyers. This said, the basic data on blacks' mortgage finance together with the known facts of redlining and the other discriminatory practices used by some building societies, do mean that blacks are at a disadvantage in their dealings with the societies. Like estate agents the societies subscribe to a value system which greatly favours 'safe' white middle-class house buyers.[42] Blacks are at a disadvantage both because they tend to be poor and because other forms of discrimination have generally limited their housing choice to older inner city properties in which the societies have little interest.

(c) *Local Authorities, National Urban Policies and the Private Market*

Legislation has given local governments in Britain a brief to meet the general housing needs of the population. Their primary function in this context is the provision of public housing, but they also have responsibility for maintaining public health and sanitation standards in private housing, for clearing areas of slum housing, and for providing mortgages for house purchase. Middle income owner occupied housing is almost completely unaffected by this legislation. It is privately rented housing and the older inner city owner occupied housing that has usually been involved. In theory, therefore, blacks should have benefited from these policies. Most observers are agreed, however, that at least as far as improving private sector housing conditions and slum clearance are concerned, this has not been the case. Overt discrimination has been rare, but racial disadvantage resulting from established practices and procedures has been common. As in other policy realms, considerable local variations exist, and the picture that emerges from research is bound to overrepresent the importance of those cities which have been the subject of research. None the less, certain general themes are clear.

One is that until the late 1960s local governments tended to go in for wholesale clearance of 'unfit' housing, but, notwithstanding some local variations, tended not to clear areas with high concentrations of blacks.[43] Why this is so is a problematical question. It may be related to the fact that many of the larger houses bought by blacks were not 'unfit' in terms of basic amenities (especially the 'plumbing criteria' of indoor toilet, hot water and bath), as were the smaller nineteenth-century artisans' cottages housing the white working class which have been the object of wholesale clearance in many cities. In fact, in terms of overcrowding and general quality, the multi-occupied housing often used by blacks has been and remains grossly inferior.[44] Also, clearing multi-occupied areas is generally more problematical and expensive for local authorities, partly because there are simply more people to rehouse in relation to the area taken up by existing units; and partly because the people in multi-occupied housing — the poor, large families, single men — are difficult to rehouse. As Chapter 6 will show, local governments' public housing policies tend to be biased against such people. Until 1973, there was in fact no obligation on local authorities' part to rehouse all families in a cleared area,[45] and if an authority did clear a multi-occupied area it may have been seen to be aggravating homelessness and the housing shortage within the private sector.

With some authorities, decisions not to clear multi-occupied housing may not have even been a conscious decision, let alone a political one. The number of actors involved in decisions on clearance is large and the process is a complex one.[46] In many instances it has been 'logical' not to clear lodging house areas, simply because of the problems involved in doing so.[47] In other cases, an awareness of the multi-occupied areas has been acute, and policies have been specifically designed to contain what has been perceived to be the spreading blight of multi-occupation. Local authorities do have considerable powers to act against the owners of housing which is a 'danger to public health'. These vary from a requirement that multi-occupied housing be registered with the council, to the issuing of orders requiring additional amenities or the reduction of overcrowding, to the wholesale takeover of the management of a property.[48] The most famous example of one of these powers concerns Birmingham. Rex and Moore's study of Sparkbrook and Elizabeth Burney's 1967 study *Housing on Trial* have assured this fame, and much research on the same city was generated by their work.[49] This is well documented and there is little need to repeat it here. However, it is important to point out that the brunt of Birmingham's registration scheme and the many orders that resulted from it fell on minority landlords. This policy, together with policies whose effects were to concentrate renewal in 'white' areas of the city and to reduce public housing opportunities for blacks, undoubtedly reduced the housing choices of Birmingham's black population.[50] Ealing, an outer London borough, has pursued a similar policy,[51] but in neither case is there extensive evidence of overt racial discrimination. It seems much more likely that the authorities were acutely aware that the spread of multi-occupation and 'black' areas would threaten the status of other neighbourhoods, aggravate housing shortage and sour race relations.[52] It is interesting to note that Birmingham and Ealing are both areas of acute housing shortage, and 'containment' policies seem much more common in such localities than in the relatively 'easy' housing markets of towns like Bradford. Perhaps, however, scholars have been far too preoccupied with the multi-occupation problem. As the number of single men in the black population has decreased so the number of single family units has increased. In future, therefore,

while multi-occupation will remain a problem, it will hardly dominate
the minority housing situation.

Since the late 1960s the emphasis of public policy towards inner
city private housing has changed. Beginning with the passage of
the 1966 Local Government Act and culminating in the 1974 Housing
Act, a series of measures have been initiated specifically to aid the
inner city. These measures have varied in scope and size and they cover
education and other areas as well as housing. However, the general
theme has been that inner city neighbourhoods suffering from
'multiple deprivation' should be improved through increased public
participation, self-help and programmes of positive discrimination.
As far as housing is concerned, this has meant a shift in policy
emphasis away from wholesale clearance and towards the
rehabilitation of individual units and the general improvement
of particular areas. Hence, in 1969, General Improvement Areas
(GIAs) were created and in 1974 Housing Action Areas (HAAs) were
introduced, both of which were designed to encourage the use of
government housing improvement grants within specific locales.
As far as blacks are concerned it does not look as though these
policies will lead to dramatic changes, however. A major reason
for this is that both programmes are underfunded. Moreover, as Murie
et al. have pointed out, 'The take up of improvement grants, the
sources of General Improvement Areas and even Housing Action
Areas, all rely primarily on the initiative of private households,
including owner occupiers, while the state provides encouragement —
and some financial support.' [53] It is fairly obvious that those
private households which are likely to show initiative in this area
will be those with resources, access to mortgage funds and general
encouragement from officials, surveyors and builders, i.e. small
middle-class white families. Indeed the GIAs have been seen to be
successful when 'gentrification' has occurred, but unsuccessful in
those areas where there has been no middle-class 'invasion'. [54]
Housing Action Areas are designed to avoid this middle-class bias,
but it remains to be seen whether or not they will make any impact. [55]

We will return to this theme later, but first a word on local
authority mortgages. As Table 4.5 showed, of those blacks with
mortgages a full 39 per cent of West Indians and 33 per cent of Asians
obtained them from their local authority. These are high figures and
apparently demonstrate the success of the local authority mortgage
scheme which was designed to provide mortgages for those people
unable to find building society support because of personal

circumstances or because they wanted finance on an older house in an inner city area.

All is not sweetness and light in this area, however. A major problem is frequent fluctuation in government policy. In 1969 Rose *et al.* proclaimed that the 'heyday of council mortgage schemes now lies in the past'.[56] Since then the number of local authority mortgages granted has, in fact, increased dramatically and reached a peak during 1973-5. However, during 1975, government financial stringencies cut them back once more, and by 1976, central government was asking building societies to put aside £100 million to lend to those who would normally qualify for local authority mortgages. It is too early to say whether or not this money will be taken up, but even if it is, it is more likely to go to small 'low risk' family units — possibly ex-council tenants — rather than to larger families, or those living in furnished accommodation. Building societies do, after all, have to look after their investors. They are not welfare organisations,[57] and they will strive to impose their values and priorities on any externally imposed policy. In the face of serious constraints imposed by central government on the level of mortgage lending, some large authorities like Birmingham have determined to give priority to older inner city areas,[58] but funds are now very limited and it is unlikely that council mortgages will cure the funding problems of many would-be black owner occupiers.

Housing and Civil Rights 1962-8

During the 1960s race and immigration became an issue in British politics for the first time. Controversy did not, however, centre on the question of racial equality so much as on the control of immigration. Between January 1961 and the passage of the Commonwealth Immigrants Act on 1 July 1962, 203,407 black immigrants arrived in Britain — almost as many as in the five years 1955-60.[59] The 1962 Act did reduce the arrival rate quite dramatically, and just 231,830 black immigrants entered the country between July 1962 and the end of 1967.[60] In spite of this, however, public opinion hardened in favour of controls during the period. A few months before the passage of the 1962 Act, 62 per cent of the public favoured controls and 23 per cent favoured free entry; by April 1968, the corresponding figures were an astounding 95 per cent and 1 per cent.

The reasons for this shift in public opinion have been thoroughly researched and documented[62] and need not be elaborated in detail. However, certain changes during this period are germane to the present study and require mention.

One is the quite dramatic shift in Labour Party and Labour Government thinking on the subject. Labour had opposed the 1962 Act with some vigour, but by 1965 they had been converted to an acceptance of immigration controls. Why this was so is difficult to say, but during the 1964 General Election campaign, the embryo of racist politics had appeared and the public seemed strongly to favour controls. Perhaps Labour perceived that a failure to support controls might not only have been damaging in electoral terms (and between 1964 and 1966 Labour had a very narrow majority), but could have also helped divide opinion on the immigration question, and thereby have raised the salience of race as a political issue. In fact, if there is a universal truth about the politics of race in Britain it is the constant, sometimes even desperate search by political leaders from the major parties to depoliticise the issue by papering over party differences.[63] Party differences do, of course, exist with the Conservatives favouring a much more active government role in reducing immigration, and a generally passive role on the question of guaranteeing racial equality in society. But these differences have never manifest themselves as major national party divisions during election campaigns. Rarely have the parties been as rigidly and openly divided on race as they have been on economic policy or indeed on housing policy. Why this should be so has already been discussed in Chapter 1, and it is a subject we will return to later. As far as the consequences of this search for consensus are concerned, however, there is little doubt that during the 1960s it produced a confusing ambivalence in Labour policy. On the one hand, Labour subscribed to the view that immigration should be controlled because immigrants placed great stress on the housing and employment situations. On the other hand, Labour supported the idea of anti-discrimination legislation in order to provide Britain's blacks with full equality of opportunity. These two policies are not inherently incompatible, but unfortunately for the Labour Governments of the 1960s, public and parliamentary debate was much more concerned with the question of immigration than with racial equality. Blacks and immigrants became synonymous in the minds of many, and this made the passage of comprehensive anti-discrimination measures that much more difficult.

A second major policy theme of the early and mid-1960s was the generally *laissez-faire* attitude of central and local governments to the social problems experienced by blacks. Tens of thousands of Asians

and West Indians had arrived in some cities, but virtually nothing had
been done to cater for the problems that many immigrants
experienced in housing, employment and education. As was implied
earlier in the chapter, many local governments (in areas of high
immigration most of them Labour controlled), behaved as though
blacks did not exist. As Elizabeth Burney put it in 1967:
'most Labour councils make a habit of resolutely ignoring immigration,
to the extent of, wherever possible, ignoring immigrants.' [64]
Central governments did little more, the most important positive
measure taken to aid blacks during this period being a special
50 per cent rate support grant made available under the 1966 Local
Government Act to local authorities within whose jurisdiction lived
Commonwealth immigrants with special language or cultural
problems. Most of this money was spent on education, but the take-up
rate by local authorities was erratic.[65] In addition, the Ministry of
Local Government and Housing had by 1968 begun to establish
housing priority areas — areas of housing stress which would receive
special central government help — and a similar scheme was
introduced in education by the Department of Education and
Science. All of these innovations were, however, relatively minor in
terms of expenditure. In fact, measures of positive discrimination
represented an advance on the attitudes embodied in the 1965
White Paper on Immigration from the Commonwealth,[66] which
(significantly) dealt both with immigration control and the
integration of blacks into British society. As far as the latter was
concerned the White Paper essentially subscribed to the view that
although immigrants did experience some problems, their needs were
'different in degree rather than kind' and the main objective should
be 'to treat them in the same way as other citizens'.[67] Blacks should,
therefore, be safeguarded against discrimination, but no attempt
should be made to discriminate positively in their favour or to remove
the racial *disadvantage* which they experienced. Indeed, there was
little understanding of disadvantage, as such; the fact that apparently
unbiased rules and procedures might result in blacks receiving
inferior treatment was not appreciated. Hence, in the housing area
the White Paper declared that the real need was to alleviate the housing
shortage and to provide for those in greatest need but said very little
about the specific needs and problems of black families and how
public policy should tackle them.[68]

    Parallel with these developments came Britain's first civil rights law,
the 1965 Race Relations Act. Given the general reluctance of the

1964-6 Labour Government to commit itself to a positive policy on race, it is perhaps, understandable that this law was a very pale affair indeed. It only covered discrimination in 'places of public resort', and while it did create a new central civil rights agency, the Race Relations Board, the enforcement powers given to the Board were limited to conciliation following investigation. Should conciliation fail and the Board consider that discrimination would continue, then the Attorney General could bring proceedings and serve limited injunctions. An emphasis on conciliation and the use of civil rather than criminal law reflects the extent to which the drafters of the law had been influenced by the American experience — although the law's coverage was very much narrower than that of the American 1964 Civil Rights Act.

Indeed, the 1965 Act's narrow coverage ensured the existence of a new campaign to extend coverage almost before it appeared on the statute books. Between 1965 and 1968 this campaign gained strength and was instrumental in persuading the government to introduce a new Race Relations Bill in 1968. Significantly, the campaign was led not by black leaders, but by white liberals — many of them with strong Labour Party connections.[69]

The bill that eventually transpired was extensive in coverage but relatively weak in enforcement provisions. Housing and employment were covered (although as with the American federal law, there was a 'Mrs Murphy' provision whereby coverage was not extended to small-scale landlords living on their own premises), but the Race Relations Board retained essentially passive enforcement powers. Following investigation of a complaint, conciliation could be attempted either centrally or by local conciliation committees. However, the law denied the Board the power to subpoena witnesses and evidence, and the ability to issue orders or injunctions. Moreover, individuals could not go to court on their own initiative and although the Race Relations Board could take cases to court, the courts could only offer plaintiffs damages for actual loss incurred (rather than punitive damages), and court orders were restricted to non-discrimination requirements. Defendants could not, for example, be ordered to release a house or apartment to a plaintiff, they could only be told not to discriminate in the future.

In some respects the weak enforcement provisions of the 1968 Act are surprising, for a year prior to the passage, the Street Report on Anti-Discrimination Law[70] had recommended that Britain adopt a civil rights law modelled on some of the stronger American

state laws. These recommendations included all the enforcement
provisions which the 1968 Act omitted, including giving the Race
Relations Board the power to subpoena witnesses, issue orders and
award damages. In addition, the Report recommended that any new
legislation specifically address discriminatory practices in the various
parts of the housing market, including estate agents, building
societies and local authorities.[71] As it turned out, the 1968 Act
failed to itemise different types of discrimination. Instead, Section 5
of the Act provided a blanket prohibition on housing discrimination.
In other words, the Act failed to take account of the complexity
of discrimination in the housing market. It also omitted to make any
distinction between racial discrimination and racial disadvantage, and
therefore was likely to be effective only against individual instances
of overt discrimination.

   1968 was, in fact, a bad year in which to enact a civil rights law
in Britain. A new and more virulent debate on immigration was in
full swing, and culminated in a further immigration control law which,
by restricting the entry of black British citizens resident abroad, but
not similarly placed whites, was patently racist in design and effect.
The tension between controlling the entry of blacks on the one hand
and, on the other, providing those already in Britain with equal
opportunity, increased perceptibly in 1968, therefore. Indeed, right-wing
extremists had played some part in the 1968 immigration debate,
and it is very likely that the Labour Government hoped to defuse
what was becoming an increasingly delicate political issue by
introducing a relatively weak Race Relations Act.[72] As Louis
Claiborne has put it:

> It was the deliberate policy of those who framed the Race Relations
> Act to eschew compulsory enforcement in favour of private
> cooperation. The hope, of course, was that by using quiet
> persuasion, one would not risk hardening attitudes, exacerbating
> prejudice, drawing battle lines. Consciously, the American
> precedents of enforcement by more drastic weapons — including
> the bayonet — were avoided.[73]

The emphasis on conciliation and persuasion was further evidenced
by the creation of a new body under the Act, the Community
Relations Commission. With its local offices, the Commission had no
powers to enforce non-discrimination; instead, its job was to educate
and inform the public on the needs and problems of Britain's

non-white communities. Admirable as this intention sounds, the fact remains that the Community Relations Commission, when coupled with a relatively weak Race Relations Board, added up to an almost exclusive emphasis on education and conciliation. 'Affirmative action', to use the American term, was almost completely absent.

Private Sector Housing and Civil Rights Since 1968: The Role of the Race Relations Board

Given the nature of the 1968 Act, it is perhaps not surprising that between 1968 and 1976, the law was judged to have made very little impact on discrimination and disadvantage in housing. The experience of the Race Relations Board's complaint procedure is, in fact, very similar to that of many American civil rights commissions administering similar laws. Table 4.6 shows that between 1971 and 1974 the Board received 404 complaints of which 90 were found to have involved discrimination. In addition, under Section 17 of the Act the Board can initiate investigations into possible discrimination. The pattern of investigations is shown in Table 4.7.

Table 4.6 Housing Discrimination Complaints Disposed of by the Race Relations Board between 1 January 1971 and 31 December 1974

Year	Opinion--discrimination (a)	Opinion – no discrimination (b)	Other* (c)	Total (d)	(a) as a % of (d) (e)
1971	14	53	19	86	16.3
1972	28	58	40	126	22.2
1973	9	37	30	76	11.8
1974	39	43	34	116	33.6
Totals	90	191	123	404	22.3

*includes cases outside the scope of the Act, complaints withdrawn, contact lost with complainant and outside the time ,imits imposed by the Act

Source: adapted from the statistical appendices of the *Report of the Race Relations Board,* 1972, 1973 and 1974

When taken together, these data reveal a familiar pattern. The number of complaints received is very small in relation to the extent of discriminatory practices. In its 1974 Report, the Board fully accepted this as fact,[74] and obviously the tiny number of investigations the Board has initiated has made little additional difference. Also, in only a minority of instances has the Board formed an opinion of discrimination – although there has been a trend towards this proportion gradually increasing.

Table 4.7 Housing Discrimination Investigations by the Race Relations Board, 1971-4

Year	Opinion – discrimination (a)	Opinion – no discrimination (b)	Other (c)	Total (d)	(a) as a % of (d) (e)
1971	2	3	8	13	15.4
1972	4	2	6	12	33.3
1973	6	5	5	16	37.5
1974	12	14	4	30	40.0
Totals	24	24	23	71	33.8

Source: adapted from the statistical appendices of the *Race Relations Board,* 1972, 1973 and 1974

As in the United States, therefore, an official civil rights agency has been unable to attract many complaints, and when it has, in only a minority of cases has it been able to detect discrimination. Moreover, the number of cases where complainants have tangibly benefited has been even smaller. In 1974, for example, just sixteen cases resulted in a cash settlement being made to the complainant (ranging from £10 to £30), although in all these cases and in a further eighteen where no settlement was made, an assurance was received by the respondents that they would not discriminate in the future.[75] Again, as in America, rental cases have dominated (in 1972, 60 per cent of all housing cases concerned privately rented accommodation)[76] as have complainants with the most housing contact with whites.

An analysis of all complaints received by the Board between 1968 and 1972 shows that complaints from Pakistanis and Bengalees, numerous groups with little contact with the 'white' housing market, represented just 7.2 per cent of cases disposed, whereas Africans, a small group which because many Africans are only temporarily in Britain, has much greater housing contact with whites, represented 19 per cent of cases disposed. There is also evidence that complainants tend to be of higher socio-economic status than the black population generally.[77]

All of the reasons put forward in Chapter 3 in explanation of the American pattern of complaints and investigations apply in Britain also. Many blacks do not know of the existence of the Race Relations Board (the 1976 PEP Report found that spontaneous knowledge of the Board ranged from 7 per cent among Asian women to 40 per cent among West Indian men),[78] and only a minority of blacks are prepared to complain. As important, the size of the complaint processing operation is small in relation to the extent of discrimination, the penalties imposed on discriminators are negligible, and the law applies only to overt acts of discrimination. Racial disadvantage — structural constraints on the opportunities available to blacks — is not covered.

On the judicial front most parallels with the United States cease. This is mainly because the British law provides so little in the way of remedies, and does not permit individuals to bring cases. Instead, the Race Relations Board can do so, but only when concilation fails and when it considers it has a sound case. The latter has occurred with relative rarity, however. If anything the standards of evidence required by British courts in race discrimination cases are even higher than in the United States. 'Scenario testing', for example which is so common in America, has not been permitted as evidence in British courts, although evidence culled by telephone testing has. In total only about fifteen housing cases have been taken to court by the Race Relations Board, most have involved rented accommodation (four of which were brought against accommodation agencies), and only two of these were of any significance in precedent setting terms. One of these involved public housing and will be discussed in Chapter 6. The other, *Race Relations Board v. Morris (Furnished Rooms Bureau)* established the fairly minor precedent that accommodation agencies must not simply assume on the basis of what they know about a particular area, that a given property is exempt under the Act; they must take steps to make sure it is exempt.[79] But as in the United States, most cases have resulted not in judgements, but in court orders. Also as in the US, judges who were initially cautious and often ill informed on the question of racial discrimination have gradually come to accept that the courts should play some role, and have gradually grown more sympathetic to a liberal interpretation of the law.[80] In Britain this applies generally to race relation litigation, however, rather than to housing cases, which, as has been stressed, have been almost insignificant in judicial terms.

A notable feature of the work of the Race Relations Board in the housing area between 1968 and 1976, was the extent to which its operations bore little relationship to other aspects of government urban policy. Like HUD's complaint procedure, the Board's complaint processing was a minor and isolated activity. It did, on occasion, catch the public eye,[81] but except in the case of blatant and publicly advertised discrimination (as had been practised by accommodation agencies), it had little effect on the basic pattern of discrimination and disadvantage. Other aspects of public policy were, however, concerned with racial disadvantage. In particular, the Urban Programme, announced in 1968, was specifically designed to ameliorate the problems of multiple deprivation in inner city areas. In essence, the programme brought together the positive discrimination measures announced earlier (see p. 96) and allocated twenty to twenty-five million pounds in additional funding for the programme's first four years. There is no doubt the problem of immigrants in inner city areas was the major spur to the programme; it was even to be administered by the Home Office which, through immigration controls, was traditionally more involved with blacks than other departments. Significantly, therefore, the positive discrimination programmes were to be administered not by the Ministry of Housing and Local Government or the Department of Education which were the 'natural' homes for most of the measures, but by the ministry responsible for immigration controls and the maintenance of public order. As it turned out the Urban Programme remained poorly funded, and a failure to coordinate its measures with those being pursued by other departments proved to be something of an embarrassment to governments.[82]

With the return of the Labour Government in 1974, new programmes of rehabilitation and general improvement based on specific locales were introduced and became the responsibility of the Department of the Environment (see p. 93 above). Finally, in 1976 the problems of racial discrimination, racial disadvantage and inner city decay were acknowledged as related by the government for the first time, and in two white papers the government proposed a series of changes which, if implemented, could have great effect on inner city private housing.

The 1975 white paper, *Race Relations and Housing*[83] was the government's reply to the report of the House of Commons Housing

Select Committee on Race Relations and Immigration which had been published in 1971. Recommendations made by the Select Committee were far reaching. Some involved public sector housing and will be discussed in Chapter 6. Others advised central and local governments to take special measures to ensure that building societies and local governments lend more in inner city areas, that discrimination in mortgage credit be eliminated, and that overcrowding resulting from multiple occupation be reduced. The government's reply to these recommendations put great faith in the provisions of the 1974 Housing Act, which introduced Housing Action Areas and Priority Neighbourhoods. However, as was pointed out earlier, it is unlikely that without greatly increased funding these will produce dramatic changes in inner city areas. In addition, the government generally promised it would encourage local authorities to take action, but it left essentially untouched the wide discretion local authorities enjoy in the housing area. Finally, the government assured the Committee that the provisions of a new race relations act would satisfy many of their recommendations.[84]

Indeed, a second white paper on racial discrimination appeared simultaneously with the race and housing white paper.[85] This document proposed dramatic changes in the administration of race relations law. Most importantly it proposed a more strategic approach to race relations by widening the law's definition of discrimination to include racial disadvantage that has resulted from present or past discrimination. Hence it stated that:

25. Legislation is capable of dealing not only with discriminatory acts but with patterns of discrimination, particularly with patterns which, because of the effects of past discrimination, may not any longer involve explicit acts of discrimination. Legislation, however, is not, and can never be, a sufficient condition for effective progress towards equality of opportunity. A wide range of administrative and voluntary measures are needed to give practical effect to the objectives of the law. But the legislative framework must be right. It must be comprehensive in its scope, and its enforcement provisions must not only be capable of providing redress for the victim of individual injustice but also of detecting and eliminating unfair discriminatory practices. The Government's first priority in the field of race relations must be to provide such a legislative framework. What is more, it is uniquely a responsibility which only the Government can discharge.

At the same time Government fully recognises that this is only a part of the subject; that the policies and attitudes of central and local government are of critical importance in themselves and in their potential influence on the country as a whole.

26. The Government recognises that what is here proposed for a further attack on discrimination will need to be supplemented by a more comprehensive strategy for dealing with the related and at least equally important problem of disadvantage. Such a strategy has major public expenditure implications, including a reassessment of priorities within existing programmes. It cannot be settled in advance of the outcome of the current major public expenditure review. The Government does not, however consider this an argument for deferring the preparation of longer-term policies or for delaying the publication and implementation of its anti-discrimination proposals.[86]

At the same time, the government acknowledged that a strategic approach would have to be related to the general problem of inner city areas:

Finally, the problems of racial disadvantage can be seen to occur typically in the context of an urban problem whose nature is only imperfectly understood. There is no modern industrial society which has not experienced a similar difficulty. None has so far succeeded in resolving it.[87]

The Race Relations Bill which followed in 1976 therefore included in its definition of discrimination acts which are discriminatory in effect, but not in intention. Taken together, the white paper and the Bill show that the government is aware of the complexities involved in trying to eliminate racial disadvantage, but they also show how it has stopped short of attempting a precise definition of what is legal and illegal under the new law. It can only be assumed that the range of practices which earlier in the chapter were demonstrated to have produced disadvantage will each have to be tested in the courts.

This is particularly likely given the greatly expanded role of the courts under the new Bill. The complaint procedure and conciliation process will be abolished but individuals will be able to take their grievances to County Courts which, in addition to having expanded injunctive powers, will be able to award unspecified damages including compensation for injury to feelings. In addition, a new body, the Commission for Racial Equality, which will replace both the Race Relations Board and the Community Relations Commission, will be responsible for more wide-ranging investigations into discriminatory practices During its investigations the Commission will be able to subpoena witnesses and evidence and should it form a judgement of discrimination it will be able to issue non-discrimination notices. Recourse to the courts is also available to the Commission, especially with regard to discriminatory advertising.

At the time of writing the Bill is going through Parliament and the final version may differ from the published Bill. Assuming the changes are small, however, it is clear that this legislation represents a quite dramatic departure from the 1965 and 1968 Acts. The courts' role is critical, and the new Commission for Racial Equality will be centrally placed to launch a strategic assault on discrimination. Because the individual complaint procedure is abolished, the new law has been attacked for failing to provide for individual redress (except through the courts).[88] Certainly, unless the Commission provides individuals with special help, few will be prepared to go through the daunting and often humiliating process involved in litigation. But the main emphasis of the new law is less on providing redress for individuals, than on establishing precedent-setting judicial and administrative decisions which will have consequences far beyond the individuals involved in particular cases.

On the face of it, a switch from individual redress to a strategic attack on institutionalised discrimination and disadvantage represents a radical change in policy. Certainly, the 1976 Bill implies much more than the symbolic or token gestures to racial equality contained in the 1965 and 1968 Acts. However, it remains to be seen whether or not it will produce meaningful change. The role of the courts will be critical, and although British courts have gradually come to accept that they have a part to play in providing individuals with redress under the 1968 Act, it is much less likely that they will adopt the sort of activist stance which the success of the 1976 Bill's strategic approach partly depends on.[89] Success will also depend on the financial resources made available to the new Commission, and generally on the government of the day's will to carry through the comprehensive attack on disadvantage which the White Paper promised. During 1976, the Labour Government seemed on the verge of fulfilling this promise by announcing a major shift in planning policy towards the reinvigoration of the inner cities, and existing housing and urban deprivation problems are likely to come under scrutiny in this general review. Fiscal constraints may prevent this shift from producing any meaningful change, however, quite apart from the enormous difficulties involved in redirecting resources into impoverished areas.

A final comment on the potential effects of the 1976 Bill relates to the motives of the government in publishing it. Is it possible to reconcile its contents with the view that there has been a deliberate attempt by élites to create a consensus on race relations? While it is too early to claim that what consensus there was has broken down, in 1976 there are signs that it is under severe strain. Conservative policies on race relations are further from Labour policies than ever before, although there are also rifts within the Labour Party on the subject. Moreover, if consensus is being sought, the 1976 Bill is a strange manifestation of it, for public debate on racial discrimination is likely to intensify should the bill be passed and implemented. Indeed, an active Commission for Racial Equality, armed with powers provided by the Bill, could increase the political salience of the race issue considerably. Rapid change may not be forthcoming, but political controversy and increasingly vocal demands for change are likely.

The motives of the government in adopting this new policy can hardly be explained in terms of a search for consensus, therefore. More likely explanations are the passage of the Sex Discrimination Act in 1975 which contained much stronger guarantees against discrimination than the 1968 Race Relations Act. To bring the official procedures in sex and race anti-discrimination law into line was a logical step. Also, the very inadequacy of the 1968 Act, and the publicity generated by its failure to tackle discrimination, contributed to a change in policy. Most important of all, however, was the increasingly sophisticated understanding of the problems of racial disadvantage and their relationship to inner city problems which Labour had acquired by 1975. As will be amply demonstrated later, in some respects government policy remains confused and incoherent on these subjects, but the advance in understanding since 1968 is unmistakable. It remains to be seen whether this new understanding will be translated into effective change.

Conclusions

Although Britain lacks the ghetto conditions prevalent in the United States, the beginnings of a dual market in private sector housing have developed in many British cities, and a major similarity between the two countries is the key role played by market intermediaries in excluding blacks from particular areas and in limiting mortgage and other housing services available to blacks. In Britain, it is much more likely that these policies result not from conscious racial discrimination (although this is not unimportant), but from the application of apparently neutral procedures whose effects are discriminatory.

Generally, British local and central governments have done little to interfere with the pattern of racial residential settlement that has developed within private sector housing. Indeed, until 1976, the British experience in civil rights law was very similar to the American. The laws were, of course, very similar in design and scope, and when implemented they resulted in the same emphasis on the processing of individual complaints, which bore little relationship to the underlying structural forces at work in producing racial discrimination and disadvantage. Also as in the United States, the British implementation experience aroused very little political conflict or controversy. As no established power positions or vested interests were challenged by civil rights law, there was no reason why it should. Property interests operating outside inner city areas, like their American counterparts, were largely untouched by the 1968 Race Relations Act, and even though government plays a much more important role with respect to inner city private housing than American federal governments, civil rights procedures were largely isolated from policies on slum clearance, multi-occupation and local authority mortgage lending.

Unlike the recent American experience, however, public debate on the relationship between race relations and the problems of the inner city received some impetus from central government initiatives. This is particularly true of the 1974-6 period during which the Labour Government proposed major changes both in civil rights law and in the general orientation of policy towards the inner city. The implementation of these policies should increase the political salience of the race and housing question, but the scope and scale of the problem will require quite fundamental changes in resource allocation before any 'solution' is found. In particular, the values and behaviour of thousands of key actors in the property industry — estate agents, building societies, surveyors, solicitors — will have to be effectively challenged. In sum, governments will have to formulate a policy towards housing and the inner city which redirects public *and* private resources towards racial minorities and the poor in general.

Commentators have been quick to point out that the vehicle for such a profound change in priorities should be public sector housing. Let us now look at the experience of Britain and the United States in the general area of public housing and civil rights.

Notes

1. See Table 2.6, Chapter 2, p.40.
2. See Alan Murie *et al., Housing Policy and the Housing System* (London: George Allen and Unwin, 1976), pp. 179-89; Harold L. Wolman, *Housing and Housing Policy in the U.S. and U.K.* (Lexington, Mass: Lexington Books, 1975), pp.47-50.
3. Quoted in Wolman, ibid., p. 50.
4. Ibid., p.54.
5. Ceri Peach, Stuart Winchester and Robert Woods, 'The Distribution of Coloured Immigrants in Britain', in Gary Gappert and Harold M. Rose (eds), *The Social Economy of Cities* (Beverly Hills: Sage, Urban Affairs Annual Review, Vol.9, 1975).
6. Ibid., pp. 408-10.
7. David J. Smith, *The Facts of Racial Disadvantage* (London: PEP Broadsheet No. 560, 1976), p. 127 and table B75. Smith's data on this subject are not complete, however and the lack of comprehensive racial records at the local level means that we do not know for sure the relationship between racial concentration within council housing and the concentration levels in the surrounding communities. However, for some pointers to this relationship, see Chapter 6, pp.158-62.
8. Peach *et al.*, op. cit., p. 405.
9. Ibid, pp. 405-6.
10. Smith, op. cit., Chapter XIII.
11. Ibid., Table B74, p. 233.
12. See for example, Peach *et al.*, op. cit., pp. 407-8; B. Dahya, 'Pakistani Ethnicity in Industrial Cities in Britain', in A. Cohen (ed.), *Urban Ethnicity* (London: Tavistock, 1974).
13. Smith, op. cit:, p. 151.
14. Ibid., Table B97, p. 242.
15. Richmond's 1965 survey of race relations in Bristol showed that 60 per cent of whites agreed or strongly agreed that 'coloured immigrants have made the housing shortage in Bristol very much worse'. Anthony H. Richmond, *Migration and Race Relations in an English City* (London: Oxford University Press, 1973), Table 10.2, p. 216.
16. David Collard, 'Price and Prejudice in the Housing Market', *The Economic Journal,* Vol. 83, June 1973, pp. 510-15; Mike Fenton and David Collard, 'Do Coloured Tenants Pay More? Some Evidence', SSRC Research Unit on Ethnic Relations, University of Bristol, 1974 (mimeo); Valerie Karn, 'Property Values amongst Indians and Pakistanis in a Yorkshire Town', *Race,* Vol. 10, No. 3, 1969, pp. 269-84.
17. Michael P. Banton, *The Coloured Quarter* (London: Cape, 1955); J. Davies, *The Evangelistic Bureaucrat: A Study of a Planning Exercise in Newcastle-Upon-Tyne* (London: Tavistock, 1972); Kenneth Little, *Negroes in Britain* (London: Kegan Paul, 1947); D. Lawrence, *Black Migrants, White Natives: A Study of Race Relations in Nottingham* (London: Cambridge University Press, 1974); Richmond, op. cit; Sheila Patterson, *Dark Strangers* (Harmondsworth, Middx.: Penguin 1965); John Rex and Robert Moore, *Race, Community and Conflict: A Study of Sparkbrook* (London: Oxford

University Press, 1967); Robin H. Ward, 'Residential Succession and Race Relations in Moss Side Manchester', Unpublished PhD Thesis, University of Manchester, 1975.
18. Rex and Moore, ibid., Chapters I, XI and XII.
19. Robin Ward, op. cit., Chapters 1-6; J. Davies and J. Taylor, 'Race, Community and no Conflict', *New Society,* 9 July 1970, pp. 67-9; Valerie Karn 'A Note on "Race, Community and Conflict: A study of Sparkbrook"', *Race,* Vol. IX, No. 1 (1967), pp. 100-104.
20. Ward, ibid., Chapters 8-10.
21. Ibid., Chapter 10.
22. Ibid., pp. 219-29.
23. In fact, multi-occupation is most common in the South East where some 35 per cent of minority heads of households live in shared dwellings, Smith, op. cit., Table A73.
24. W. W. Daniel, *Racial Discrimination in England* (Harmondsworth, Middx.: Penguin, 1968), Table 14, p. 155.
25. Smith, op. cit., Table A86, p. 159.
26. Ibid., Table B104, p. 244.
27. Ibid., Table B81, p. 236.
28. See Daniel, op. cit., Chapter 9.
29. Smith, op. cit., p. 159.
30. A preliminary report on the Bristol Household Survey Analysis, published in 1975, found that 62 per cent of New Commonwealth origin respondents used estate agents as their primary source of housing information – the same figure as for the white population. Mike Fenton, 'Bristol Household Survey Analysis', SSRC Research Unit on Ethnic Relations, University of Bristol, mimeo, 1975, p. 5. In November 1975 the Department of Prices and Consumer Protection was working on a consultative document on the regulation of estate agents (which did not, significantly, cover accommodation agencies). However, by 1976 no legislation had been generated by this initiative.
31. Neil McIntosh and David J. Smith, *The Extent of Racial Discrimination* (London: PEP Broadsheet No. 547), p. 19.
32. Daniel, op. cit., Chapter 10; E. J. B. Rose *et al., Colour and Citizenship* (London: Oxford University Press, 1969), pp. 242-3; Elizabeth Burney, *Housing on Trial* (London: Oxford University Press, 1967), Chapter II.
33. David Collard, 'Exclusion by Estate Agents – An Analysis', *Applied Economics,* Vol. 5, 1973, pp. 281-8; Stuart Hatch, 'Constraints on Immigrant Housing Choice: Estate Agents', SSRC Research Unit on Ethnic Relations, University of Bristol, 1971 (mimeo).
34. The Monopolies Commission, *Estate Agents: A Report on the Supply of Certain Services by Estate Agents,* HMSO, 1969.
35. Hatch, op. cit., pp. 1-55.
36. See Stuart Hatch, 'Estate Agents as Urban Gatekeepers', Paper before the BSA Urban Sociology Group, University of Stirling, 1973.
37. See Burney, op. cit., pp. 45-9.
38. Smith, op. cit., Table A67, p. 130.
39. Burney, op. cit.
40. For a good summary of building societies' activities and a review of the scant literature on the societies, see Camilla Lambert, *Building Societies, Surveyors and the Older Areas of Birmingham,* University of Birmingham, Centre for Urban and Regional Studies, Working Paper No. 38, 1976, pp. 9-21.
41. Stuart Weir, 'Redline Districts', *Roof,* Vol. 1, No. 4, July 1976, pp. 109-14, and sources cited.

42. Lambert, op. cit., pp. 16-21 and sources cited.
43. Daniel, op. cit., Chapter 11; Rose, *et al.,* op. cit., pp. 236 *et seq.*
44. For a general discussion of this question, see David J. Smith and Anne Whalley, *Racial Minorities and Public Housing,* (London: PEP Broadsheet No. 556), Chapter V.
45. The 1973 Land Compensation Act requires local authorities to rehouse all those living in a clearance area at the time a clearance order is made. See Smith, ibid.
46. See J. B. Cullingworth, *Problems of an Urban Society, Vol. 2. The Social Content of Planning,* (London: George Allen and Unwin, 1973), Chapter 3.
47. As was the case with Bradford, see Rose *et al.,* op. cit., pp. 252-4.
48. See Smith and Whalley, op. cit., pp. 100-101.
49. See in particular the publications of the Centre for Urban and Regional Studies at the University of Birmingham.
50. Rex and Moore op. cit., Chapter XI; Rose *et al.,* op. cit., pp. 246-50.
51. Community Relations Commission, *Housing in Multi-Racial Areas,* Report of a Working Party of Housing Directors (London: CRC, 1976), p. 45; Smith and Whalley, op. cit., Chapters III and V.
52. Smith and Whalley, ibid.; Rex and Moore, op. cit., Chapter 1; Burney, op. cit., Chapter 1.
53. Murie *et al.,* op. cit., p. 173.
54 Ibid., pp. 252-3.
55. On the attitudes of building societies and surveyors towards improvement schemes see Lambert, op. cit.
56. Rose *et al.,* op. cit., p. 244.
57. Officially, building societies are non-profit making friendly societies. However, as they have grown in size so they have adopted commercial operating criteria. They still do not distribute profits to shareholders as do strictly commercial organisations, but they *do* make profits. See Lambert, op. cit., pp. 9-21.
58. See Valerie Karn, *Priorities For Local Authority Mortgage Lending: A Case Study of Birmingham,* Centre for Urban and Regional Studies, University of Birmingham, Research Memorandum No. 52, 1976. Karn also points out that Birmingham's policies have tended to help the better off residents of the inner city.
59. Rose *et al.,* op. cit., Table 8.1, p. 83.
60. Ibid.
61. From Gallup polls, quoted in Rose, *et al.,* ibid., Table 28.24, p, 595.
62. See particularly Rose *et al.,* Chapters 16, 26, 27 and 29 and sources cited; Anthony Lester and Geoffrey Bindman, *Race and Law* (Harmondsworth, Middx: Penguin, 1972), Chapters 2 and 3.
63. For a discussion of the political consensus on race relations in Britain, see Alan Brier and Barrie Axford, 'The Theme of Race in British Social and Political Research', in Ivor Crewe (ed.), *British Political Sociology Yearbook, Volume 2: The Politics of Race* (London: Croom Helm, 1975), pp. 2-25.
64. Quoted in Rose, op. cit., p. 237.
65. Ibid., pp. 346-7.
66. Cmnd 2739, August 1965.
67. Quoted in Rose, op. cit., p. 346.
68. Ibid., p. 232.
69. Ibid., Chapters 26 and 27; Lester and Bindman, op. cit., Chapter 3.
70. Harry Street, Geoffrey Howe, Geoffrey Bindman, *Anti-Discrimination Legislation* (London: PEP, 1967).

71. Ibid., Part IV.
72. For accounts of the debate surrounding the 1968 Commonwealth Immigrants Act, see N. Deakin, 'The Politics of the Commonwealth Immigrants Bill', *Political Quarterly,* Vol. 39, No. 1, 1968; D. Steele, *No Entry: The Background and Implications of the Commonwealth Immigrants Act, 1968* (London: Hurst, 1969).
73. Louis Claiborne, *Race and Law in Britain and the United States* (London: Minority Rights Group, Report No. 22, 1974), p. 13.
74. *Report of the Race Relations Board For 1974* (London: HMSO, 1975), p. 12.
75. Ibid.,Table 8, p. 33.
76. *Report of the Race Relations Board for 1972* (London: HMSO, 1973), p. 29.
77. Ibid., Appendix V, p. 27.
78. *The Facts of Racial Disadvantage,* Table A87, p. 166.
79. Reported in *Rented Accommodation and the Race Relations Act 1968,* Race Relations Board, London, 1974, p. 5.
80. Interview with Geoffrey Bindman, Legal Adviser to the Race Relations Board, May 1976.
81. The most famous case came to a head in 1976 when, following action by the Race Relations Board, a Mr Robert Relf refused to remove a sign proclaiming that his house was 'for sale to an English Family'. Relf defied a court order to remove the sign and was jailed. The case attracted widespread publicity, which was just what Relf, an activist in racist politics, wanted. See 'Robert Relf — "bring back Hitler" — Joins the National Front Campaign', *The Sunday Times,* 4 July 1976, p.6.
82. Generally on the Urban Programme, see J. B. Cullingworth, *Problems of an Urban Society, Vol. 2: The Social Content of Planning* (London: George Allen and Unwin, 1973), Chapters 4 and 5.
83. Cmnd 6232 (September 1975).
84. Ibid., pp. 11-23.
85. *Racial Discrimination,* Cmnd 6234 (September 1975).
86. Ibid., p. 6.
87. Ibid., p. 4.
88. 'Critics Line up for Race Row.' *The Guardian,* 7 February 1976, p. 4: *Racial Discrimination: A Guide to the Government's White Paper* (Runnymede Trust, 1975).
89. For a discussion of the role of the courts under the Bill, see Geoffrey Bindman, 'Law and Racial Discrimination: the New Procedures', *New Community,* Vol. IV, No. 3 (Autumn 1973), pp. 284-90.

5 SUBSIDISED HOUSING POLICIES AND RACE IN THE US

Although in terms of public expenditure governments play a minor role in housing and urban affairs in the US, they are critically important within parts of the housing market, in providing support for the private sector, and in providing protection for local communities intent on preserving the class and racial homogeneity of their neighbourhoods.

Almost all those aspects of housing policy which involve expenditure — as opposed to regulation and political protection for the private market — are within the federal government's domain. The most prominent (and most notorious) of these is the public housing programme, but the federal government also operates other programmes most of which involve federal subsidies for the developers of low and 'moderate' income apartments and owner occupied housing. While the federal government is concerned with the regulation of mortgage finance, most of the important decisions affecting land use and the control of building quality and design are strictly local prerogatives. The extent of local government autonomy in the US has already been noted, and in no aspect of policy is this autonomy more jealously guarded than with respect to private property. Hence, local zoning laws and building codes effectively determine local land use. Comprehensive planning machinery based on jurisdictions wider than the locality or the county is rare, and although, in theory, local governments are merely elements within unitary state systems (as are British local governments in relation to central government), states generally defer to local judgements in the land use and property areas. Within the federal system, therefore, the federal government which hands out largesse to local governments and private interests via the various housing and urban programmes is potentially in conflict with any local government or private interest which wants to pursue a land use or housing policy based on values incompatible with those embodied in federal legislation.

Historically, such conflict has not occurred, either because general agreement on the principle and practice of programmes existed or because the federal government was willing to let local or state governments dictate the shape of federally financed

112

programmes. Between 1934 and the mid-1960s the mortgage insurance
guarantee programme run by the Federal Housing Administration
(FHA) was a good example of agreement between the federal
government and the private property market on basic principles.
There was little controversy over a programme aimed to assist
property ownership for middle income families and which, it
eventually transpired, provided finance for 19 per cent of all owner
occupied non-farm dwellings between 1935 and 1969.[1]

This is not to say that controversy over the detail of legislation,
together with lobbying and bargaining, did not exist; it is merely to
claim that conflict over fundamentals was absent. In contrast,
controversy has always accompanied the two main spending
programmes, Public Housing and Urban Renewal, created respectively
in 1937 and 1949 — although criticisms of the programmes rarely
inspired national debate or political conflict between governments.
For example, at least until the mid-1960s public housing was
controversial not because local governments were pursuing policies
disliked by the federal government, but because, as a redistributive
welfare programme, public housing was unpopular with almost all
governments, whatever the level. One commentator summed up the
situation well in 1957 by pointing out that 'public housing after more
than two decades, still drags on in a kind of limbo, continually
controversial, not dead, but never more than half alive'.[2] In fact
between 1937 and 1970 just 800,000 units of public housing
accommodating 2.5 million people were built.[3] Congresses,
Presidents and state and local governments were not prepared to
support a programme which was based on principles incompatible
with the American ethic of self-reliance and individualism.

Like public housing, the Urban Renewal programme did not,
during its first fifteen years, produce great conflict between
governments. As is so often the case, Congress left much discretion to
local and state government as to how they could use Urban Renewal
money. Moreover, because the programme provided subsidies to
clear and develop land for commercial and speculative investment,
it was quite strongly supported by Congress. There was, however,
considerable controversy over how local interests and governments
were using the programme. Rossi and Dentler's account of urban
renewal in Chicago demonstrates this,[4] as do a host of other case
studies which flooded on to the market in the mid 1960s.[5]
Most of these studies demonstrated how, at the local level, political
élites, with at least the tacit approval of Washington, were using the

programme for exclusively economic ends, the by-product of which was the destruction of old neighbourhoods containing low income housing, and the removal of inconveniently located populations mostly poor and often black.[6]

Down to the mid-1960s then, federal housing and urban programmes while not without controversy were not a cause of great political conflict and were in no way part of a broader national debate on poverty and urban problems. Several events during the 1960s were, however, to transform the situation; among the most important of these was an increasing tendency to see urban problems as synonymous with racial problems.

Race, Housing and Federal Urban Programmes in the 1960s

Perhaps the most prominent characteristic of the 1960s was the greatly expanded role played by governments in social and economic life. Aided by the dominance of the Democrats in Congressional and Presidential politics, this tendency reached its peak during the later years of the Johnson Administration by which time all government spending accounted for some 22.4 per cent of GNP.[7] In the urban area, several new programmes were created including, in 1966 the Model Cities Programme for Community Development, and in 1961 and 1968 new subsidised housing programmes. In addition, some existing programmes were given a new lease of life via increased appropriations and congressional amendments. These new programmes were, from 1965, organised and directed by a new federal agency, the Department of Housing and Urban Development (HUD) created specifically to deal with national urban problems. Fresh government activity in this area was in many respects a response to a new political and economic urban context. Mass migration of Southern blacks to Northern and Western cities, together with an intensification of inner city decay and the flight of the economically productive white population to the suburbs had begun in the 1940s and 1950s, but it was not until the 1960s that these phenomena attracted national attention, and then as a result of increasing racial tension and racial violence. At the same time the 1964, 1965 and 1968 Civil Rights Acts, together with various Supreme Court decisions, outlawed virtually every type of racial discrimination.

Finally, the 1960s witnessed the 'rediscovery' of poverty, and the 1964 Economic Opportunity Act encouraged increased public participation and community action to eradicate poverty. As far as the cities were concerned, this legislation focused further attention on urban problems and went some way towards raising the political consciousness of deprived groups — especially urban blacks.[8]

As a result of these events, during the late 1960s federal urban programmes came under a new kind of scrutiny based not so much on whether they were properly funded or efficiently managed, as whether they were racially discriminatory in design or in effect. As we shall see, this raised the level of political conflict over federal resource allocation considerably. Before analysis of attempts to control discrimination in the public sector is made, it will be useful to look at how the various housing programmes acquired a reputation for racial discrimination.

(a) *Public Housing*

The history of public housing since its inception in 1937 has been adequately documented elsewhere,[9] but for present purposes it is important to note that as the programme developed it acquired three distinctive characteristics: unpopularity among government élites and among a general public who increasingly associated public housing with housing for what they saw as an 'inadequate' lower class; concentration of public housing tenants among two main groups — poor blacks and the white elderly; and strict segregation of the programme along racial lines.

The near universal unpopularity of public housing can only be partly attributable to ideological factors; it is also a result of the programme's relegation from what was originally conceived as housing for the industrial working class to housing for the near destitute. So, reflecting various governments' antagonism to the idea of public housing as a social service for low paid industrial workers, the occupants of public housing have gradually changed from those with (albeit inadequate) incomes from employment, to those who have virtually no income from employment but who are either wholly or partially on relief. Hence, by 1970, nearly 40 per cent of all public housing families had family heads aged 65 or over (elderly public housing) and virtually all of these were receiving either public assistance or social security payments.[10] Of the tenants with family heads under 65 (family public housing), 50 per cent were receiving public assistance or social security benefits and nearly all were desperately poor.[11] In 1970 the median family income of tenants under 65 was \$3,636 p.a.,[12] making public housing tenants among the poorest of any group in the US (in 1970 the Social Security

Administration official poverty income was $3,968).[13] Moreover, income limits are placed on public housing tenants, who are obliged to vacate units should their income rise above a certain level. This assures that public housing is, indeed, housing for the poor. However, public housing tenants, while strikingly poor, by no means constitute a majority or even a large proportion of the poor — a fact which has had important consequences. As Henry Aaron has pointed out:

> The number of families eligible for public housing on the basis of income so vastly exceeds the number of units available for occupancy that local housing authorities have broad discretion in screening applicants. How these powers are exercised determines the characteristics of public housing tenants, the size of federal subsidy required, and the distribution of benefits.[14]

Generally, local authorities have divided the public housing population by age and race. In 1970, 74.3 per cent of non-elderly public housing units were occupied by non-white families and of these 82 per cent were families of three or more and 46 per cent were families of five or more.[15] Most of these families were headed by women and 39 per cent had no labour force earners.[16] Many local authorities were, therefore, reserving most family public housing for one of the least economically productive family units in the US: the large female headed poor black family.[17]

In addition, most big city family public housing has been of poor quality and rigidly segregated along racial lines. Given the small number of public housing units and the large number of poor people eligible for public housing, it is perhaps not surprising that local authorities have channelled the most disadvantaged of the poor — the large black family with a low earning potential — into public housing. In smaller towns, where land costs are relatively low, this has been achieved with fewer harmful effects than in large cities where land costs are high. In cities under 100,000 population (where some 47 per cent of all public housing had been constructed),[18] low costs have allowed projects to remain relatively small, and although racial segregation has occurred public housing projects have, as small developments, blended into existing communities with comparative ease. However, in cities over 500,000 population, where 28 per cent of all public housing had been built,[19] opposition to public housing from low cost suburban areas, and high land costs in central areas, have combined to force local authorities into constructing large high-rise segregated projects in highly populated ghetto areas. These massive public housing projects have been aptly named 'federal slums'.[20] Most of them, occupied almost exclusively by highly disadvantaged large black families, and built cheaply to compensate for high central city costs, have become rife with vandalism and crime and have assumed the general social and economic pathology of the slum dwelling.[21]

Opposition to public housing from more affluent white neighbourhoods is both a cause and a result of the big city federal slum. As Steiner points out there has always been middle-class opposition to low income public housing,[22] and this has helped channel public housing in large metropolitan areas into the inner city areas. However, as these projects became racially exclusive, they became associated in the minds of whites with delinquent teenagers, drugs, crime and civil disorder. By the 1960s, therefore, to most white suburbanites and to whites living in the outer central city areas, *all* family public housing was synonymous with poor blacks, and proposals to build even small projects in white areas met with intense social and political opposition.

It was politically and economically impracticable, therefore, for big city governments to integrate public housing, and at least until the late 1960s the federal government's role in this context was simply to defer to local opinion. Not only public housing, but also federal Urban Renewal funds were used by local authorities to reinforce ghetto areas, for families uprooted by Urban Renewal development were often relocated in segregated public housing.[23] During the 1940s and 1950s there was some public housing site selection controversy, but it was almost entirely local. The few strings which were attached to federal public housing grants were mostly technical (involving such things as cost effectiveness and building standards); where public housing was built was determined by the outcome of local political battles.

(b) *Other Housing Programmes*

Apart from public housing which, until the creation of HUD in 1965, was the responsibility of the Public Housing Administration, federal housing programmes were traditionally run by the FHA. Until the 1960s this effectively meant the mortgage insurance programme, and throughout this period the FHA allowed — even encouraged — segregation in its programmes. Indeed, until the late 1940s segregation was official FHA policy. The 1938 FHA Appraiser's Underwriting

Manual prescribed: 'If a neighbourhood is to retain stability, it is necessary that properties shall continue to be occupied by the same social and racial classes.'[24] Appraisers were therefore instructed to achieve the 'prohibition of the occupancy of properties except for the race for which they are intended'.[25] The Underwriting Manual has since been modified and now uses more cautious language, but until very recently FHA (and VA) practices remained largely unchanged.

In 1967 the National Committee Against Discrimination in Housing (NCDH) produced a report entitled *How the Federal Government Builds Ghettoes,* which attacked the FHA and other federal housing agencies for failing to interfere with the private property market forces. So deferential to the market did the FHA become, that it 'redlined' by prohibiting the granting of mortgages in certain 'poor risk' inner city areas. This practice severely reduced the housing choice of middle income non-whites. The NCDH report commented:

FHA and the VA together have financed more than $120 billion-worth of new housing since World War II. Less than 2 per cent of it has been available to non-white families, and much of that on a strictly segmented basis. 'It is one thing', declares Gunnar Myrdal in *The American Dilemma,* ' when private tenants, property owners and financial institutions maintain and extend the pattern of racial segregation in housing. It is quite another matter when a Federal agency chooses to side with the segregationists.'[26]

Probably a major explanation of the FHA's policies is related to the agency's original brief which required the FHA to support the private mortgage market. Originally, FHA staff were recruited from real estate and lending agencies and not surprisingly they took established values and practices with them when they moved to the new federal agency. The FHA soon developed as an agency geared to servicing the needs of the property market. Its bureaucratic culture was programmatic; production and cost effectiveness figures were all important while social objectives (such as racial integration) were seen as incompatible with the main programmatic objectives of the agency.[27]

When, in 1965, the FHA officially became part of the new federal housing agency, HUD, it retained considerable autonomy. The merger of the agency into what was a Great Society housing administration did not, therefore, immediately affect the FHA's operational values.

But, in spite of this, during the late 1950s and 1960s the FHA acquired responsibilities for administering new subsidised housing programmes and was obliged to consider broad social criteria for the first time. The first of these programmes (Section 202 of the 1959 Housing Act and Section 221 (D) (3) of the 1961 Housing Act) provided low interest loans for developers of low income elderly and family apartments, but neither programme was particularly ambitious and between 1959 and 1969 only about 187,000 202 and 221 (D) (3) units were built. Things changed dramatically after 1968, however, for the Housing Act of that year introduced two new interest subsidy schemes, Section 235 and 236 housing, which for the first time directly involved the federal government in the provision of housing for low income families on a mass scale.

The 235 programme was designed to help less well off families buy their own homes, but instead of providing private developers with direct loans, the programme created a new type of interest subsidy. Under the scheme, the home buyer has to find a mortgage on the private market (insured, as are many mortgages, by the FHA) at the current market interest rate. The federal subsidy consists of the smaller of either the difference between 20 per cent of the mortgagee's monthly income and the required monthly payment for interest, taxes, principal and insurance, or the difference between the total actual monthly debt and what this would be at an interest rate of 1 per cent. Limits are placed on the cost of homes which can be bought under the scheme and on the incomes of buyers. New, existing or rehabilitated homes qualify under the programme, and generally the Act was aiming at houses in the $10,000-$25,000 price range and purchasers in the $4,000-$10,000 p.a. family income range depending on geographical location and family size.[28]

The 236 programme, designed to replace both the 202 and the 221 (D) (3) schemes, provides subsidies for the developers or mortgagors of low income apartments. Assistance payment cannot be more than either: (i) the difference between the FHA 'market rent' (which is based on the market interest rate) and a mortgage interest rate of 1 per cent; or (ii) the difference between the 'market rent' and 25 per cent of the tenant's income. Whichever of these is the smaller constitutes the subsidy. To qualify as a sponsor of 236 housing, a developer has to be part of a 'non-profit, cooperative or limited dividend organisation'. As with the 235 scheme, rules limit occupacy of the housing to families in the $4,000-$10,000 income range. Both programmes, therefore, aid low and moderate income families

by stimulating the private property market into increasing the supply
of cheaper housing. It was hoped that HUD and the FHA would heed
the past mistakes of the public housing programme by integrating
projects racially and economically, and by avoiding building large
estates in blighted and central city areas. Above all, the two
programmes (and particularly the 235 scheme) were expected to aid
minority families by giving them decent housing. As the US Commission
on Civil Rights has noted:

> Witness after witness appeared before Congressional committees to
> express their support for the new home ownership programmes
> as a vitally needed answer to the housing problems of black
> Americans and as a means of relieving a principal cause of racial
> unrest. Congress itself expressed the expectation that the 235
> programme would be of special benefit to minority group
> families. In fact in 1968 nearly three of every five non-white
> families had incomes that fell within the range of eligibility
> for participation in the 235 programme.[29]

In terms of number of units built, the programmes were, initially, a
startling success. Table 5.1 shows how by 1970 federally subsidised
housing starts accounted for almost 30 per cent of the total — a
remarkable total in historical perspective — and of these more than
80 per cent were being built under the 235/236 programmes.

The decline from 1970 was a result of a healthier private market
(between 1969 and 1971, high interest rates and recession had caused
a slump in the private market), but more importantly by President
Nixon's decision in January 1973 to impose a moratorium on all
subsidised housing programmes. The ban was later lifted by President
Ford, but the moratorium is particularly relevant to our purposes
because it was partly inspired by the relationship that had developed
between the programmes and patterns of racial residence.

While comprehensive data on the programmes are not available, it
is possible to build up a picture of the location and racial composition
of 235 and 236 housing. Within urban areas and with very few
exceptions, 235 housing has been built on a segregated basis with
black families confined to 'blighted' and deteriorating central areas.
In November 1971 the US Commission on Civil Rights concluded:

> *All* new 235 homes constructed in 'blighted areas' are being

purchased by black families, while 70 per cent of all new 235 homes
constructed outside 'blighted areas' are being purchased by white
non-minority families. The data for the Section 236 programme . . .
show that 2/3rds of all units are occupied by white non-minority
families and that 120 out of 389 projects reporting (30 per cent)
are totally segregated by race and ethnic group. 80 projects are all
white, 38 are all black, and 2 are all Spanish American. Of the 269
projects remaining only 100 are more than 15 per cent integrated.
That is, 142 projects are more than 85 per cent white and 27
projects are more than 85 per cent black[30] [emphasis added].

Table 5.1 US Housing Starts, 1961-1973 (thousands)

	Federally subsidised starts (including public housing)	Private non-subsidised starts (excluding mobile homes)	Subsidised starts as a % of total
1961	36.2	1328.8	2.7
1965	63.7	1446.0	4.2
1966	70.9	1124.9	5.9
1967	91.4	1230.5	6.9
1968	165.5	1379.9	10.7
1969	199.9	1299.6	13.3
1970	429.8	1039.2	29.3
1971	430.0	1654.5	20.6
1972	338.8	2039.7	14.2
1973	181.1	1878.3	8.8

Source: US Department of Housing and Urban Development, *Housing in the
Seventies* (Washington D.C.: HUD, 1973), pp. 4-7.

These conclusions are based on very limited HUD data, but a more
detailed analysis of at least the 235 programme has been carried out
by the Civil Rights Commission in Denver, Little Rock, St Louis and
Philadelphia. A sample of 286 Section 235 cases were examined.
Of these, 102 were black buyers and all but three of these bought
existing (rather than new) houses in all black or racially transitional
central city neighbourhoods. All but two of the new financed houses
were built in suburban areas.[31]

The absence of comprehensive data makes generalisation in this area
difficult, but the evidence suggests that the 235 programme has been
used to help extend the ghetto. But it has also, it should be added,

helped black families buy houses in areas previously excluded from all federal help by 'redlining'.[32]

During the early 1970s the administration of Section 235 housing began to acquire a reputation for poor management and corruption. In particular, FHA staff in collusion with real estate and building interests appeared to be financing and selling inferior homes at inflated prices to blacks who could hardly afford the mortgage payments, let alone high (often prohibitive) maintenance costs. Massive foreclosures and shoddy homes seemed to be the fate of 235 housing.[33] Certainly foreclosures and low quality housing were a problem and it was black families who suffered most. But the reports were almost certainly exaggerated and tended to obscure the more important fact that both 235 and 236 housing were, potentially, a major means of increasing the low and moderate income housing supply in the ghetto, and of providing blacks with good housing in attractive areas, including the white suburbs.[34] Section 235 housing *did* have serious financial and management problems,[35] but if via Congressional amendment these could be ironed out there seemed no reason why federal subsidies could not be used to improve dramatically the housing stock and housing opportunity. Moreover, the 236 rental programme tended *not* to experience these problems,[36] but, as the Civil Rights Commission data earlier showed, and as Table 5.2 shows for the Chicago area, Section 236 units located in the central city have been used to a much greater extent by black families, and have largely been confined to black areas.

Table 5.2 Section 236 Units in Chicago: Location by Racial Composition of Community Area, 1972

	%			%
% 236 sites in areas <	10	non-white residence		.... 7.3
" " " " " <	10-30	"	"	"	.... 8.7
" " " " " <	31-50	"	"	"	.... 10.2
" " " " " <	51-70	"	"	"	.... 0.0
" " " " " <	71-90	"	"	"	.... 35.9
" " " " " >	90	"	"	"	.... 37.8
Total number of units = 9,853				99.9

Source: Computed from data provided by Economic and Market Analysis Division, HUD Area Office, Chicago

Most of the suburban Section 236 housing constructed has been located on low-cost vacant land on the periphery of towns and cities, and while many working class whites have benefited from the programme, 236 housing has become the major battleground in the struggle to build low income housing for blacks in the white suburbs,[37] but more of this later. In the meantime, it is important to stress that financially and administratively 236 housing was successful and represented a major breakthrough in terms of providing housing for those with 'moderate' increases. It is in this context that President Nixon's moratorium should be considered.

Subsidised Housing and Civil Rights 1964-76

President Nixon's 1973 moratorium on federal housing programmes was, in fact, the culmination of a period of mounting political conflict over race and publicly funded housing in the US. By 1964, an Executive Order and a Civil Rights Act proscribed certain forms of discrimination in federally funded programmes. Section 101 of President Kennedy's 1962 Executive Order 11063 directed

all departments and agencies in the executive branch of the Federal Government, insofar as their functions relate to the provision, rehabilitation, or operation of housing and related facilities to take all action necessary and appropriate to prevent discrimination because of race, colour, creed or national origin.

Title 6 of the 1964 Civil Rights Act proclaimed that 'no person in the United States shall, on the grounds of race, colour or national origin, be excluded from participation in, be denied the benefits of, or be subjected to discrimination under any programme or activity receiving federal financial assistance'. Neither provision was quite as comprehensive as the wording implies, however, and neither covered the private market. It took the passage of the 1968 Civil Rights Act and the 1968 *Jones v. Meyer* Supreme Court decision to provide a comprehensive ban on racial discrimination in housing. The sections of the 1968 Act relevant to federal programmes are 808 (d) and (e) which respectively require that 'all executive departments and agencies shall administer their programmes and activities relating to housing and urban development in a manner affirmatively to further the purposes of this title', and that the Secretary of HUD 'administers the programmes and activities relating to housing and urban development in a manner affirmatively to further the purposes of this title'.

However, none of these provisions was specific in providing federal agencies with clear instructions on how to pursue non-discriminatory policies. Indeed, the law was and is remarkably vague on this score. It is not surprising, therefore, that since the mid-1960s political and judicial debate has focused on clarification, and when clarification has come it has usually followed a political battle. This debate has been dominated by the question of site selection which has produced conflict at several levels: between federal and local governments, within and between local governments, between private individuals and groups and various governments, and within the federal government. If there is a basic unit suitable for analysis in this area, it is the *community* — city, suburb or neighbourhood. For either in the form of accepting federal aid (for public housing, for example) or through the use of zoning ordinances, or through the direct exercise of political power (via a local referendum, for example), the community has to make a conscious decision to accept or reject low income or public housing, and then decide on where to site it.

Political scientists and sociologists have devoted much effort to examining the American community, its ecology, society and political-economic system. Most recently attempts have been made systematically to compare communities along political, demographic and economic dimensions in order to identify recurring patterns of social activity.[38] Unfortunately, the result has not been the creation of a new body of knowledge establishing a comparative theory of American communities, but rather a flood of facts and statistics, some interesting findings, but little theory building.[39] What, above all, this work has demonstrated is that beyond simple descriptions of basic relationships, the extraordinary variety and complexity of American communities has so far limited the utility of sophisticated comparative analysis. When extraneous factors, such as the role of the federal government, are added, the picture becomes even more complex.

In the race and housing area, the situation is no less complex. Each community displays unique social, economic and political characteristics, and appears to respond to the prospect of low income housing in a slightly different way. Haar and Iatridis' study of five Boston suburbs shows this.[40] Their work also demonstrates how difficult it is to identify correlations between the political response to low income housing and general political, social or economic variables. For example, higher income communities, claimed by the literature[41] to be more innovative and 'public regarding', do not appear more amenable to low income housing than some less well off communities.[42]

While a systematic analysis of the response to low income housing is not feasible, it is possible to discern some general patterns of activity both on the part of local communities and by federal institutions.

(a) *Most communities adopt defensive measures against low income housing*

Whether the motive is the preservation of race or class exclusivity, most communities resist low or moderate income housing. Zoning laws may be invoked to exclude multi-family dwellings, building codes enforced in a way which makes certain buildings expensive to construct or run, local referenda may specifically exclude certain housing types, local assemblies, mayors, or planning committees may simply veto a proposal.[43] Opposition to proposals may come from the political élite, the community at large, or from a special interest, but in almost every instance it comes and in most cases it prevails. With suburbs, the opposition is usually against any low or moderate income housing plan within the jurisdictional area of the community. In cities, it is as likely to manifest itself as opposition to housing within specific (usually white) neighbourhoods. The only communities which have not resisted low income housing have been those already in the ghetto or those which can geographically isolate developments from the rest of the community. As will be shown, controversy has centred on attempts to disperse low income housing from lower income to higher income communities.

(b) *In almost all instances the federal government is involved, but its role has varied according to the historical period and according to local conditions*

Virtually all low and moderate income housing schemes receive federal subsidies; this assures federal involvement. Until about 1968, however, the federal role was passive; since then it has been more active. It has involved threats to cut off funds (and sometimes these have been carried out), negotiations and bargaining with local officials, and, often after a struggle, acceptance of local preferences. Under the Nixon Administration, conflicts within HUD and between HUD officials and the President were common, with the President and his political appointees advocating a passive federal role against HUD liberals who favoured an active integrationist federal role.

(c) *Where local civil rights or other integrationist groups have*
    engaged in conflict with defensive communities or with the
    federal government the courts have usually been involved

Recourse to judicial redress is a basic strategy adopted by American
reformist movements, and this has been no less the case in the race and
housing area. With the 1964 and 1968 Civil Rights Acts on the statute
books together with the Equal Protection clause of the 14th
Amendment, civil rights reformers had the ammunition at least to test
local and federal actions in court. Generally, the courts have played
a major role, and as will be shown have been instrumental in moulding
federal policy during the 1970s.

These three broad generalisations derive from case studies conducted
by the author and by others both of local reactions to low income
housing proposals, and of particular judicial decisions. Some of these
pinpoint the main public policy issues and controversies and are
worth discussing at length.

1. *Stoughton, Mass.*   In Haar and Iatridis' study of low income housing
plans in five Boston suburbs, only in Stoughton were the plans fully
accepted and the housing built.[44] In the four other localities,
political opposition either in the form of restrictive zoning ordinanees,
and/or direct political veto prevented the plans from being approved,
or, in one instance, opposition delayed and reduced the number of
housing units built. Moreover, these four suburbs varied in socio-
economic characteristics quite dramatically. Some were high or middle
income and exclusively white, one was low income and had a fair sized
black minority. In none of the four cases, however, were the federal
courts involved, and in none did HUD appear to play an active
integrationist role.

Stoughton is a middle income blue-collar Boston suburb with in
1970 a population of 23,450, and a black population of just 1.6 per
cent. In 1967, a group of local liberal and church leaders formed the
Citizens Housing Corporation (CHC) which, together with the Boston
based Interfaith Housing Corporation (IHC) proposed a 104 unit
221 (D) (3) family apartment complex. From the start the proposal
met with little political opposition, partly because it derived from
within the community, but also because the proposed site was
separated from existing residential development. However, there was
opposition from the local planning board and the proposal was
experiencing financial problems.

The 104 unit site was eventually approved, however, largely

because HUD held a trump card in the form of federal Public Works and Facility-Type funds. Stoughton had a serious water storage problem which was hampering further growth, and following negotiations, HUD agreed to grant federal funds to ease this problem on the condition that the low income housing project (now to be funded under the 236 programme) was built.

There was not, it should be added, much political conflict surrounding these events, and while Haar and Iatridis characterise the HUD offer as a 'great trade-off', the community had very little to lose and a great deal to gain from it. The housing was geographically isolated so shared no interface with existing social groups, it was a small low-rise development and the community badly needed the public works money. As it turned out, only 13 per cent of the apartments were to be occupied by black families. Moreover, there was no conflict within HUD over the offer, and the courts were not involved. It would be fair to say that Stoughton is a very typical suburban community, but as far as low income housing was concerned it displayed an unusual set of circumstances. Stoughton cannot be regarded as a breakthrough, therefore, either as a precedent setter, or even in terms of achieving a new social mix within the suburb. The development is, after all, tiny in relation to Stoughton's total population.

2. *Chicago Heights.* Chicago Heights is a low income working-class township in Southern Cook County ranked 151st out of 200 Chicago suburbs in socio-economic status and with a black population in 1970 of 14 per cent.[45] On the east side of the town, surrounded by chemical industrial development and separated from the rest of the community by railway tracks, is the black ghetto — a run down area recently vacated by working-class people of Italian origin. Within the ghetto, 3 public housing projects totalling 72 units had been constructed by 1968. In addition, two new projects were planned in 1968: a 56 unit low income public housing project in the ghetto and a high-rise 84 unit project for the elderly in the industrial area between the ghetto and the downtown area of the city.[46] Had the low income project been built, the ghetto area would have been further 'impacted' racially. On hearing of this plan, Frank Fisher, then Regional Administrator for the Chicago Region, personally intervened. Local civil rights and community leaders were demonstrating considerable opposition to HUD's plans and were threatening legal action. The political leadership in Chicago Heights, monopolised by an ethnic

Democratic machine, was uncompromisingly opposed to scattered site public housing. Fisher suggested a compromise. He agreed that the public housing and elderly project could go ahead, but only if 110 235 units were built outside the ghetto area on farmland at the edge of the town.

This was a considerable gamble for Fisher — the 1968 Housing Act containing the 235 programme was still going through Congress at the time, and he still would have to persuade the FHA to sanction the housing. In fact, Washington objected to the arrangement which for 1968 was considered progressive and innovative, but they finally agreed. Agreement was also reached with the City and with the CCHA (the Cook County Housing Authority who were to build the public housing). The contracts were let and everything was ready to go, when in September 1969 Fisher heard that the local FHA insuring office had recently approved, contracted and completed 250 units of 221 (D) (3) housing right in the heart of Chicago Heights' ghetto area between the existing public housing and the proposed 56 unit project. Until then, Fisher and HUD had no knowledge of the project, but its existence altered everything. Once the situation was revealed to the public, a local civil rights group, Cook County Legal Aid, sued HUD for contravening the 1964 and 1968 Civil Rights Acts, claiming that HUD and FHA were deliberately concentrating blacks in the ghetto area. To complicate things further, CCHA wanted to lease most (and possibly all) of the 221 (D) (3) housing and use it for public housing.[47] If this happened it would be occupied by poor black families, and the impression that HUD/FHA were conspiring to concentrate poor blacks in the run down area of Chicago Heights would be strengthened.

Realising that to build the 56 units of public housing would now be politically (and legally) inexpedient, Fisher quickly withdrew his compromise offer to the City and the CCHA. Backtracking further, he decided to invoke the Workable Programme requirement attached to the Urban Renewal funds which the town was receiving to force the City to move the 56 units of public housing to a white area. Section (101) (v) of the 1949 Housing Act makes assistance under Urban Renewal programmes subject to a Workable Programme requirement — a feasibility plan provided by local authorities which must be submitted to HUD for approval before funds are released. For certification of such programmes HUD requires that Urban Renewal schemes take into account the effects of renewal on the surrounding community. Effectively, therefore, Fisher threatened to cut off Urban Renewal funds which were scheduled for downtown redevelopment unless the City reassessed the siting of the public housing. There then followed a fierce political battle, with the City, under the leadership of Mayor Maurino Richton, remaining totally intransigent. Indeed, Richton appealed to Senator Percy of Illinois, to Edward T. Derwinski, the local Representative, and direct to Washington, but to no avail.

The final outcome was that the Urban Renewal funds were terminated, the public housing was not built and Cook County Legal Aid's case against HUD failed. (Cook County Legal Aid attacked HUD's public housing policy in Chicago Heights — a policy which, because of HUD's use of the Workable Programme requirement and the subsequent cut-off of funds, was quite defensible in court. Had they attacked the siting of the FHA 221 (D) (3) scheme, they might have been more successful.)[48]

The Chicago Heights case illustrates how HUD, in spite of some horizontal integration in 1965, continued to experience considerable internal confusion, especially between those HUD officials (like Fisher) appointed during the Great Society period and the FHA whose values and orientations were geared more to production criteria than to social reform objectives. Chicago Heights also demonstrates just how strong and intransigent local opposition to integrated subsidised housing can be. The town was prepared to sacrifice Urban Renewal money rather than receive more low income housing. Of course, unlike Stoughton, Chicago Heights already had a substantial ghetto area, and like many of the suburbs in Southern Cook County, was in desperate fear of being absorbed into the encroaching ghetto of Chicago's South Side. This is not an atypical response of lower income communities near the ghetto periphery, or of those with a substantial minority black population.[49]

Although judicial action was taken in Chicago Heights, it did not have far reaching consequences. Certainly, the new civil rights legislation, potentially of great significance, was not utilised to the full. Moreover, HUD's role, while vital did not involve overt conflict between HUD officials at the grass roots and political bosses in Washington. For such scenario we will have to return to the inner city and to the most celebrated controversy of all, that over Chicago's public housing.

3. *Chicago and the Gautreaux Case.*   Chicago's public housing programme gained public attention in the 1950s both because of its

size (more than 30,000 units), and because of the fierce controversy, recorded by Meyerson and Banfield, over its siting.[50] It had, in fact, been strictly segregated and consisted of ugly high-rise blocks riddled with social problems. It was not surprising, therefore, that in August 1966 the American Civil Liberties Union (ACLU) acting on behalf of disgruntled public housing tenants, brought two suits in Federal Court charging the Chicago Housing Authority (CHA), and separately HUD, with violations of Title 6 of the 1964 Act and the Equal Protection Clause of the 14th Amendment. The cases, filed in the District Court, North East Division of Illinois, Eastern Division were allocated to Judge Richard Austin. Austin decided to deal with the case against the CHA *(Gautreaux v. CHA)* first. Austin argued that if the CHA was found guilty, it would be then logical to pursue the case against CHA's financial backer, HUD *(Gautreaux v. Weaver, Secretary of HUD,* later *Gautreaux v. Romney, Secretary of HUD).* *Gautreaux v. CHA* proved to be a highly complex and controversial case. After thousands of pages of argument from both sides had been studied by Judge Austin, judgement was found for the plaintiffs in January 1969, and was followed by a judgement order in July 1969. The court found that the City Council had vetoed 99.5 per cent of the public housing sites proposed for white areas, but had vetoed only 10 per cent of those proposed for black areas. While fully aware of this the CHA had gone on to build on segregated sites and was, therefore, the court maintained, guilty of violating the Equal Protection Clause of the 14th Amendment. Further, by categorising tenants as either white or negro and then proceeding to allocate them on a segregated basis, the CHA was found guilty of breaking Title 6 of the 1964 Civil Rights Act.[51] The July judgement order was far reaching and required the CHA to take specific action to 'prohibit the future use and to remedy the past effects of CHA's unconstitutional site selection' by building the next 700 units of public housing outside the ghetto and by requiring that future projects house not more than 120 people, with family housing restricted to low rise development.[52]

This act of judicial interventionism provoked a smug reaction from the City who delayed publishing any plans for two years. Not until after the court had issued a further order, were plans published. However, the plans were impracticable as they involved numerous small high cost developments, and were in any case strongly opposed by the City Council. The Chicago political machine, supported by most of the city's white residents, was, in fact, vociferously opposed to public housing in white areas. To most white Chicagoans such developments signalled further extensions of a ghetto which had already spread rapidly in the South and the West of the City.[53]

Meanwhile, HUD, itself still under the threat of judicial action, hoped to defuse the situation by seeking an administrative solution. Again, it was the liberal Fisher who attempted to invoke the Workable Programme requirement attached to Urban Renewal funds in order to persuade the city to comply with Austin's Order. HUD and the City commissioned a joint study which revealed a serious deficit of 6,198 housing units caused by City Urban Renewal development. The study further recommended that 1,500 units for which sites were by then available should be built as soon as possible in compliance with the *Gautreaux* order.[54]

The choice for the city now seemed clear: either they comply with the order, or they could lose what amounted to $46 million in Urban Renewal and Model Cities funds which were up for recertification. However, in early 1971 Fisher was replaced as Regional Administrator by the conservative Republican George Vavoulis — a man who was in no way committed to integration and wanted a solution fast. Therefore on 12 May 1971 Vavoulis signed a letter of intent with the Mayor and the CHA agreeing to release the HUD funds if the City Council approved, within 8 months, sites for 1,700 units to be built by the CHA.[55] The City agreed, and HUD released some of the Model Cities money amounting to $12 million. This is significant, for Model Cities funds were *not* covered by a Workable Programme requirement. Urban Renewal funds were, and federal regulations effectively prevented Vavoulis from releasing these funds as well. Meanwhile, the Council had, by September, approved just 288 sites, and appeared determined to approve no more. Vavoulis, however, intent on settling the dispute, said and did nothing.

During September 1971 the drama returned to the courts. Judge Austin had dismissed the *Gautreaux v. HUD* case, but on 10 September Judge Duffy, the Senior Judge on the 7th Circuit Court of Appeals, reversed Austin by proclaiming HUD, through its funding of the CHA, guilty of violating the Due Process clause of the Fifth Amendment and Title 6 of the 1964 Civil Rights Act.[56] Judge Duffy referred the case back to Austin for resolution and on 1 October Austin delivered further judgement on the case stating:

> It is obvious from the evidence in this case that the drafters and signers of the Letter of Intent knew, or should have known, the improbability of compliance with the undertakings [of the Letter

of Intent] . It is becoming increasingly clear that there was no
intention by each of the above parties to comply with their
undertakings. The Court finds that the sole purpose of the Letter
was to induce HUD to grant $26m. for funding the Model Cities
Programme . . . It is apparent that the planned release of the Model
Cities funds was conditional. It is also perfectly clear that the
conditions set forth have not been met, and it is becoming
obvious they never will be.[57]

Austin then proceeded to enjoin HUD from releasing any further Model
Cities funds. The funds would be released, Judge Austin promised, when
the City Council approved at least 700 new housing units in white
areas — less than half of their original undertakings in the Letter of
Intent. When this was achieved, the Council should proceed to approve
the balance of the 1,700 units.[58]

This decision was appealed by HUD, and the Appeal Court
reversed Austin, claiming that Model Cities was not really a housing
programme, and therefore HUD was justified in releasing the
funds.[59] However, the discriminatory acts of both HUD and the CHA
had been established, and the plaintiffs had yet to receive relief. On
remand, therefore, the District Court entered a summary judgement
against HUD, consolidated the two cases and ordered all parties to draw
up a 'comprehensive plan' to remedy the past effects of public
housing segregation, including 'alternatives which are not confined
in their scope to the geographic boundary of the City of Chicago'.[60]
In other words a *metropolitan* solution to a problem hitherto perceived
only in terms of the City of Chicago was advocated.

When, in August 1974, this new issue was heard by the Appeal
Court, HUD and the CHA were in full agreement that the solution
should be strictly confined to within the City boundaries, and both
agreed that the solution embodied in the five year old Letter of Intent
between HUD, the City and the CHA should be implemented This
was a particularly cynical strategy adopted by HUD, given the near
insuperable political barriers to building public housing in Chicago.
The Appeal Court, however, opted for a metropolitan solution. Justice
Clark of the 7th Circuit Appeal Court argued that local boundaries
could be 'bridged' but not 'basically ignored'.[61] Unlike the celebrated
school desegregation case, *Bradley v. Milliken,* which upheld suburbs'
right to resist bussing to achieve integration across metropolitan
boundaries,[62] there was no tradition of local control in public
housing which was very much a federal programme. In such

circumstances, the violation of the basic rights of blacks could be remedied via metropolitan-wide solutions. Finally, in April 1976 the Supreme Court upheld the Appeal Court in an 8-0 decision. However, the Court acknowledged that local communities *might* be able to continue excluding low income housing via zoning laws, and the final metropolitan-wide plan was to be left to the local District Court which would have wide discretion over details.[63] The *Gautreaux* saga is by no means over, therefore, even after ten years of litigation and political battles, and six years after the death of the original plaintiff, Mrs Dorothy Gautreaux!

Several important lessons can be drawn from the case, however:

i. It confirms the findings from the Chicago Heights case that HUD has only limited powers when it comes to persuading local governments to integrate housing. Rarely do communities *depend* on HUD support (in this respect Stoughton was an exception), and they can often muster political forces effectively in opposition to federal agencies.
ii. National political leadership can be a vital influence on local events. Fisher's replacement by Vavoulis reflected the Presidents' political preferences and it transformed relations between HUD and the City. From 1971 they were no longer protagonists, but allies against the ACLU and increasingly active courts.
iii. Judicial action can lead to *immobilism* (ten years is a long time), but it can also publicise and nationalise an important reform issue. *Gautreaux* started as an essentially local issue affecting the City of Chicago. It ended in a Supreme Court decision setting national precedent not only for inner cities, but for whole metropolitan areas. Federal and local political forces will now be obliged to heed the decision. They may, up to a point, be able to avoid it, delay it or compromise it, but *Gautreaux* has helped establish a new policy framework within which future political conflicts will occur.

Gautreaux does, of course, only apply to public housing, but a parallel case, *Shannon v. HUD,* found HUD guilty of discrimination in a 221 (D) (3) project in Philadelphia.[64] *Shannon,* while immediately relevant only to the central city, does extend the logic of *Gautreaux* to all subsidised housing programmes. There remains, however, the vital *caveat* entered in the *Gautreaux* decision concerning the ability of local governments, via zoning ordinances and other local expediencies, to exclude low income housing.

4. *Land Use and Zoning Cases and the Suburbs.* Any zoning ordinance, local regulation or referendum supporting exclusionary land use could not, following the 1968 *Jones v. Meyer*[65] decision, contain explicit racial classifications. Until 1971 the courts had also held that if exclusionary zoning or referenda approving exclusion had racial *effects*, then it was illegal and unconstitutional. Thus in *Hunter v Erickson*,[66] the Supreme Court in declaring a local referendum prohibiting the passage of any open housing law unconstitutional and a violation of the Equal Protection clause, concluded: 'Although the law on its face treats negro and white, Jew and gentile in an identical manner, the reality is that the law's impact falls on the minority.'[67] In *Kennedy Park Homes Association v. City of Lackawanna*,[68] the city of Lackawanna was found to be divided into three wards, one of these, the First, had 98.9 per cent non-white residence. Kennedy Park Homes (a cooperative housing association) wished to build integrated housing in the (white) Third Ward which prompted the local Council to zone the land in the vicinity of the site for open space park areas, and bar all new land subdivisions for new projects on the grounds that the city's sewage system could not cope. While the District Court acknowledged that the City may have had racial motives or purposes behind its actions, it held that the important point was that its actions had discriminatory *effects*. Therefore, the appeal court judge in finding the City's policy to be a denial of the Equal Protection clause of the 14th Amendment, ordered that sewage facilities be provided immediately and declared:

> Even if we were to accept the City's delegation that any discrimination here resulted from thoughtlessness rather than a purposeful scheme, the City may not escape responsibility for placing its black citizens under severe disadvantage which it cannot justify.[69]

In addition, both the *Gautreaux* and *Shannon* cases looked at the effects of local and federal government action on local minority communities. The courts have also found that racial motivation alone is sufficient to qualify as an illegal act. In *Dailey v. City of Lawton* (Oklahoma)[70] a 10th Circuit Court of Appeal held that the city had denied a zoning change to permit the construction of low income integrated housing. Without looking to the effects of this act, the Court found it constituted a violation of Title 8 and of the 14th Amendment because it was racially motivated.[71]

Until 1971, the courts seemed almost united in moving towards
opposing local autonomy in the low income housing area. However, in
that year the Supreme Court appeared to reverse this trend in *James v.*
Valtierra, where the Court held that Article 34 of the California State
Constitution, requiring a referendum to be held before public housing
could be constructed in a community, did not violate the Equal Protection
Clause of the 14th Amendment.[72] By allowing communities to
exercise their democratic right via the referendum in this context,
the Court effectively sanctioned economic discrimination.
Considerable debate has surrounded the permissibility of economic
discrimination under the 14th Amendment, and the implications of
including economic discrimination within its orbit are profound —
taken to extremes such as extension of the Equal Protection clause
might render unconstitutional the whole American system of free
enterprise![73]

However, while *Valtierra* did represent a retreat from the principles
of looking at the motivation and effects of local action, it applied
only to public housing and to local referenda. Since *Valtierra,* at least
one District Court *has* looked at the effects of an apparently neutral
act and concluded that the Cleveland suburban community of
Cuyahoga, by failing to agree with a federal directive requiring the
suburb to come to an agreement on local low income housing needs
with the City, was acting in a discriminatory manner against all blacks
in the metropolitan area.[74] The logic here is that if the effects of the
referendum in *Valtierra* were to be shown to be racially discriminatory,
then the referendum would indeed be unconstitutional.

Moreover, the 1976 Supreme Court *Gautreaux* decision must be
regarded as a threat to local autonomy because it advocates
metropolitan wide solutions to low income housing site selection.
But the Supreme Court has yet to decide on the constitutionality of
certain types of exclusionary practices, including many zoning laws,
so nothing is settled. Indeed, a 1975 Supreme Court decision
dismissed an appeal challenging a Penfield, N.Y. (a Rochester suburb)
zoning ordinance, because, the Court agrued, the plaintiffs (Rochester
residents and non-profit housing organisations) lacked standing.[75]
This decision will undoubtedly make it more difficult to challenge
exclusionary zoning ordinances. However, the decision was a narrow
one (5 to 4), and while in the face of changing judicial styles and
circumstances it is impossible to predict the future behaviour of the
courts, their involvement in low income housing site selection is now
firmly established. And if the most recent *Gautreaux* decision is

anything to go by, they could continue to be agents for change in this area.

Finally, it is interesting to note that the groups and organisations responsible for bringing most of these cases are essentially middle class and integrationist in orientation. Many have been church or libertarian groups, or non-profit corporations set up specifically to build integrated housing with the help of federal 236 funds. Most of these organisations have the support of or have been initiated by blacks, but they also usually receive white institutional and corporate support. Their aims and policies are certainly not based on exclusively racial considerations. Their main objective is the provision of housing for the poor (or moderately poor) in middle-class white areas, although this usually means attempting to house blacks in white suburbs.

The Political Response to Judicial Action

It should be recalled that the first Nixon Administration showed considerable antipathy to integrated low income housing. President Nixon's 'New Federalism' involved delegating power to states and localities.[76] As far as social policy was concerned this almost always meant leaving local judgements free from federal control or 'interference'. Whether this was part of the President's electoral strategy or whether it had its roots in a conservative philosophy of government is difficult to say, but in the race and housing policy area it produced clear results.

First, the Civil Rights Division of the Department of Justice, in spite of a directive in the 1968 Civil Rights Act requiring Justice to sue when there was evidence of a 'pattern or practice' of discrimination (Section 813 (a)), showed great reluctance to bring action against discriminating local governments. John Mitchell and Richard Kleindienst, the Attorneys General during the period, and Jerris Leonard, Head of the Civil Rights Division, warned Division lawyers to steer clear of such cases because of the 'political sensitivity and legal complexity' involved.[77] It was left to Civil Rights groups and private individuals to bring such cases, which as has been shown, they did with some effect.

Second, regulations clarifying how the 1964 and 1968 Civil Rights Acts were to be implemented were not forthcoming. As was shown in the Chicago Heights and *Gautreaux* cases, without these, HUD officials had to rely on other more coercive methods of persuading local governments to integrate housing, which were not

always successful. Regulations would have had the effect, if
implemented, of establishing uniform criteria as to how HUD should
act with respect to low income and other subsidised housing. They
could, therefore, have focused further attention on the question of
local autonomy and the relationship between HUD programmes and
local political power.

Third, President Nixon attempted to fill the key positions in HUD
and Justice with personnel sympathetic to his point of view. In Justice
this produced a passive federal role. In HUD the situation was more
complex. Until 1972 George Romney was secretary of HUD and he
was known to approve an activist, integrationist federal role. From
1970 he was, however, an increasingly isolated figure in the
Administration, and many appointments were made against his
wishes. Most of these resulted in incumbents favouring a passive
federal role, as did George Vavoulis in Chicago, where by 1971 HUD
and the City appeared to be in general agreement.

From 1971, however, a discernible change in federal policy occurred.
In that year the President issued a comprehensive statement on race
and housing, the Department of Justice sued a local government for
violating the 1968 Act, and in 1972 comprehensive regulations
specifying site selection criteria for HUD and the FHA were published.

By making a distinction between economic and racial
discrimination, the President's statement tried to please everybody.
On the one hand he proclaimed that 'it will be the firm purpose of
this Administration to carry out all the requirements of the law fully
and fairly. Racial discrimination in housing is illegal and will not be
tolerated'.[78] President Nixon went on to say that HUD and Justice
should be given full means to implement the law, and that local
authorities and communities found practising discrimination should
have federal funds withheld or should be sued. On the other hand,
Nixon determined that 'this Administration will not attempt to impose
federally assisted housing upon any community', and 'we will not
seek to impose economic integration upon an existing community'.[79]
It is almost certain that the President's statement was precipitated by
the flurry of judicial decisions between 1969 and 1971. *Shannon* and
Gautreaux had put HUD in an embarrassing position, and unless the
federal government was to become embroiled in dozens of other
similar cases, some action was necessary.

Immediately following the statement, the Civil Rights Division of
the Department of Justice sued the City of Black Jack Missouri (a
St Louis suburb) for zoning land so as to exclude a 236 development.

Pressure had been building for action against Black Jack for some time.[80] Its policies seemed blatantly racist and HUD funds were involved. After three years of litigation, a federal appeal court found the City guilty of racial discrimination under the 1968 Civil Rights Act.[81]

In January 1972 HUD issued new project selection criteria which apply to *all* subsidised housing (including public housing). Under the new Project Selection Criteria, each project is tested on the basis of eight criteria and then rated 'superior', 'adequate' and 'poor'. Priority in the funding of projects is determined by the rating system, but if any proposed project receives a 'poor' rating on any one of the criteria it is not approved. Of the eight, numbers 1, 2 and 3 are the most important as far as race and housing are concerned. Criterion 1's objective is to 'identify the proposed projects which will best serve the most urgent needs for housing for lower income households'. The objectives of Criterion 2 are:' 1) . . . to provide minority families with opportunities for housing in a wide range of locations, and 2) to open up non-segregated housing opportunities that will contribute to decreasing the effects of past housing discrimination.' Criterion 3 and 4's objectives are:

1) . . . to avoid concentrating subsidised housing in any one section of a metropolitan area or town;
2) to provide low(er) income households with opportunities for housing in a wide range of locations;
3) to locate subsidised housing in sections containing families and services that are typical of those found in neighbourhoods consisting largely of standard unsubsidised housing of a similar market value;
4) to locate subsidised housing in areas reasonably accessible to job opportunities.[82]

Therefore, the construction of low income housing is a major objective — minority families should be especially looked after — the housing should be built in a variety of areas, and should particularly aim to decrease the past effects of discrimination. The message of the three criteria is clear: low income housing should be integrated and should not be concentrated in ghetto and transitional areas. It is also clear that the regulations failed to specify *precise* instructions. For example, what is an area of minority concentration? Or, if housing is to be dispersed, in what sort of ratio?

An analysis of administrative interpretation of these regulations in Chicago in 1972 showed that they caused considerable confusion.[83] FHA staff, unwilling to provoke property interest and local communities, adopted a conservative interpretation of the regulations, considering a one to one ghetto non-ghetto distribution of units satisfactory. More liberal HUD staff opted for a one to three ratio (as had Judge Austin in the original *Gautreaux* order), and the Nixon-appointed area office Director John Waner, hoping to avoid conflict of any kind, tried to preserve the *status quo* by pursuing a no-change policy (in other words building most 235 and 236 housing in ghetto areas). Paradoxically, however, this latter policy was supported by a third group within HUD, the black radicals. who believed that HUD should redress the mistakes of the past by encouraging investment in ghetto areas. This viewpoint highlights what in the future may be a major policy dilemma: should effort be concentrated on dispersing the black population into white areas, or into reinvigorating the inner cities. During the 1968-74 period public attention and political conflict centred on the former problem — possibly because no Republican Administration was likely to provide the funds which would be necessary to tackle the latter problem. It may be, however, that when a more interventionist national administration comes to power, this dilemma will be raised once more. Certainly 'dispersal' carries with it unfortunate connotations of compulsion, and also implies that homogeneously non-white communities are *ipso facto* a bad thing. Also, increased investment in the inner city is more likely to be proposed by a Democratic rather than Republican administration and given the desire among some blacks to retain the cultural solidarity of the ghetto, and the considerable political problems involved in dispersal, a Democratic federal government might find inner city investment a more palatable solution. This is a problem we will return to later, but it should be emphasised that the whole question of site selection and low income housing is likely to remain an important issue, whichever government is in power. The existence of the regulations, the judicial interpretation of civil rights law to date, and the existence of many independent civil rights groups intent on challenging the class and social exclusivity of many suburbs, assures this.

Many of the difficulties raised by HUD's site selection regulations were partly removed by President Nixon's moratorium on all low income housing, which came within a year of their publication. It seems probable that the moratorium was inspired by the fact that continuing controversy over 235/6 site selection, especially following the new regulations, was slowly but surely raising the salience of race and housing as a political issue. Moreover, from 1971 it was the Nixon Administration (or at least HUD and Justice) who appeared to be enforcing integrationist law in this area.

The moratorium greatly reduced low income housing production (see Table 5.1) and helped defuse the race and housing issue. However, the moratorium was lifted by President Ford in 1974, and a new programme of public and 235/6 housing was launched.[84] Also in 1974 came a new law requiring localities to create area-wide planning authorities which must take into account housing needs in the metropolitan area before Urban Renewal funds are awarded (now called Community Development Grants).[85] In theory, this legislation provides a framework for comprehensive metropolitan housing plans, and given an activist federal government, could have important implications for dispersed low income housing. However, the legislation also increased the discretion available to localities in their use of federal funds, so it is doubtful whether, when implemented, it will result in enhanced federal power.[86]

So far, discussion has concentrated on the role of federal institutions and how they have interacted with localities in the race and housing area. A few States and metropolitan authorities have also initiated attempts to break down the exclusivity of white suburbs. In particular, New York State's Urban Development Corporation, and metropolitan governments in Dayton Ohio, Minneapolis-St. Paul and Washington D.C. have harnessed federal housing subsidies (mainly under the 236 programme) in efforts to build low income suburban based housing. However, as Michael Danielson has shown in a comprehensive review of these programmes, indifference on the part of the federal government, conservative state legislatures, suburban power and weak metropolitan authorities have combined to prevent these efforts from being translated into effective change. At the most, subsidised housing for poorer suburbanites has resulted. Suburban housing for inner city blacks has been blocked at almost every attempt.[87]

Subsidised Housing and Civil Rights: Some Conclusions

Between 1968 and 1976, race and housing controversy was dominated by one issue: the dispersal of low and moderate income federally subsidised housing into white areas, and particularly into the suburbs. There was, by contrast, much less preoccupation with tenant selection and the use of racial integration quotas discussed in Chapter 3. Site selection problems dominated because they represented, very vividly, the conflict between income and social classes in American metropolitan areas.

During the 1960s federal urban policies had failed to eradicate the problems of the ghetto and the inner city – problems which, with a lower rate of economic growth and developing fiscal crises, have increasingly revealed the racial and class rift in urban areas. In addition, the departure of an activist federal government in 1968 and the advent of the conservative and cautious Nixon Administration, removed the last hope that government could, in the immediate future, help solve the problems of the inner city.

It is not surprising, therefore, that reformers within and outside government turned their attention to breaking down the class and race residential barriers which had been erected around the inner city and within some of the larger cities. The main agents for change in this process turned out to be private groups utilising federal civil rights law in the federal courts. Gradually, the courts have expanded the application of civil rights law and the 14th Amendment, and have helped create a new public policy agenda within which metropolitan wide solutions to housing inequalities are widely discussed – although judicial decisions have by no means always worked to reduce exclusion, and much uncertainty on the constitutionality of many exclusionary practices remains. The courts also helped oblige a reluctant federal government into taking actions which it would otherwise not have taken. The official civil rights procedures set up under the 1968 Act and discussed in some detail in Chapter 3, were of little relevance to these events, although the general and vague directives to the federal government contained in both the 1964 and 1968 Civil Rights Acts did prove important in provoking the publication of site selection regulations following judicial interpretation.

However, in terms of breaking down the class and race homogeneity of communities, these efforts produced very little change during the period. Most blacks remain in the inner city; most cities are segregated, and most middle and upper income suburbs remain exclusive. However, the policy agenda has changed, housing poor blacks in white areas has become a vital political issue, and the return of an activist Democratic Administration intent on expanding housing programmes could produce more tangible results. It would also, inevitably, increase the level of conflict between defensive communities and any agents of change, especially the federal government, and whether, given the considerable electoral importance of the suburbs, *any* federal government would be willing to tolerate such conflict remains to be seen. Quite apart from such obviously political constraints, all national administrations now seem fated to pursuing policies of fiscal caution, if not fiscal conservatism. If this is to be, America's already small federal involvement in housing is unlikely to increase, and until it does, it is unlikely that fundamental changes in social and class segregation, possibly spurred on by judicial imperatives, will occur.

Britain, of course, has had and continues to have a sufficiently large public involvement in housing and urban affairs to ensure, at least in theory, that government policies can produce fundamental changes. What, then, has been the British experience in this area?

Notes

1. Henry J. Aaron, *Shelter and Subsidies: Who Benefits From Federal Housing Policies* (Washington, D.C.: Brookings, 1972), p. 77. The Veteran's Administration runs a similar programme, which also inspired little controversy.
2. Catherine Bauer, quoted in Gilbert S. Steiner, *The State of Welfare* (Washington, D.C.: Brookings Institution, 1971), p. 135.
3. Aaron, op.cit., p. 108. For accounts of the American public housing programme see Robert Fisher, *Twenty Years of Public Housing* (New York: Harper, 1959); Leonard Freedman, *Public Housing: The Politics of Housing* (New York: Holt, Rinehart and Winston, 1969); Lawrence Friedman, *Government and Slum Housing* (Chicago: Rand McNally, 1968); Steiner, op. cit., Chapter Four; Robert Taggart, *Low Income Housing: A Critique of Federal Aid* (Baltimore: Johns Hopkins, 1970), Chapter Three; Harold L. Wolman, *Housing and Housing Policy in the U.S. and U.K.* (Lexington, Mass.: Lexington Books, 1975).
4. Peter A. Rossi and Robert A. Dentler, *The Politics of Urban Renewal* (New York : Free Press, 1961).
5. See in particular the collection of essays edited by Jewell Bellush and Murray Hausnecht, *Urban Renewal : People, Politics and Planning* (New York: Anchor, 1967).
6. Between 1949 and 1967 the programme destroyed 400,000 housing units, almost all of which were low and moderate income, but replaced them with 107,000 units, only 42,000 of which were for low and moderate income families, Michael Stegman, *Housing Investment in the Inner City* (Boston, Mass.: MIT Press, 1972), p. 227.
7. For the 1966-70 period, compared with 12.8 per cent in 1945-50. Quoted in James O'Connor, *The Fiscal Crisis of the State* (New York: St Martin's Press, 1973), p. 97.
8. See Peter Bachrach and Morton S. Baratz, *Power and Poverty* (New York: Oxford University Press, 1972); J. David Greenstone and Paul E. Peterson, *Race and Authority in Urban Politics: Community Action and the War on Poverty* (New York: Russel Sage Foundation, 1973).
9. See note 3.
10. Aaron, op. cit., Table 7-3, p. 117.

11. Ibid.
12. Ibid., p. 15.
13. Non-farm, for a family of four, *Statistical Abstract of the U.S.* 1974, American Almanac Edition (New York: Grosset & Dunlap, 1973), Table 547, p. 335.
14. Aaron, op. cit., p. 113.
15. Ibid., Table 7-3, p. 117.
16. Ibid.
17. Although there has been a tendency to exaggerate the extent to which the American welfare crisis is synonymous with the black welfare mother (see Martin Rein and Hugh Heclo, 'What Welfare Crisis? A Comparison Among the U.S., Britain and Sweden', *The Public Interest,* No. 33 (Fall 1973), pp. 61-83). Indeed, publicity about the difficult position of black mothers in *public housing* may have helped project a false impression concerning the *general* position of black women.
18. Aaron, op. cit., Table 7-4, p. 120.
19. Ibid.
20. Lee Rainwater, *Behind Ghetto Walls: Black Families in a Federal Slum* (Chicago: Aldine, 1970). Rainwater's book is an account of family life in the Pruitt Igoe public housing project in St Louis.
21. See Rainwater, op. cit.; Robert J. Forman, *Black Ghettoes, White Ghettoes and Slums* (Eaglewood Cliffs, N.J.: Prentice Hall, 1971), Chapter 9; Lawrence Friedman, op. cit., pp. 117-46.
22. Steiner, op. cit., p. 160.
23. A 1965 survey conducted by the US Housing and Home Finance Agency showed that 13 per cent of families uprooted by Urban Renewal were relocated in public housing, and three quarters of these were non-white. Quoted in Jewell Bellush and Murray Hausnecht (eds), *Urban Renewal: People, Politics and Planning* (New York: Anchor, 1967), p. 357.
24. Quoted in Davis McEntire, *Residence and Race* (Berkeley and Los Angeles: University of California Press, 1960), p. 301.
25. Ibid.
26. National Committee Against Discrimination in Housing, *How the Federal Government Builds Ghettoes* (New York: NCDH, 1967), p. 19.
27. See Daniel J. Baum, *Toward a Free Housing Market* (Coral Gables, Florida: University of Florida Press, 1969), Chapter 3; Forman, op. cit., pp. 69-72; McEntire, op. cit., Chapter 7.
28. For fuller details of the schemes see Taggart, op. cit., pp. 63-73; Wolman, op. cit., pp. 36-9; US Congress, *Housing Subsidies and Housing Policies,* Hearings before the Joint Economic Committee, 92nd Congress, 2nd Session (Washington, D.C.: US Government Printing Office, 1973).
29. US Commission on Civil Rights, *Homeownership for Lower Income Families: A Report on the Racial and Ethnic Impact of the Section 235 Programme* (Washington, D.C.: Government Printing Office, 1971), p. 8.
30. US Commission on Civil Rights, *The Federal Civil Rights Enforcement Effort: One Year Later* (Washington, D.C.: US Government Printing Office, 1971), p.45.
31. US Commission on Civil Rights, *Homeownership for Lower Income Families,* op. cit., p. 15.
32. In 1967 and 1968 the FHA issued regulations requiring FHA staff to encourage lending in high risk inner city areas.
33. See Congressional Quarterly, 'Federal Low Income Housing Programmes Under Scrutiny', *C.Q.,* Vol. 30, No. 20 (13 May 1972), p. 100; 'U.S. Now Big Landlord in Decaying Inner City', *New York Times,* 2 January 1972, pp. 1 and 26; '13 Indicted by U.S. for Shoddy Homes', *Chicago*

Daily News, Thursday 27 July 1972; 'HUD Scandal Profited all but Taxpayer', *Detroit Free Press,* p. 3, Section A, 19 March 1972; Erwin Knoll, 'Fellow Slumlords', *The Progressive,* Vol. 36, No. 7 (July 1972); Tom Ricke, 'Stories of Hope, Broken Vows, and a lot of FHA Money: How Two Black Families Got Taken in the Home Scandal', *Detroit Free Press,* Magazine Section, 18 June 1972, pp. 18-21.

34. See US Congress, *Housing Subsidies and Housing Policy,* op.cit., especially testimony of Henry Aaron and Anthony Downs, pp. 275-92.

35. See Wolman, op.cit., pp. 37-8.

36. US Congress, *Housing Subsidies and Housing Policy,* testimony of Anthony Downs, pp. 287-92.

37. See in particular, Charles M. Haar and Demetrius S. Iatridis, *Housing the Poor in Suburbia: Public Policy at the Grass Roots* (Cambridge, Mass.: Ballinger, 1974).

38. See, for example, Terry Clark, 'Community Structure, Decision Making, Budget Expenditures and Urban Renewal in 51 American Communities', *American Sociological Review,* Vol. 33, No. 4 (August 1968), pp. 576-93; Amos M. Hawley, 'Community Power and Urban Renewal Success', *The American Journal of Sociology* Vol. 60, No. 4 (January 1963), pp. 422-31; Thomas R. Dye, 'Urban School Desegregation: A Comparative Analysis', *'Urban Affairs Quarterly,* Vo. 55, No. 2 (December 1968), pp. 141-84.

39. For critiques of this literature, see Herbert Jacob and Michael Lipsky, 'Outputs, Structure and Power: An Assessment of Changes in the Study of State and Local Politics', in Richard Hofferbert and Ira Sharkansky (eds), *State and Urban Politics* (Boston: Little Brown, 1971), pp. 14-40; David H. McKay, 'Political Science and Urbanism in Europe: Some Lessons From the American Experience', *European Journal of Political Research,* Vol. 3 (1975), pp. 303-17.

40. Haar and Iatridis, op. cit., Chapter 11.

41. See James Q. Wilson and Edward Banfield, *City Politics* (Cambridge: Harvard University Press, 1963), Conclusions.

42. Haar and Iatridis, op. cit., Chapters 4-8.

43. For a good description of the powers of suburban communities see Thomas P. Murphy and John Rehfuss, *Urban Politics in the Suburban Era* (Homewood, Illinois: Dorsey Press, 1976), Chapters 2-3.

44. Haar and Iatridis, op. cit., Chapters 4-8. All of the following analysis of Stoughton is based on Haar and Iatridis' Chapter 8.

45. 'Kenilworth Still Leads Status Derby', *Chicago Daily News,* Monday 14 August 1972, pp. 1 and 10.

46. The following analysis is based on interviews with HUD officials conducted during 1971 and 1972.

47. Under the Housing Act of 1965 local authorities can lease units from private owners for use in public housing programmes.

48. Following the failure to build the 56 units of public housing, the case was declared moot, *Lorraine Cooper v. CCHA and HUD* No. 70 C 595 (N.D. Ill), Order of Dismissal, 9 November 1971.

49. In Haar and Iatridis' study, East Providence was in this category, it fought hard (and in the main successfully) to exclude low income housing, op. cit., Chapter 7.

50. Martin Meyerson and Edward C. Barfield, *Politics, Planning and the Public Interest* (New York: Free Press, 1955). The following analysis is partly based on interviews with HUD officials and spokesmen for the CHA and ACLU, all conducted during 1971 and 1972.

51. 296 F. Supp. 908 (1969) at 910-914.

52. 296 F. Supp. 907 Judgment Order at 1.

53. See *Urban Crisis Monitor,* Vol. IV, No. 9 (15 May 1971), pp. 14-15.
54. HUD/City of Chicago Research Team, *Preliminary Report on Chicago Housing Supply* (Chicago: City of Chicago, mimeo, 1970), pp. 42-52.
55. HUD/City of Chicago Letter of Intent, 12 May 1971, p. 2 (mimeo).
56. 448 F. 2nd at 737-40.
57. 332 F. Supp. at 369.
58. Ibid., at 370.
59. 457 F. 2nd 124 (1972).
60. Quoted by Justice Clark, *Gautreaux v. CHA and James T. Lynn, Secretary of HUD,* 503 F. 2nd 930 (1974) at 934.
61. Ibid., at 935.
62. 418 US 717 (1974).
63. *Hills v. Gautreaux* U.S. (1976).
64. 436 F. 2nd 809 (1970).
65. 392 US 409 (1968).
66. 393 US 385 (1969).
67. Ibid., at 391. See also *Reitman v. Mulkey,* 387 US 369 (1967).
68. 318 F. Supp. 669 (1970). Affirmed 436 F. 2nd 108 (1970). *Certiorari* denied 401 US 1010 (1971).
69. 436 F. 2nd 108, at 710.
70. 425 F. 2nd 1037 (1970).
71. Ibid., at 1040. Although in *Southern Alameda Spanish Speaking Organisation v. Union City (California),* 424 F. 2nd 291 (1970), a Ninth Circuit Appeal Court found that the motivation behind Union City's referendum excluding a Mexican American housing project was not relevant because it was not possible to measure motivation. The court denied SASSOs plea for an injunction against the referendum, and referred the case to the District Court for resolution. In *Ranjel v. City of Lansing,* 417 F, 2nd 321 (1969), a similar request for an injunction was also refused because motivation was judged irrelevant. For a discussion of the problems involved in trying to distinguish racial motives and effects, see Robert Freilich and G. Allen Bass, 'Exclusionary Zoning: Suggested Litigation Approaches', *Urban Lawyer,* Vol. 3, No. 3 (Summer 1971); Donna M. Murasky, 'James v. Valtierra: Housing Discrimination by Referendum?', *Chicago Law Review,* Vol. 39 (1971), pp. 129-42.
72. 402 US 137 (1971).
73. For a discussion of the 14th Amendment's coverage, see Donna Murasky, op.cit., pp. 119-29, and Footnote 20; 'Developments in the Law — Equal Protection', *Harvard Law Review,* Vol. 82 (1969), p. 1065 (Note); 'The Equal Protection Clause and Exclusionary Zoning After Valtierra and Dandridge', *Yale Law Journal,* Vol. 81 (1971), pp. 61-86 (Note); Ralph K. Winter, 'Poverty, Economic Equality, and the Equal Protection Clause', in Philip B. Kurland (ed.), *Supreme Court Review,* 1972 (Chicago: University of Chicago Press, 1973), pp. 41-102.
74. *Mahaley v. Cuyahoga Metropolitan Housing Authority,* 355 F Supp. 1257 (1973); on this case see 'Civil Rights', *Fordham Urban Law Journal,* Vol. 11, No. 2 (Winter 1974), pp. 349-62.
75. *Warth v. Seldin* 422 U.S. 490 (1975). This followed a 1974 decision, *Village of Belle Terre v. Borass* 416 US 7 (1974), which upheld certain exclusionary practices.
76. On Nixon's New Federalism see Rowland Evans and Robert Novak, *Nixon in the White House* (New York: Vintage, 1972), pp. 241-4.
77. From interviews with Department of Justice Civil Rights Division Lawyers conducted in 1971.

78. Office of the White House, Press Release, *Statement of the President on Federal Policies Relative to Equal Housing Opportunity*, 11 June 1971, p. 9.

79. Ibid., p. 11.

80. The National Committee Against Discrimination in Housing had demanded action in 1970, see NCDH, *Open Housing and Open Communities, NCDH Recommendations to the President of the United States* (New York: NCDH, 1970), p. 9.

81. *US v. City of Black Jack, Missouri*, 508 F. 2d 1179 (1974).

82. HUD, Office of the Assistant Secretary for Housing Production and Mortgage Credit, FHA Commissioner, 'Project Selection Criteria', *Federal Register*, Vol. 37, No. 4 (7 January 1972), pp. 205-9.

83. Based on interviews with HUD staff conducted during 1971 and 1972.

84. Under the *Housing and Community Development Act 1974.*

85. Also under the *1974 Housing and Community Development Act* as reported in Wolman, op. cit., pp. 97-8.

86. Reported in *Congressional Quarterly Almanac* (Washington D.C.: Vol. XXX, 1974), pp. 345-63.

87. Michael N. Danielson, *The Politics of Exclusion* (New York: Columbia University Press, 1976), Chapters 9 and 10.

6 PUBLIC HOUSING POLICIES AND RACE IN THE UK

In comparison with the United States, the most striking feature of the British housing market is the size and resilience of the public sector. In 1971, 31 per cent of all British households rented from a local authority,[1] compared with just 13 per cent in 1947,[2] and while there have been considerable fluctuations in public housing building, the sector continues to account for over one third of all housing starts.[3] The size of the public housing sector reflects the fact that successive British governments have viewed housing as an area where the state should play a leading role in providing a basic need which the free market has failed to satisfy.

Housing, therefore, is considered a social service and a central part of social policy.[4] Hence, Section 91 of the 1957 Housing Act states that 'it shall be the duty of every local authority to consider housing conditions in their district and the needs of the district with respect to the provision of further housing accommodation'.[5] So, as was stressed in Chapter 4, local governments have a *general* responsibility for housing, not just public housing. Where there is overcrowding or insanitary conditions in the private sector, the local authority has the power to clear the area or to enforce public health regulations. While public housing is undoubtedly meant to cater for the particular needs of the disadvantaged, it has been understood, at least since 1949 that local governments should also provide 'general needs' housing for the population both through the public housing programme and to a lesser extent by providing mortgages for house purchase.

Unlike the United States, then, public housing in Britain is designed for a large and quite varied section of the population. Indeed, as Table 6.1 shows, in 1972 just 0.5 per cent of US public housing households had a gross income in excess of the national median and 36.5 per cent earned less than 25 per cent of the median. Comparable figures for the UK were 40.1 per cent and 8.1 per cent. Table 6.1 also shows, however, that few British public housing tenants are well off. The largest single group is, in fact, 'the respectable working class' — skilled workers, foremen and the like who account for about 40 per cent of tenants. Unskilled, semi-skilled and service workers account for about 25 per cent, as do the retired.[6] Public housing, then, while not exclusively housing for the poor, caters in part for the poor but predominantly for the gainfully employed working class.

Table 6.1 Public Housing Households in the United States and the United Kingdom, by Income Distribution, 1972

Gross Household Income as a % of Gross Median Income	% of Total Households Residing in Public Housing	
	UK	US
Less than 25% of Median	8.1	36.5
Between 25-50% of Median	18.2	40.6
Between 50-75% of Median	15.6	15.4
Between 75-100% of Median	17.8	7.0
Between 100-125% of Median	14.7	.5
Between 125-150% of Median	10.3	—
Between 150-200% of Median	10.1	—
More than 200% of Median	5	—

Source: Reprinted by permission of the publisher, from Harold L. Wolman, *Housing and Housing Policy in the US and the UK* (Lexington, Mass.: Lexington Books, D. C. Heath and Company, 1975), Table 3-5, p. 34

Another notable feature of British public housing is the extent to which its management and quality is controlled by local rather than central governments. Via substantial grants, central governments do subsidise public or council housing, and national legislation determines the main direction of policy. Moreover, central governments can, at least in theory, legislate to control all aspects of public housing. By tradition, however, they have left the day-to-day management of housing very much to local governments.[7] So, as far as the allocation, location and quality of units are concerned, local governments exercise wide discretion.

A third important feature of Britain's public housing is the extent to which it has been incorporated into a comprehensive planning system. During the 1940s it was envisaged that most urban growth would be channelled to new towns and growth towns outside the major conurbations and that public housing would dominate the housing market.[8] Neither has transpired in its totality, partly because economic growth and a concomitant increase in the size of the private sector has been much greater than expected, and partly because changes in government have produced considerable deviations from the policies conceived by Labour in the 1940s. What is important to note, however, is that governments and bureaucrats have generally accepted macro-land use planning as both legitimate and necessary. In this context, publicly financed housing in new towns[9] and in 'overspill' estates around London have become part of the overall planning system. In addition, another major aspect of post-war urban policy, slum clearance, has been achieved via national policy, and public housing units have been erected in their hundreds of thousands on sites cleared by local authorities under the guidance of national legislation. What the United Kingdom has, therefore, which the US so patently lacks, is a system which incorporates public housing into a planning structure with stated social objectives such as urban containment or the relief of overcrowding. Sometimes these objectives are not precisely defined, and often policies are not implemented effectively, but the highly intrusive role of government and especially of central government is accepted, and the potential for further 'engineering' to achieve social objectives is great.

It is against this background that discussion of the relationship between racial minorities and public housing in Britain must take place. Unlike the United States, public sector housing in Britain has not been reserved for a particular class or racial group, it caters for a wide section of the population and it is part of a generally much more active public sector. Also, when Britain's black immigrants arrived in the 1950s and 1960s they constituted a relatively small group in desperate housing need which faced a public sector already established as a major housing provider for the industrial working class. In the US, public housing and the more recent subsidy programmes have virtually been shaped by racial factors. So much so that family public housing is looked on as synonymous with black housing. As a result, public controversy has centred on the question of siting 'black' public sector housing in white areas. In Britain, this has not (at least so far) been the central issue. Instead, debate has dwelt on minority families' *access* to public housing, and on local authorities' *allocation* policies – the location and quality of housing provided for non-whites.

As was pointed out in Chapter 4, the British housing market is not as readily divided into private and public sectors as is the American. Government influences the private sector in a variety of ways, and as was shown, this is particularly true of inner city private housing which has been profoundly influenced by the enforcement of public health regulations, and by slum clearance and council mortgage lending policies. The following analysis, however, will be mainly confined to public housing policies, and especially to the problem of housing access and allocation.

Race and Public Housing 1961-8

In 1966, after the main period of immigration was over, and after the first immigration controls had been introduced, very few black British lived in council housing. A 1966 Political and Economic Planning (PEP) survey found less than 1 per cent of the sample lived in council housing, compared with 26 per cent for the white population.[10] PEP's sample tended to concentrate on areas of minority concentration and therefore excluded the newer council estates, but the 1966 census showed only 4.2 per cent of non-whites in the London area renting from a local authority compared with 22.2 per cent for whites.[11] Given the poor housing conditions of most black families, this reflected badly on a programme whose major objective was to relieve housing need and hardship. However, these figures are not at all surprising given the allocation policies adopted by most local authorities.

It was earlier pointed out that British public housing is meant to provide 'general needs' housing for the population, but that local authorities have to give reasonable preference to large families and to those living in overcrowded, insanitary or unsatisfactory housing conditions. The relevant legislation (1949 and 1957 Housing Acts) says little more than this, however, so local governments have great discretion in deciding on which sort of family should be given priority. Given the situation of acute housing shortage that has existed in Britain since the war (and which, if anything, intensified during the 1960s), this discretion puts considerable power into the hands of those local housing officials responsible for running the system. The system is, of course, discriminatory in the sense that it rations housing between different groups. As the Cullingworth Report put it 'certain applicants are selected, given a particular priority and allocated specific houses. As a result, other applicants are refused, given lesser priority or denied particular houses'.[12]

Any person applying for council housing has to go on to a waiting list — unless his or her family are eligible for council housing because they live in a clearance area or because they have been evicted or are homeless. How local authorities determine priorities between different sorts of applicants, or between those on the waiting list, varies from authority to authority and many highly complex formulae are used.[13] Generally speaking, however, local authorities give priority in terms of time to those in greatest need: the homeless and those whose desperate housing circumstances demand very rapid solution. Such families are usually prepared to accept lower quality housing, simply because they are so desperate. Similarly, among those who are rehoused from cleared areas, the most disadvantaged groups in terms of housing circumstances will be those most dependent on local authority help, and therefore able to exercise least housing choice. Among waiting list applicants, need is also a criterion, but so also is 'desert', in particular how long an applicant has been resident in the area, and how long he or she has been on the list.

Quite dramatic variations in housing quality exist within the public sector, especially between post-war 'cottage estates' of semi-detached single family houses built in suburban or near suburban contexts, and pre-war inner city overcrowded apartment buildings.[14] Councils also acquire 'shortlife' property in clearance areas, which can be used as temporary council housing and which is often of very low quality. What sort of public housing a family is allocated, can, therefore, be of great importance.

The allocation of council housing is, then, based on principles of rationing, where the needs and deserts of particular families have to be matched with what is available in terms of the quality and quantity of the existing public housing stock. Rationing principles derive only in part from national legislation which, it should be recalled, is remarkably vague in this area. They derive also from the values, prejudices and traditions of the housing management departments. Generalisation in this area is difficult, but most departments are geared to serving the needs of the 'respectable' or 'deserving' working class, rather than to providing a welfare service for the very poor.[15] They display, therefore, a bias in favour of clean, orderly small families. This is reflected in the size of units built,[16] in the attitudes of housing visitors who grade potential tenants according to housekeeping standards,[17] and in the tendency to segregate housing estates along class lines. 'Problem families' — those with large families and social problems — are allocated to particular estates usually inferior in quality, while 'respectable' families are allocated to the better estates.[18]

Given these practices and values it is not surprising that the scope for systemic bias against non-white families is considerable. Two observers of current housing practices and race relations have

summarised the ways in which the system can lead to racial
disadvantage thus:

1. Eligibility qualifications — particularly those depending on
   periods of residence — will tend to work to the disadvantage of
   all newcomers, including minority groups.
2. Priority systems may work to the disadvantage of minority
   groups, who may, for example, be concentrated among those
   sources of applicants which are given a low priority,
   particularly in terms of quality of accommodation; thus there
   is a high concentration of West Indians among the homeless in
   London. Again, where points are awarded to waiting list
   applicants for length of residence or for length of time on the
   list, this may tend to work to the disadvantage of newcomers.
3. The administration of the matching procedure might be racially
   biased even though this was not the result of any set policy.
   However formalised the procedures are, they must involve some
   element of personal judgement, guesswork or apparently random
   selection, and there is always the possibility that these
   judgements might be made by prejudiced people, with the
   result that racial discrimination occurs.
4. The pool of available accommodation might be unsuited to the
   needs of the minority groups; for example, it might include too
   few of the large properties which tend to be needed by the
   minority groups. Again, the properties in central areas which are
   close to the previous homes of Asians and West Indians, and
   also to their places of work, might tend to be of an inferior
   quality.
5. The assessment of housekeeping standards by housing visitors
   might be racially or culturally biased.
6. The element of choice in the allocation procedure might tend
   to work to the disadvantage of the minority groups; for
   example, white applicants might tend to fall among those
   categories which are able to exercise a relatively greater choice,
   and in exercising their choice, they might tend to restrict the
   remaining scope for choice by the minority groups.
7. The minority groups might suffer a range of disadvantages
   because of poor communication; they might tend to be ignorant
   about council housing, and fail to apply for it even when in
   need; they might be handicapped in their dealings with the
   council by ignorance of the system and how to work it; and

communication between minority applicants and housing
visitors or other council officers might be so poor that the
applicants fail to make their wishes understood.[19]

By 1969 several studies had confirmed that some of these factors
were at work and at that time were in particular responsible for the
exclusion of blacks from public housing.

So, the findings from a 1967 PEP study of six local authorities'
housing practices[20] can be summarised thus:

i.   There was little evidence of overt discrimination.
ii. In one of the areas studied there was little demand for housing
     among blacks, but in all the others few were housed because they
     simply did not qualify under the system. In particular, waiting lists
     with residential time qualifications were effectively excluding
     minorities from public housing.
iii. Slightly larger numbers were rehoused via clearance
     programmes, but generally, local authorities claimed not to have
     cleared many areas of high residence, or when they had cleared
     The latter was especially true of houses in multi-occupation
     where local authorities would rehouse the owner and his family
     but not other tenants in the house.
iv. There was a marked and near universal tendency not to keep
     records containing racial data. In some authorities this was
     accompanied by a reluctance to accept that there was a 'colour
     problem'. Indeed, many officials were afraid that publicity
     highlighting the housing problems of blacks might make life very
     difficult for them.[21]

The PEP findings were substantiated by further evidence published in
1967 in Elizabeth Burney's *Housing on Trial*. Burney's study of several
large local authorities in London, the Midlands and the North revealed
that some of the allocation practices generally recognised as invidious
were having particularly injurious effects on black applicants. For
example, good housekeeping standards are recognised by most local
housing officials as a major criterion for being given a good quality
house. As Burney puts it: 'The principle is simple: a clean person gets
a clean house, and dirty person gets a dirty house.'[22] Housing visitors'
subjective reports on housekeeping usually worked to the disadvantage
of future black tenants resulting in their being sent to lower quality,

older, inner city estates. Indeed this seemed to be a general policy adopted by many authorities, and is also noted by the 1967 PEP Report.[23]

However, the central finding of these early studies was that biases within the system were denying blacks access to council housing. One common defence employed by local government spokesmen was that blacks did not want council housing; their preference was for owner occupied housing. Certainly the statistics revealed a remarkably high degree of owner occupation among minority groups (see Chapter 4, Table 4.2) and especially among Asians. However, the evidence strongly suggests a relatively high level of demand for council housing among West Indians (the 1967 PEP data showed that 23 per cent of West Indians had considered applying for council housing, compared with 9 per cent among Pakistanis and 10 per cent among Indians).[24] Moreover, some blacks were poorly informed about their eligibility for council housing, or considered the waiting lists hopelessly long. The PEP survey showed that 47 per cent of respondents had not applied for council housing because the waiting period was too long, while a full 20 per cent thought they were not qualified for council housing.[25]

There was little evidence in these studies that blacks were being deliberately excluded from council housing on racial grounds. Nor was there much evidence that local government officials and politicians perceived race and housing as a political or social problem. Certainly, there was nothing equivalent to the American practices of deliberate exclusion from white areas, or of the segregation of public housing projects. It is much more likely that local officials assumed that blacks would gradually melt into British society, and as they slowly became eligible for facilities such as public housing, so they would be helped towards this goal. No special provision for blacks, including the keeping of records, was necessary, therefore. For such views to be held suggests a high degree of ignorance and indifference among politicians and officials concerning both the nature of the black communities and the ways in which official rules and procedures affect their housing and other opportunities. Research by Katznelson, Thomas and Newton has conformed that such ignorance is widespread.[26]

Judging by the 1965 White Paper on Immigration from the Commonwealth, central government shared this ignorance and indifference, for the White Paper rather glibly assumed that any problem that there was would gradually melt away through the normal working of the system:

> As time goes on, immigrants will qualify for rehousing by local
> authorities either by virtue of residential qualifications or through
> being displaced by slum clearance or other redevelopment. Thus it
> will become commonplace for Commonwealth immigrants to be
> rehoused by local authorities in pursuance of their normal
> statutory responsibilities. This in itself will tend to break up
> excessive and undesirable concentrations.[27]

Such official attitudes together with the inadequacies of the 1965
Act inspired new debate on race relations, and during 1967 a campaign
to enact a more comprehensive race relations bill got underway. A
major element in the campaign was the publication in 1967 of the
Street Report on anti-discrimination legislation.[28] Chapter 13 of
the Report concerned itself with municipal housing and made several
recommendations as to how any new legislation should affect local
authority housing policies. In particular, heeding the evidence of the
PEP report on racial discrimination, Street called for more central
control of local authority housing allocation practices. The wide
discretion exercised by local authorities in allocating families
displaced by clearance or those in acute housing need had, the report
claimed, led to discriminatory effects, even if policies were not
motivated by racial discrimination. Only more central control
could fundamentally change this situation:

> . . . over large areas of their housing activities, local authorities
> have an uncontrolled discretion how they carry out their
> obligation to rehouse and their powers of providing housing.
> The Ministry of Housing and Local Government do not record
> information about how these powers are in fact exercised by the
> various authorities. If the present system for the control and
> management of public housing is to continue it does not seem
> to us possible to eliminate discrimination without making
> provision for much more detailed control, which would have the
> specific purpose of requiring local authorities to satisfy the
> ministry about the non-discriminatory nature of all their
> policies.[29]

Accordingly, the report recommended that the Ministry together
with the Race Relations Board should play a much more active role

in monitoring local authorities' waiting lists and general allocation policies. The report even went so far as to recommend that where rehousing from cleared areas was involved, local authorities should submit a plan to the central government showing which categories of occupants were being rehoused where. By so doing, the common practice of rehousing minority families in poor quality estates in the inner city could be avoided.[30] In other words, the Report was recommending that central government take a lead in guiding plans to disperse minority families from inner city estates.

As it turned out, the 1968 Race Relations Act completely failed to include special references to local authority housing. Instead the new law provided blanket prohibitions on discrimination practised by private or public authorities. It is worth repeating the point made in Chapter 4 that the eventually rather weak 1968 Act resulted at least in part from political opposition to a strong anti-discrimination law, and to the continuing tendency among civil servants and politicians of all parties to assume that the stronger any anti-discrimination law was, the more likely it would be to politicise the race issue and therefore lead to a deterioration in race relations.[31]

Race and Public Housing 1969-76

In spite of the 1968 Act's failure to make special provision for council housing, an authoritative statement on race and public housing did appear in 1969 when the Central Housing Advisory Committee for the Ministry of Housing and Local Government reported (the Cullingworth Report).[32] Cullingworth devoted a whole chapter to housing minority families much of which confirmed the findings of earlier studies of local authority housing practices. The report also noted that without comprehensive records it was difficult to make recommendations as to how policy should develop.[33] However, it did plunge into one controversial area with some conviction: dispersal. The extent to which minorities were concentrated in certain towns and neighbourhoods was well known in 1969, and some evidence existed showing how local authorities were tending to concentrate minority families in certain inner city estates. Probably more energy has been expended on discussing dispersal than on any other aspect of race relations. It provokes heated debate because so many fundamental liberal principles are involved. On one side the concentration of racial minorities in certain areas, even if it is a result of market forces rather than of compulsion, tends to

compound their disadvantaged position, especially in housing and
education, and can lead to the emergence and growth of ghetto-like
communities. Concentration also increases the sense of separateness
between the different communities and might, therefore, damage race
relations. Dispersing concentrations of blacks, so the argument runs, can
therefore only serve the best interests of both minority and host
communities. On the other side, concentration enhances the cultural
solidarity of communities, and dispersal carries with it notions of
compulsion incompatible with free choice. The Cullingworth
committee was concerned with what public sector housing could do
to aid dispersal. The broader question of dispersing non-whites *en
masse* from certain geographical areas was not discussed, nor has it been
part of the general debate on dispersal.

Cullingworth accepted that compulsory dispersal in public housing
would be unacceptable. Quoting from the Birmingham Community
Relations Commission, the committee agreed that 'this would involve
treating people as things and would destroy the cultural and social
links that exist between people of a similar background'.[34] However,
the committee was convinced that concentration was inimical to
minority families' interests because it led to an intensification of their
disadvantaged position. Accordingly the committee recommended that
'voluntary' dispersal should be an objective but not the overriding
purpose of policy:

> Dispersal is a laudable aim of policy, but this policy needs
> pursuing with full respect for the wishes of the people concerned.
> Dispersal of immigrant concentrations should be regarded as a
> desirable consequence, but not the overriding purpose, of housing
> individual immigrant families on council estates. The criterion of
> full, informed, individual choice comes first.[35]

Unfortunately, Cullingworth failed to show how, in the formulation
of policy, dispersal and individual choice were to be reconciled. The
report acknowledged that there would be 'problems of management'
and that white tenants may show great resistance to minority families
as neighbours,[36] but it said no more.

In fact, between 1969 and 1976 much more concrete evidence of
local authorities' allocation practices was published which provides
a more rational basis on which to discuss the question of dispersal.
Two major trends appeared. First, while still under-represented in
relation to their housing needs, the number of minority families in

council housing rose quite sharply; and second, the concentration of blacks in certain inner city estates appeared to be increasingly common practice. Let us look at each of these in turn.

By 1974 26 per cent of West Indians and 4 per cent of Asians rented from the council compared with 28 per cent in the population as a whole (see Chapter 4, Table 4.2). According to the PEP 1976 Report, the *Facts of Racial Disadvantage,* these still quite low figures partly reflect a lack of awareness of public housing opportunities. Only about 50 per cent of Asians and two thirds of West Indians answered positively to the question 'Does the local council in your area provide houses or flats to rent?', compared with 85 per cent of whites.[37]

Table 6.2 shows, however, that there is considerable pent-up demand among non-white private tenants for council housing, among whom 49 per cent of West Indians and 38 per cent of Asians (compared with 25 per cent of whites) were, in 1974, on a waiting list. Table 6.2 also shows that among Asians renting privately there has been a recent increase in council house applications, with 13 per cent having been on the waiting list for one year or less. Further PEP survey data of all those who have ever applied for council housing shows that in 1974 51 per cent of whites were eventually successful in obtaining tenancies compared with 37 per cent of West Indians and a mere 4 per cent among Asians.[38] Of course these figures partly reflect the fact that many blacks (and especially Asians) have only recently applied for council housing and are, therefore, more likely still to be on the waiting list. But it may also reflect a continuing bias in the system which makes it more difficult for minority families to obtain council tenancies.

That such bias continues to exist is confirmed by the 1975 PEP report *Racial Minorities and Council Housing,*[39] which is easily the most comprehensive analysis of the subject to date. In this report, David Smith and Anne Whalley studied the practices of ten (anonymised) local authorities with high proportions of blacks among their population. While considerable local variations were discernible, the report found that allocation systems continued to discriminate against minorities. Residential qualifications (in London, it is five years), the exclusion of owner occupiers from waiting lists, and the general practice of giving residential qualifications and time on the waiting list as much weight as 'need' in the allocation process tended to work to the disadvantage of minorities.[40] Moreover, in the matching process, minority families continued to come off worse because the pool of available property was often inappropriate to

Table 6.2 Applications for Council Housing by Tenure — Whites and Minorities Compared, 1974

Heads of household	Owner Occupiers			Owner Occupiers		
	West Indians	Asians	Whites	West Indians	Asians	Whites
	%	%	%	%	%	%
Have applied for council housing at some time	17	7	25	57	43	45
Now on council waiting list	3	3	2	49	38	25
Have been on list for:						
1 year or less	—	1	1	9	13	5
2 years	—	1	—	14	13	4
3-4 years	—	—	—	18 ⎱ 26	9 ⎱ 12	12 ⎱ 17
5 years or more	3	1	1	3 ⎰	3 ⎰	5 ⎰
Period not stated	—	—	—	1	—	—

Source: David J. Smith, *The Facts of Racial Disadvantage* (London: PEP Broadsheet No. 560, 1976), Table A79, p. 151.

their specific needs. In particular, large black families often could not be allocated housing or were forced to wait because of large units.[41]

This last point indicates the real 'Catch 22' in the system: minority families suffer greater housing stress, have larger families than white, and are, therefore in the greatest housing need. However, the allocation process means they have less access to council housing, and, as important, are more likely to be allocated inferior property. The latter occurs for a variety of reasons. For one thing those rehoused via clearance schemes, or because they are homeless or in an emergency housing situation, are much more likely to be rehoused in inferior inner city estates, partly because these are more likely to be immediately available, are more likely to house larger families, and because clearance tenants are often rehoused locally, i.e. in the inner city.

Table 6.3 shows that Asians and West Indians are more likely to be rehoused via these routes, than by their presence on the waiting list with a full 68 per cent of Asian tenants and 52 per cent of West Indians being rehoused other than by the waiting list compared with just 31 per cent for whites.

Comprehensive data on the relationship between minority density and the quality and geographical position of council housing are not

Table 6.3 The Route to Council Housing —
Asians West Indians and Whites, 1974

Council tenants (Heads of Household)	*West Indians*		*Asians*		*Whites*	
	%		%		%	
How came to be rehoused:						
From clearance area	21		42		20	
Homeless	10	} 31	11	} 26	3	} 11
Because of some emergency	21		15		8	
Waiting list	47		14		60	
Other ways	1		12		7	
Not stated	—		6		3	

Source: David J. Smith, *The Facts of Racial Disadvantage* (London: PEP
    Broadsheet No. 560, 1976), Table B.101, p. 243

available, but there is enough evidence to come to some broad
conclusions. Table 6.4 is based on a Runnymede Trust analysis of
1971 census data and shows that in Greater London Council housing
there is a marked tendency towards the concentration of minority
families (corresponding to the census category Both Parents Born
New Commonwealth — BPBNC) in lower quality older estates located
in those inner city areas with a high percentage of blacks in the general
population. Indeed, in the least attractive category of GLC housing
(pre-war high density estates), is found the highest percentage of
minority families — 13.7 per cent, while in the most attractive housing
category (pre- and post-war cottage estates) a mere 0.6 per cent of
tenants were black. The Runnymede Trust report found a similar
pattern for housing operated by the London boroughs, especially in
those boroughs with a high percentage minority population. For
example, in Lambeth, Newham and Wandsworth, all of which are areas
more than 10 per cent black, black council tenants were heavily
concentrated in pre-war flats.[42] Smith and Whalley's study further
substantiates this general trend. In only two out of the ten boroughs
studied was there evidence that black families had not been
concentrated in inner city housing, and in five the evidence of
concentration was overwhelming.[43] Moreover, in four of these five
boroughs blacks had been concentrated in inferior older property.
In the fifth, 'Midtown', while 23 per cent of central city tenants

were black, and just 0.9 per cent of outer area tenants were black,[44] blacks were being allocated to good quality property. However, the city had pursued a massive redevelopment programme including the construction of good quality two storey housing in the inner area, so little relationship between racial occupancy and quality of housing was found.

Table 6.4 GLC: Distribution of BPBNC by Type of Estate, 1971

Estates in Inner Boroughs	(1) Total Population	(2) Persons with BPBNC	(3) % BPBNC	(4) ED with highest % BPBNC
Pre-war: high density	38,095	5,218	13.7	43.7
low density	22,434	364	1.6	8.3
1945-60: high density	37,094	1,806	4.9	29.0
low density	43,136	1,505	3.5	20.9
1961-71: high density	23,437	779	3.3	20.9
low density	10,773	326	3.0	13.0
Estates in Outer Boroughs				
Pre- and post-war cottage estates	135,855	805	0.6	6.6
Estates built since 1960	3,787	79	2.1	3.5
TOTAL	314,611	10,882	3.5	43.7

Source: *Race and Council Housing in London* (Runnymede Trust, mimeo), 1975, Table 1, p. 5

Not all the inferior council owned property consists of pre-war apartments. Indeed, the lowest quality council houses are the acquired properties awaiting redevelopment. Some of these are shared dwellings, and blacks have found themselves allocated to such properties in numbers proportionately vastly greater than white tenants. 1974 survey figures show that 10 per cent of West Indians and 18 per cent of Asian council tenants live in shared dwellings compared with 0.6 per cent of white tenants.[45]

Smith and Whalley's study shows that a planned policy of racial discrimination was rarely responsible either for racial concentration or for blacks being allocated inferior properties. Instances of racial discrimination were detected in several boroughs, but they were usually the result of the prejudices of lower grade officials whose activities were often unknown to housing managers.[46] Indeed, a general problem in housing departments is a lack of professionalism and strictly adhered-to operating standards, which result in poor administration and inconsistent policies. But these factors pall beside the basic fact that blacks receive unfavourable treatment because of the existing relationship between type and intensity of demand for housing among blacks and the available housing supply.

These findings indicate the very small extent to which the Cullingworth Report's cautious advice on dispersal has been heeded since 1969. They also show how wildly inaccurate were the predictions of the 1965 White Paper which claimed that high concentration of blacks in council housing would be avoided by the normal working of the system. How have local governments responded to this increasingly obvious concentration of blacks in certain estates? Smith and Whalley found that most of the boroughs' housing departments in their study claimed to have dispersal policies, but only one had been implemented. Other sources confirm, however, that some localities have operated dispersal policies, the aim of most being to prevent the build-up of 'black estates' with serious social problems. Birmingham, for example, has operated a policy of restricting the ratio of blacks to whites in particular streets to 1 in 13. Some commentators have argued that such a policy, whatever the motive, may be both illegal and unfair.[47]. To understand why this is so, it will be useful to look at dispersal policies in some detail. The dispersal policy of one locality, the London Borough of Lewisham, has been partly documented, and therefore is appropriate for closer analysis.

The Lewisham Case

Lewisham is an inner London borough with, in 1971, a black population of 8.3 per cent, and a minority council tenant population of 7.2 per cent.[48] Following the publication of the Cullingworth Report and the rapid growth of the black population of the Borough's northern estates (by 1971 one of these had a black population of 45.6 per cent − the highest of any estate in London),[49] the Borough decided to adopt a dispersal policy. In future, once the number of blacks in any tower block or street had reached 50 per cent, they would be steered away from the northern estates and towards the 'white' estates in other parts of the Borough.[50] However, by 1974 it was obvious that the effect of this policy was to reduce considerably the housing opportunities of black families. Blacks with high points scores on the waiting list were being denied housing because the only available and suitable units occurred in the already integrated northern estates. This was because most of the properties which did become available were too small or were high-rise (West Indian families showed great reluctance to move above the fifth floor). So, white families with low points scores were being housed, while the blacks had to wait.[51] A report on this policy published by the Borough strikes right at the heart of this problem by pointing out that: 'A policy of dispersal is only viable and effective when there is somewhere to disperse to — when there is a reasonable expectation of a steady flow of vacancies scattered throughout the Borough.'[52] In other words dispersal policies are extremely difficult to operate in the context of serious housing shortage. If minority families are prohibited from certain areas, suitable housing must be available for them elsewhere. This was not the case in Lewisham, but even if it was, their policy would have violated two important liberal principles. First, the policy was compulsory. Once the quota was reached blacks *could not* move to the northern area; they were being treated as a separate population group for whom entry to particular estates was forbidden. Second, had they been allocated housing in more attractive areas the principle of equity would have been violated, for unless the better housing was available in unlimited supply (which is never the case) white families in similar or greater housing need than blacks would have been denied housing opportunity to make way for blacks. In fact, the housing was not available, but equity was violated anyway, because blacks were denied housing to make way for whites. These last points are vital, because they illustrate that unless local authorities are willing to abandon completely the criteria used for allocating families, a policy of *voluntary* dispersal will never work. Voluntary dispersal would involve giving minority families an element of choice which is at present denied to all housing applicants in great housing need. Large families, the homeless or those living in desperate housing conditions have virtually no choice under the present system; they simply accept what is offered. Voluntary dispersal would discriminate positively in favour of black families in this situation by greatly extending their choice.[53] It seems extremely unlikely that housing managers set in established rules and procedures would tolerate this dramatic departure from traditional practice. Voluntary dispersal also implies considerable changes in the housing stock — in particular the construction of large family units in 'white' probably suburban locales so as to provide black families with a realistic choice. Again, to do this for the specific purpose of dispersing black families would be a fundamental departure from existing policies which tend to concentrate black and white 'problem' families into particular inner city estates. It would also be expensive, and it might well produce the sort of defensive tactics by white communities so familiar in the United States.

Following a complaint to the Race Relations Board in 1974 claiming that blacks were being treated unfairly, Lewisham's policies were investigated by the South Metropolitan Conciliation Committee of the Board. In February 1975, the Committee reported and found that the Borough's policy contravened the 1968 Race Relations Act. (Birmingham's dispersal policy has also been found to be illegal). However, the Committee agreed that the Borough's policy was well intentioned, its aim being to prevent the growth of ghetto-like conditions with their attendant social problems. No litigation ensued, but the Borough agreed to adopt a 'solution' which dispensed with compulsion, and effectively returned to the *status quo ante* of 1969:

> The current policy is very much more flexible in that when the opportunity for dispersal presents itself this is offered to black applicants, although there is no compulsion to disperse, but the lack of this opportunity is no longer in any way a barrier to an offer being made. In practice this approach achieves much the same rate of dispersal as the earlier policy without the inequitable side effects, but it does not solve the longer term problems of the large and growing potential ghettoes in the north of the Borough. The solution of this latter problem is clearly a matter of great and growing concern both to the Council and to the whole community.[54]

The last two sentences suggest that the authors accept that this is not a solution at all, for given the existing housing stock very few black families can be dispersed under this policy.

The Lewisham case highlights the general difficulties involved in adopting dispersal policies and also points to the role that the law could play in such cases. It is perhaps not surprising that most local authorities have declined to adopt dispersal policies, and even have shown some hostility towards them.[55] A 1976 report prepared by the housing directors of some of the largest cities and of the London Boroughs confirms that opposition to dispersal is widespread.[56] It is interesting to note that while this report called for more information on the consequences of allocation policies, and pleaded for more and clearer communication with black tenants, it declined to face up to the formidable problems involved in pursuing a genuinely voluntary dispersal policy.[57] In other words, the housing managers did not recommend the complete overhaul of allocation procedures which would be necessary to implement such a policy.

We will return to the question of dispersal later, but first it is important to establish the views of black minority families themselves on the subject of dispersal. Surveys have not specifically addressed dispersal policies, but they have established that black public housing tenants are much less satisfied with their housing than are white tenants. Hence, the 1974 PEP survey found that only 26 per cent of minority men were very satisfied with their council housing, compared with 45 per cent of white men.[58] A preliminary report on the 1975 GLC letting survey found a similar pattern. Thirty-seven per cent of non-whites were dissatisfied or very dissatisfied with their GLC housing compared with 25 per cent of whites.[59] Moreover, more blacks than whites had thought of moving, and more blacks than whites were interested in living in semi-detached housing as opposed to flats.[60] All these findings indicate that minority families in council housing are not happy in the inner city apartment blocks to which they are largely confined. However, the GLC survey also showed that 63 per cent of blacks compared with 35 per cent of whites were interested in remaining in Inner London. Christopher Duke's study of colour and rehousing in Leeds found a similar pattern in that city — blacks wanted good housing, but were reluctant to move from the inner city area.[61] It is difficult to gauge the significance of this pattern. It may be related to employment opportunities, to community ties or even to ignorance of areas outside the inner city. Certain facts are clear, however. Minority families are generally not happy with their inner city council properties, but they appear to show a preference for living in the inner areas. In sum, the evidence on minority preferences fails to support conclusively any assertion that blacks want to be dispersed to the outer areas.

Race, Public Housing and the Law

It is obvious from the pattern of council housing allocation documented above that between 1969 and 1976 very little had changed from the previous period. An increasing number of minority families were being housed, but the allocation procedure continued to result in disadvantage. In particular, blacks continued to be concentrated into inner city, often inferior estates. While the 1968 Race Relations Act made no distinction between private and public sector housing, Section 5 of the Act makes racial discrimination in housing by *any* party unlawful. Moreover Section 5(b) makes it unlawful to discriminate 'against any person occupying any such accommodation, premises or other land, by deliberately treating him differently from other such occupiers in the like circumstances'. Clearly this prohibits any form of compulsory dispersal or quota system, and the Lewisham case showed how the law was interpreted in just this way. Quite apart from anything else, therefore, compulsory dispersal or the use of quotas is illegal under the 1968 Act.

The Race Relations Board has recognised this both by acting over Lewisham's and Birmingham's quotas, and by publishing, in their 1974 Report, a special memorandum on local authority housing which states that compulsory dispersal is illegal.[62] This memorandum highlights the problems of the Race Relations Board in this area. Most of the advice offered by the circular states quite simply that for local authorities to treat minorities in anything but an equal manner would be discriminatory. This applies to treatment of tenants, waiting lists and general allocation policy. On quality of housing, the memorandum advised that: ' . . . it would be unlawful to offer coloured applicants inferior accommodation, or place them on less desirable or older estates on irrelevant grounds such as their colour, race or origins.'[63]

The Board has, in fact received several dozen complaints concerning local authorities during the 1970-76 period, but in almost all, no unlawful discrimination was found. In only a handful were local authorities found to be acting illegally and in two this was because they had treated 'immigrants' unfairly. Hence, in 1970 Wolverhampton was found to be operating a waiting list rule which required people born outside the UK to wait longer than British born applicants. After investigation, Wolverhampton agreed to drop this rule, but replaced it with a rule discriminating against any applicant who had not lived in the country for ten years. After further investigation this rule was dropped.[64]

The second case is more significant, for it is the only major instance of judicial involvement in the race and council housing area in Britain. In 1969, a complaint from the London Borough of Ealing was received, alleging that the Borough's policy of excluding all non-British and non-Commonwealth citizens from council housing was a contravention of Section (1) of the Act which prohibits discrimination on grounds of national origin.[65] The Board found for the complainant, and the Borough appealed to the High Court. Eventually, in 1972, the House of Lords heard the case and determined that current nationality was not within the scope of the

Act and therefore Ealing's rule was lawful.[66] The 1976 Race Relations Bill amends this position, but it is interesting to note the contrast between the British and the American judicial role in this area.

In Britain, the law gives little scope for anything but very narrow judicial interpretation. There are no provisions equivalent to the American 'affirmative action' provisions which require governments to act to reduce racial disadvantage. Without these, the Race Relations Board can act only when there is a clear instance of discrimination. The morass of local authority practices which are not explicitly discriminatory but which have discriminatory effects go untouched.[67]

Calls for such affirmative action, in particular for central government guidelines standardising local authority allocation policies, have been frequent. They first occurred, as earlier noted, in the Street Report, and in 1971 the House of Commons Select Committee on Race Relations and Immigration argued for Department of the Environment guidance on dispersal.[68] However, when in 1975 the government published its reply to the Select Committee's recommendations,[69] it steadfastly refused to take action in this area. As far as dispersal is concerned the reply to the Select Committee sums up the government's position on this issue. After agreeing that dispersal was an important and complex question, the reply went on:

> The Government does not at this stage consider it appropriate to go beyond this statement of policy, or to issue further guidance to local authorities on this issue. The pattern of settlement of coloured people, particularly as it changes over time, calls for consideration by authorities in the light of the housing and other social conditions in their area, including the number of coloured people there, their cultural, social and family patterns, and their wishes. The Government recognises that the position can differ greatly between one area and another. But it expects local authorities in whose area the issue is a material one to formulate a balanced view on it; and to take it into account as one factor in their general management policies and in the day-to-day allocation of their housing stock, in planning forward programmes of building, redevelopment and improvement. If, for instance, a Housing Action Area, General Improvement Area or Priority Neighbourhood is declared in an area where coloured people have settled these issues might come to the fore and an authority which has declared such an area will want to ensure that the declaration is not seen as an attempt to enforce 'dispersal' against the wishes of those concerned.[70]

So, the government will not use its powers to encourage dispersal, but it has not really given good reasons why it will not do so. Certainly, in government statements on this question there is more than an element of reluctance to interfere with local authority discretion. Perhaps also, the government is aware that any guidelines on dispersal and allocation would immediately raise the issues of equity and need in the current allocation process, which were discussed earlier.

As a result, current practice would be fundamentally challenged, and in all likelihood the political salience of the race and public housing issue would be raised dramatically. Housing is the most jealously guarded policy area in local government, mainly because it combines great spending power with great discretion, and some local governments may well attempt to resist any central government attempt to change the *status quo.* Constitutionally, of course, they have to operate within the confines of national legislation. But it is difficult to imagine national directives in this area which would remove all discretion from the locality. The precise meaning of regulations and the extent of discretion would be hotly debated, and could well end up being decided in the courts.[71]

Given the already noted reluctance of British governments to take any action that would politicise the race question in Britain, it is perhaps not surprising that the government has failed to issue directives standardising allocation procedures. Moreover, new allocation guidelines, by recognising the inequities in the present system, would virtually demand of government some increase in public spending on public housing in order to ease the shortage which makes the present rationing system necessary.

On questions other than allocations, the central government has pledged itself to taking a more active role. Hence, the Department of the Environment has promised to issue guidance on the keeping of racial records, and it is encouraging local authorities to consider their housing needs not just in terms of immediate demand, but in terms of the total social and economic environment as it affects housing supply and demand.[72] Moreover, the government now recognises that the policy of siphoning population to new and expanding towns has had the effect of further aggravating the problems of the inner city by accelerating the outward movement of the economically productive. Accordingly, there is a chance that in future new towns will be required to rehouse some families in housing stress, which would include many black families.

In addition, since 1966, the government has made efforts

through the setting up of Housing Action Areas, General Improvement Areas and Educational Priority Areas, to help the inner city areas via positive discrimination programmes. However, these programmes are poorly funded, often have confused and conflicting aims and are unlikely dramatically to change the face of the inner city. Similarly, the other measures taken or promised on record keeping and new towns policy are likely to change very little, and requesting local authorities to take a more comprehensive view of their housing situations, although helpful, will produce few changes unless the government aids them in tackling housing shortage.

Finally, during 1976 the government announced a complete reappraisal of the post-war planning policy of directing growth away from the central cities and towards the new towns and growth towns. In future, the government promised, the inner cities should be the recipients of new investment. This was, it should be stressed, only the promise of a change in policy; no new programmes were announced. But if greater emphasis on the cities means concentrating public housing construction in the inner city, it could have the important effect of easing housing shortage and therefore removing some of the obstacles to the implementation of more flexible allocation policies.

Whether or not such a policy is pursued, the implementation of the new Race Relations Bill going through Parliament in 1976 is likely to raise the political salience of race and public housing, for the Bill specifically proscribes action whose effects are discriminatory, even if they are not racially motivated. Clearly, the role of the courts in interpreting a new race relations act will be vital, especially given the expanded role of the courts under the Bill. It is possible, therefore, that the policies and procedures of local government housing policies will, as in the United States, be publicised and possibly challenged as a result of judicial action.

Conclusions

Unlike the United States, Britain has a large public housing sector specifically designed to meet the needs of significant sections of the working class. However, in spite of this social service orientation, British public housing has not adequately served the black population. Until the late 1960s, 'colour blind' local allocation policies resulted in few blacks gaining access to council housing, and when, during the 1970s, the number of black families on council estates did increase significantly, most found themselves living in the less attractive inner city flats and houses. There is little evidence either that the limitations on black access to council housing, or the concentration of blacks in the inner city, has resulted directly from overt discrimination. Instead, the operation of rationing principles, and a general bias in many housing departments against certain types of family unit have worked to the disadvantage of many black families.

Attempts at correcting the pattern that has emerged have been few. Because of the many social and political problems involved, most local authorities have preferred not to attempt dispersal or to impose quotas, and the experience of Birmingham and Lewisham's dispersal policies indicates that, quite apart from their questionable legality, dispersal policies that are anything but compulsory cannot work. Meaningful voluntary dispersal would give blacks a degree of choice that is presently denied similarly placed white families, and if such a policy was implemented, the reaction of the white community might be vociferous. It is in any case unlikely that local officials would agree to operate such a system. However, without central government help to ease the housing shortage, the alternative is a continuing concentration of blacks in certain low quality estates often located in areas with a high concentration of blacks in private sector housing. So, whether wittingly or not, existing policies have tended to place blacks among those considered by housing departments as 'problem families' who live on the authorities' 'problem estates'. No doubt some local variations exist, but this is the general pattern.

Central governments, both in their race relations policies and in their general urban policies, have done little to interfere with local discretion in this area. This is in marked contrast to the American experience where even conservative federal governments have attempted to impose scattered site selection policies on reluctant local governments. American federal governments have, it is true, been goaded into such activity by the courts. Moreover, the American experience has been shaped both by the dramatic economic and social contrasts that exist between the ghetto and myriad independent white communities, and by a generally much smaller government involvement in urban affairs. Britain does not have ghettoes, and the British public sector is, at least in theory, sufficiently large to bring about important changes in the pattern of minority settlement that has developed within the private sector. But British central governments, fearing the political consequences of challenging local discretion, have failed to use the public sector to this effect. This was and remains government policy. Recent initiatives on race relations law and on the reinvigoration of the inner city should bring some reappraisal of this policy, but as will be discussed in the next chapter economic and political constraints may prevent any fundamental changes from taking place.

Notes

1. *Social Trends,* No. 3, 1972 (London: HMSO, 1972), Table 102, p.137.
2. Quoted in David Donnison, *The Government of Housing* (Harmondsworth, Middx.: Penguin, 1967), p. 186.
3. Although depending on government policy and the state of the private market, this figure can be over 50 per cent in any one year.
4. See Harold L. Wolman, *Housing and Housing Policy in the US and UK* (Lexington, Mass.: Lexington Books, 1975), Chapter 2.
5. Quoted in Pat Niner, *Local Authority Housing Policy and Practice,* University of Birmingham, Centre for Urban and Regional Studies, Occasional Paper No. 31, (Birmingham, 1975), p. 20.
6. Ibid., Chapter 4.
7. See Alan Murie *et al., Housing Policy and the Housing System* (London: George Allen and Unwin, 1976), Chapter 4; Pat Niner,ibid., Chapter 2.
8. See Peter Hall, *Urban and Regional Planning* (Harmondsworth, Middx.: Penguin, 1974), Chapters 5-7.
9. Housing in New Towns is owned not by local authorities but by the New Town Corporations and in 1974 around 170,000 units were involved. See Alan Murie *et al.,* op. cit., pp. 100-101.
10. Political and Economic Planning, *Racial Discrimination* (London: PEP, 1967), p. 69.
11. Quoted in Community Relations Commission, Discussion Paper No. 1, *Allocation of Council Housing* (London: Mimeo, 1974), p. 1.
12. *Council Housing Purposes, Procedures and Priorities* (Cullingworth Report) (London: HMSO, 1969), p.117.
13. This is confirmed by the first really comprehensive study of local authority housing policies and practices, Pat Niner, op.cit. See also Alan Murie *et al.,* op.cit., Chapter 4.
14. See Alan Murie *et al.,* ibid., pp. 108-14, Cullingworth Report, op. cit., Chapter 1. '
15. This was recognised by the Cullingworth Report, ibid., pp. 18-25; also by the Seebohm Report on the *Local Authority and Allied Personal Social Services* (London: HMSO, 1968),quoted in Cullingworth, ibid.
16. Ibid.
17. See Elizabeth Burney, (London: Oxford University Press, 1967), Chapter III.
18. Ibid.
19. David Smith and Anne Whalley, *Racial Minorities and Public Housing* (London: PEP Broadsheet No. 556, 1975), pp. 12-13.
20. W. W. Daniel, *Racial Discrimination in England* (Harmondsworth, Middx.: Penguin, 1968).
21. Ibid., Chapter 11.
22. Burney, op. cit., p. 71.
23. Ibid., pp. 72-4; Daniel, op. cit., pp. 187-92.
24. Daniel, ibid., p. 194.
25. Ibid., p. 195, see also, Cullingworth Report, op. cit., pp. 125-9.
26. Ira Katznelson *Black Men, White Cities* (London: Oxford University Press, 1973), Chapter 10; Kenneth Newton, *Second City Politics* (London: Oxford

University Press, 1976), Chapter 9; Graham Thomas, 'The Intergration of Immigrants: A Note on the View of Some Local Government Officials', *Race,* Vol. IX, (October 1967).

27. Cmnd. 2379 (1965), p. 18.
28. Harry Street *et al., Anti-Discrimination Legislation* (London: PEP, 1967).
29. Ibid., p. 79.
30. Ibid., para. 131.7, p. 81.
31. On this tendency, see particularly, Ira Katznelson, op. cit., Chapters 8 and 9.
32. Cullingworth Report, op. cit.
33. Ibid., pp. 138-9.
34. Ibid., p. 135
35. Ibid., p. 136.
36. Ibid.
37. David J. Smith, *The Facts of Racial Disadvantage* (London: PEP Broadsheet No. 560, 1976), p. 150.
38. Ibid., Table A80, p. 152.
39. Smith and Whalley, op. cit.
40. Ibid., Chapters III and IV.
41. Ibid., Chapter IV.
42. Runnymede Trust *Race and Council Housing in London* (London: Runnymede Trust, mimeo, 1975), Table 3, p. 8.
43. Smith and Whalley, op. cit., Chapter IV.
44. Ibid., p. 88.
45. Smith, op. cit., Table A77, p. 143.
46. Smith and Whalley, op. cit., p. 108.
47. 'Birmingham's Black Dispersal Illegal', *Roof,* Vol. 1, No. 1 (Jan. 1976), p 4; see also Nicholas Deakin and Clare Ingerson, 'Beyond the Ghetto: The Illusion of Choice', in David Donnison and David Eversley (eds), *London: Urban Patterns, Problems and Policies* (London: Heinemann, 1973), pp. 238-45.
48. *Race and Council Housing in London,* Table 2, p. 6.
49. Ibid., p. 9.
50. Reported in Race Relations Board, *Annual Report of the South Metropolitan Conciliation Committee of the RRB,* RRB, mimeo, 1976, pp. 3-4.
51. John G. Stunnell, *An Examination of Racial Equity in Points Scheme Housing Allocations,* London, Borough of Lewisham, mimeo, 1975, pp. 2-5.
52. Ibid., p. 4.
53. For illustrations of how little choice most disadvantaged families being rehoused enjoy, see Sidney Jacobs, *The Right to a Decent Home* (London: Routledge and Kegan Paul, 1976).
54. Stunnell, op. cit., p. 4.
55. See Donnison and Eversley, op. cit.; House of Commons Select Committee on Race Relations and Immigration, Session 1970-71, *Housing, Vol. 2, Evidence* (London: HMSO, 1971), pp. 45-8.
56. *Housing in Multi-Racial Areas: Report of a Working Party of Housing Directors,* London, Community Relations Commission, 1976.
57. Ibid., Chapter 5.
58. Smith, op. cit., Table B 97, p. 242.
59. Greater London Council, *Race and Council Housing – Preliminary Report of the GLC Housing Lettings Survey,* GLC, mimeo, 1976, p. 7.
60. Ibid.
61. Christopher Duke, *Colour and Rehousing – A study of Redevelopment in Leeds* (London: Institute of Race Relations, 1970).

62. *Report of the Race Relations Board for 1974* (London: HMSO, 1975), pp. 42-3.
63. Ibid., p. 42.
64. *Report of the Race Relations Board for 1970-1971* and for *1971-1972* (London: HMSO, 1971 and 1972), p. 11 and p. 10.
65. *Report of the Race Relations Board for 1969-1970* (London: HMSO, 1970), p. 12.
66. *Ealing London Borough Council v. Race Relations Board* (1972), AC 342. Smith and Whalley's study shows that Ealing's rule was having an adverse effect on housing applicants, not least because some housing officials were unsure which countries were in the Commonwealth and which were not. Smith and Whalley, op. cit., pp. 16-17.
67. For a discussion of this issue, see Lester and Bindman, op. cit., pp. 243-6.
68. House of Commons Select Committee on Race Relations and Immigration, Session 1970-71, *Housing, vol. 1 Report* (London: HMSO, 1971), pp. 25-7.
69. *Race Relations and Housing, Observations on the Report on Housing of the Select Committee on Race Relations and Immigration*, Cmnd. 6232 (1975).
70. Ibid., pp. 9-10.
71. One interesting precedent of judicial activism in Britain was established in July 1976 when the Court of Appeal upheld the Conservative controlled Tameside District Council's refusal to comply with a central government directive to adopt comprehensive secondary schools, *The Times*, 27 July 1976, p. 1.
72. *Race Relations and Housing*, op. cit., pp. 3-8.

7 CONCLUSIONS

The Consequences of Civil Rights Laws

Although there are problems involved in establishing clear causal links between particular civil rights laws and particular consequences, what can be said with certainty is that in neither country has the law transformed the housing opportunities of racial minorities. Indeed, discrimination in the private sector seems hardly to have been affected at all. Some of the more obvious discriminatory tactics have disappeared, and most of those property market actors who have been directly involved in litigation and administrative action have ceased to discriminate — if in many instances only temporarily. However, very few individuals and institutions *have* been directly involved, and the basic pattern of discrimination and disadvantage persists.

What is remarkable is the extent to which the private sector patterns are similar in the two countries. Greenstone and Peterson's comment that 'if institutional racism is to make a useful distinction, rather than merely become a redundant label for anti-black prejudice, it should refer not to personal attitudes, but to constraints imposed by certain social structures'[1] is highly relevant in this context, for the social structures supporting the property industry in Britain and America are, in the final analysis, incompatible with the provision of equal opportunity in housing. In both countries, estate agents and mortgage lending institutions operate in similar ways within similar property markets whose primary motivating force of profit is at least partly dependant on social segregation. With the market divided along class lines, property interests can channel their resources into those middle-class parts of the market which are the safest investment risks. Less stable parts of the market receive less favourable treatment and, as redlining and other policies show, this makes buying or renting properties in these sectors much more expensive and difficult. Essentially then, this discrimination, which can affect individuals or areas, is economic in nature, and exists irrespective of the presence of racial minorities in British and American cities. The presence of blacks aggravates the situation by adding racial to economic discrimination. Many blacks are poor, and along with similarly placed white people suffer from economic discrimination. But to many whites, and certainly to most white property interests, *all* blacks are perceived as a threat to the economic integrity of properties and neighbourhoods. They are believed to lower property values and to lack the future-oriented financial prudence of middle-class whites. As a result, middle-class blacks are excluded from the large, varied and highly advantaged middle-class housing markets.

Of course some important differences do exist between the two countries in this area. In particular, in the United States the racial factor dominates to the extent that ghettoes prevail, and a dual property market based on race has emerged. As a result, in many American cities racial minorities are seen by property interests and many whites as the primary agents responsible for blight and the deterioration in the social and economic status of neighbourhoods. There can be little doubt that numbers are a critical factor here. With, in many cities, a majority of the poor being black, both ghetto conditions and racial discrimination are more likely. In Britain, while racial concentration is marked, it is not possible to talk of a dual property market, although the beginnings of one are appearing, especially in cities such as Birmingham which have large numbers of blacks concentrated in private sector housing.

The discriminatory tactics employed by property interests also differ between the two countries. In the US, the stark totality of racial separation in combination with housing shortage within the ghetto have produced (and are a result of) explicit discriminatory tactics on the part of estate agents intent on excluding blacks from favoured white neighbourhoods. In Britain, where the black population and the extent of separation is smaller, and where many blacks have not attempted to move from inner city areas, overt discrimination has been less necessary. However, the (admittedly limited) evidence does suggest that discrimination within private rental housing has been pervasive and that estate agents have engaged in exclusionary practices when blacks have attempted to move from the inner city. Significantly, private rental sector discrimination seems to have decreased in recent years, not because of the spread of more liberal attitudes, but because housing contact between whites and blacks has declined in this sector. In other words, a separate 'black' market not unlike that existing in many American cities *is* developing. Moreover, what we have called racial disadvantage, or the operation of apparently neutral rules and procedures whose effects are discriminatory, has been widespread, especially in mortgage finance.

In sum, while the differences between the two private sectors are important, the central fact remains that in both countries the similar 'social gatekeeping' roles played by property interests have had similarly disadvantageous effects on the black populations. What is more, if left to their own devices, there seems little doubt that in Britain market forces will produce a higher and higher degree of racial concentration and separation.

Administrative and judicial remedies under civil rights laws have not had much impact on the private property markets in either country because they fail to challenge the social structures responsible for succouring those values and practices which result in discrimination and disadvantage. Civil rights laws providing remedies for individuals are based on principles of equity deriving from English Common Law. As such, they prevent the problem of discrimination from being perceived in terms of broad structural forces, such as the fundamental economic interest which property industries have in social segregation. Instead, the law portrays discrimination in terms of individual instances of interpersonal conflicts of interest. The detail of the law can be of marginal importance. By any standard the 1968 Race Relations Act is a weak civil rights act, and both this law and the American 1968 Civil Rights Act are weak in relation to some American state laws. With wide coverage, the use of injunctive powers by administrative and judicial agencies and the capacity to impose damages and other sanctions, such laws have, on a local basis, probably been more effective than the federal law. But as Duane Lockard and others have pointed out, they have not made anything but a small dent on the general pattern of discrimination.[2]

Governments can, of course, affect the operations of the private sector in ways other than by civil rights laws. Urban renewal and other urban policies as well as public sector housing policies are obviously relevant. In the United States urban renewal policies have, if anything, reinforced the patterns of discrimination imposed by the private sector, and in the United Kingdom, although the evidence on slum clearance policies is patchy, it is unlikely that they have greatly eased the position of blacks buying and renting property in the private sector.
Similarly, local authority policies towards multi-occupied housing have not eased the housing shortage among blacks, and may even, as in the case of Birmingham, have aggravated it. Insensitive local authority policies in Britain derive in part from the 'colour blind' orientation of local officials and politicians, and from a widespread ignorance about the needs of the black population and the effects of official rules and procedures on black people. Such ignorance is typical of

institutional racism, which has been defined as 'the unintended, unanticipated consequences of social structures not primarily oriented toward racial concerns'.[3]

There are few parallels between the two countries' experiences of race and public sector housing. Britain has a large public housing stock catering for wide sections of the white population, while in the US public housing is an almost marginal part of the housing market, and is viewed as virtually synonymous with housing for poor blacks. Moreover, in the US controversy in both public housing and the quasi-public subsidised housing programmes (of which there are no equivalents in Britain) has centred on the question of siting black or potentially black housing in white areas. In other words, the existence of the ghetto together with political fragmentation has shaped the politics of public sector housing in the United States. In contrast, the main issues in Britain have been the extent to which blacks have been given equal access to public housing, and the extent to which high racial concentrations have built up on particular estates.

While American civil rights laws have not directly addressed public sector and land use questions, they have, together with the 14th Amendment, been used in the courts by civil rights and community organisations to challenge exclusionary zoning and segregation in the public sector. These efforts have not achieved notable success, but they have shifted the focus of policy debate away from the provision of redress for individuals and towards broader challenges to racial and class segregation in the United States. Moreover, judicial imperatives were influential in persuading a conservative federal government into taking, if not an actively integrationist position, then certainly a less segregationist position than would have been the case without such decisions as *Gautreaux* and *Shannon*.

The concentration of public debate on the question of integration does not necessarily reflect the 'liberal' or 'assimilationist' views of the reformers, for the obvious alternative to dispersing the black population, greatly increased investment in the ghetto, was hardly a politically achievable alternative in the 1968-76 period. The Nixon Administration failed to increase federal government involvement in housing and urban affairs, and historically, federal programmes have been the main agents of social reform in urban areas. None the less, the dilemma of whether to invest more in the ghetto or to disperse the black population, remains, and will once more be highlighted should an activist liberal federal administration be elected.

The relationship between race and public sector housing has been a much less politicised issue in the United Kingdom, partly because the black population is less visible and has fewer political resources than have American minorities (of which more later), but also because, in the absence of ghetto conditions, consciousness of any problem on the part of local government officials and national élites is lower than in the United States. Interestingly, the increasing awareness which did come during the 1974-76 period resulted not from litigation inspired by private groups, but from a change in government and the publication of detailed academic evidence on the relationship between race and housing policies. While racial disadvantage has been widespread in Britain public housing policies, the 1968 Race Relations Act has been almost completely inappropriate for dealing with it. An awareness of this fact was possibly important in persuading the Labour Government to introduce a new Race Relations Bill in 1976.

Given this apparent catalogue of failure in both private and public sectors in both countries, it might seem odd to claim that civil rights laws have produced any significant changes at all. Clearly they have not changed the objective housing conditions and opportunities of blacks in any dramatic fashion. Yet there is evidence that the laws have altered the frame of reference within which problems of race and housing are discussed. In the United States, challenges to the economic and racial exclusivity of middle and upper income white communities stem directly from civil rights legislation. So far, such challenges have been largely unsuccessful, but the very fact that they occur at all is a significant change from the 1950s and early 1960s when racial problems were perceived largely in terms of the need to provide legal equality for minorities. Open housing litigation has, therefore, begun an assault on spatial political fragmentation − a phenomenon which is widely regarded as a primary cause of inequality and a major barrier to social reform in American urban areas.[4] Moreover, litigation was largely responsible for mobilising federal resources, namely HUD's housing programmes, behind attempts to site low income housing in white areas. Should housing programmes grow in size and importance, the issue of race and site selection will have to be confronted and could result in HUD pursuing policies specifically designed to overcome the inequalities resulting from political fragmentation.

Finally, the more publicity that civil rights law implementation inspires (whether it be over land use or any other issue), the more conscious black and white populations become that serious conflicts of interest not only exist, but can be confronted via constitutionally sanctioned measures. Potentially, this gives black and other minority communities a hitherto unavailable power resource, although as will later be argued, it may be a resource more easily utilised by middle class rather than by poor blacks. In sum, the implementation of the law has had the effect of creating a new political agenda, or in Bachrach and Baratz' terms, of bringing certain issues into the central arena of decision-making, even if, so far, most of the decisions taken have not directly benefited blacks.[5]

In Britain, civil rights implementation has not aroused the same degree of political controversy. A weak law, and the low mobilisation of black interests and articulation of their demands is partly responsible for this. When agitation to change the law and housing policies did occur, it did so not as a result of litigation or the efforts of the black community, but through academic and other reports produced by white liberal élites. Much social reform in Britain has derived from the interaction of governmental and academic élites, and race relations law appears to have been no exception.[6] The main impetus to reform in the 1970s seems to have been recognition among élites of the inadequacies of the 1968 Act and of the continuing social and economic inequalities experienced by British blacks. This recognition was important in producing the 1976 Race Relations Bill whose contents should provide black groups and individuals with the legal armoury necessary to challenge (if not to defeat) those discriminatory rules and procedures which are partly responsible for the disadvantaged housing position of minorities.

It seems highly unlikely that changes in consciousness and particularly in the way different groups perceive power relations in society were consequences specifically intended by the framers of civil rights laws. In both the British and the American cases the content of the laws was partly determined by the coalitions and compromises of the legislative process, so clear and specific intentions are hard to identify. Generally, however, the liberal impulse behind civil rights agitation assumed that legal equality together with redress against individual acts of discrimination would reduce and eventually remove discrimination. Beyond this, intentions as such are hard to identify. Certainly the complex interactions between institutions and the social and economic environment which have characterised civil rights implementation processes in both countries could not possibly have been accurately predicted by legislators or executives.[7] This complexity is reflected in myriad, and sometimes confused public policies. As was shown, some policies, such as those designed to revitalise central cities, may be incompatible with others which aim to break down patterns of segregation and disperse blacks to outer areas. Policy makers do not plan such incompatibilities; much of the time they are reacting rather than initiating, or as Hugh Heclo has put it: 'Politics finds its sources not only in power but also in uncertainty'.[8]

It would be wrong, however, to leave the impression that uncertainty and complexity prevent the identification of general patterns of activity which have been responsible for particular policy consequences, and which constitute clear constraints on the achievement of policy objectives. The next section identifies some of these constraints, and, on a comparative basis, provides some general pointers to the limits to what can be achieved by civil rights legislation and other policies designed to reduce racial inequality in housing.

Patterns of Political and Economic Power

By now it should be clear that 'traditional' civil rights laws which proscribe individual acts of discrimination have not and never will remove racial discrimination and disadvantage. In both Britain and the United States, the position of urban blacks is intimately related to the social and political economies of urban areas, and dramatic reductions in existing inequalities can only be achieved by policies which attempt not only to remove discrimination but which also redistribute resources in favour of the black population either by massively increased spending on the inner city, or by moving disadvantaged populations from unfavourable to favourable economic environments. Any 'solution' to racial disadvantage must, then, involve highly interventionist government policies. For if there is a clear thread running through this study it is that if left unaffected by governments, housing market forces will produce an intensifying pattern of racial segregation and inequality in housing. It would appear to follow, therefore, that the more intrusive is government in any one society the greater is the potential in that society for upsetting and correcting market forces. If this is so, Britain is much more favourably placed than the United States. Hence, Peach, Winchester and Woods note that:

Perhaps the most critical way in which the British and American situations differ is in the availability of local authority housing. With one-third of the housing controlled by local municipalities and with a substantial section of the suburban peripheral housing development controlled by the council's allocation of points, rather than the money market and income, Britain possesses, in incipient form, the most powerful levers for the sociospatial engineering of society.[9]

Additionally, Britain lacks the extensive jurisdictional fragmentation which in the United States tends to reduce still further the reformist role of government by inhibiting the growth of broad tax bases which are a prerequisite for the formulation and implementation of redistributive policies. As Kenneth Newton has put it:

> The most important economic consequence of fragmentation is that each jurisdiction is forced by the logic of the situation in which it finds itself to use the full array of zoning regulations, subdivision controls, building regulations, and tax and service differentials and a good measure of old-fashioned social prejudice, in order to protect its tax base, which enables it to aim for that combination of public and private goods which enables it to maintain its quality of life at the highest possible level. In other words fragmentation, and its concomitant zoning, building and tax laws, helps to create a rigid social structure which prevents the free mobility of different social strata and ethnic groups. Only the wealthiest are in a position to survey the full range of packages of goods and services produced in different jurisdictions and to choose freely the combination they prefer. By then deploying the powers of their chosen local government unit in order to protect this combination of goods and services, they automatically limit the choices available to the not so wealthy who, in their turn, use their power to limit the choice of lower social strata, and so on down to the bottom of the social pile where there is virtually no choice whatsoever.[10]

Add to this pattern of metropolitan fragmentation, further fragmentation deriving from the federal system, and the potential for comprehensive, responsive, redistributive policies is further reduced. It is this institutional structure which also explains why the government with the broadest electoral and tax base, the federal government, has been the most innovative in the social policy and civil rights areas, and has in the process come into constant conflict with myriad near-autonomous local governments.

On the face of it, Britain's system, being unitary and lacking strong localist traditions, is the very antithesis of this. Moreover, the ideology of economic individualism which partly explains both anti-statist and localist sentiments in the United States is much less influential in the United Kingdom. Instead collectivist notions supporting equality of condition and the redistributive policies necessary to achieve this, have been influential in British society. These factors help explain why Britain has a large public housing sector, and why she has adopted comprehensive planning legislation. Yet as previous chapters have shown, free market forces have been instrumental in determining the housing opportunities of Britain's black population, and *within* the public sector blacks have received much less than equal treatment.

However, except perhaps to those who believe that America's urban problems would vanish with the adoption of a unitary system and increased government activity, this is no conundrum, for centralised government and a large public sector do not *necessarily* produce an enfeebled private sector or just and equitable public sector policies. As has been shown, Britain's centralised system has not prevented the growth of extensive local discretion in housing matters, a discretion which, given entrenched interests and bureaucracies, any central government would find extremely difficult to remove. And as long as local discretion persists, racial disadvantage in local authority housing allocation procedures is likely to continue. Moreover, public sectors serve some interests or constituences more than others, and Britain's public housing has been and continues to be geared to the 'respectable' working class, rather than to the economically marginal or to a black population largely unloved and possibly feared by many white public housing tenants. While acknowledging that evidence on this subject is scant, it is but a short step to infer that the often unsympathetic attitudes and policies adopted by local authorities towards blacks are related to a perceived interest in serving the mainstream working-class white population. Like American blacks, British minorities lack a strong political power base and in spite of Britain's reforming social democratic tradition this has intensified their disadvantaged position. Indeed, there are signs that the notions of universalism in social policy which were so influential in the immediate post-war period are on the wane in contemporary Britain. A more instrumental brand of politics has emerged which places more emphasis on the power resources of individual groups and classes. If this is so, Britain's black populations may be poorly placed to improve their existing low status in society.

Yet it would be misleading to imply that Britain's centralised system, reformist tradition and extensive public sector are of little significance. Clearly, these factors *have* influenced policy and *do* provide greater potential for change than does an American system characterised by political fragmentation and limited government involvement in society. The point being made is, rather, that Britain's apparently 'favourable' arrangements need not result in policies in some sense *opposite* to those produced by 'unfavourable' arrangements. Much depends on historical circumstances, the issue in question, and, not least, the political power of the groups and classes most directly involved.

Further constraints on redistributive policy are imposed by what can broadly be called fiscal disparity. In the American context the relationship between political structure and fiscal disparity has already been noted. Britain's unitary system does, in theory, facilitate the broadest possible tax bases and therefore the potential for a more equitable distribution of public goods. However, the structural economic forces responsible for central city decline and the concomitant growth of the suburbs, are present in both countries. In the United States political arrangements have aggravated intra-metropolitan inequalities. In Britain, they have probably reduced them. There are, none the less, limits to the redistributive urban policies which can be achieved in Britain. Private capital and the free market remain of critical importance in determining the pattern of British urban change, and as the experience of Britain's regional policies shows, government has not been able totally to control and direct the movement of capital. Pronouncements, such as those made in 1976, that central government intends to 'reinvigorate' the central city should therefore be treated with some circumspection. Britain's fiscal crisis is, moreover, national in nature, and increased spending on inner city housing and other services, or even on urban manufacturing industry, is hardly reconcilable with the now dominant policies which direct resources away from the service sector and towards those manufacturing industries with the highest investment yields (which tend to be located in suburban rather than inner city areas).[11]

In addition, as in both countries the economically productive population desert the central city for suburbs and smaller towns, so they take their political resources (not least their electoral resources) with them. This presents reformist political parties with one of the greatest dilemmas of all, for increasingly, Democratic and Labour Party power bases are not in the inner areas of cities, but in more affluent outer areas whose populations have little to gain from policies designed to aid the inner city poor. There can be no doubt that redistributive policies must come from governments formed by these reformist parties. Earlier chapters showed how both in the formulation and implementation of social reform policies they played the leading role. But fiscal and electoral factors inevitably put some limit on what they can achieve.

Clear limits also exist on governments' ability to control transactions in private sector housing. The American state experience in this area suggests that the meaningful regulation of property interests is a chimera. In Britain, the public licensing of estate agents and accommodation agencies would probably help eliminate some of the more outrageous discriminatory practices, and a tighter regulation of mortgage finance would ease house purchase for some blacks. But neither would transform those market values and operating standards responsible for discrimination and disadvantage. To do this would require policies which would effectively put paid to the free market, for as was argued earlier, the thousands of discrete actors in the market thrive on the profits to be reaped from class and race segregation. It is these phenomena that governments have to attack, and removing segregation can only be achieved by pursuing redistributive policies across wide jurisdictions. The obstacles to such policies in both countries have already been noted.

Finally, is it possible that constitutional and legal imperatives can overcome all these obstacles and achieve a meaningful redistribution of resources? In the United States the experience both with bussing and with court-ordered integrated housing suggests that the courts can force changes in the policy agenda, and, more rarely, in resource allocation. With a written constitution and judicial review, the United States is much better placed to facilitate such changes than is Britain. Even if the 1976 Race Relations Bill with its expanded judicial role is passed in full, it is extremely unlikely that British judges will indulge in the sort of activist political decision-making of which *Gautreaux* was such a typical example in the United States.

There are, however, limits to constitutional solutions. Courts lack enforcement powers and are obviously constrained by political and economic environments. Their main function is one of focusing attention on particular issues, and possibly on politicising issues[12] – always remembering that such activity can be to the detriment as well as to the benefit of the disadvantaged.

The Policy Alternatives

Given all these constraints it is not possible to talk in terms of
'solutions' to the problem of racial discrimination and disadvantage
in housing. There is no prospect in either country of some sudden and
dramatic improvement in the living conditions of urban blacks. On the
contrary, the immediate prospect in Britain is for the continuing
growth of largely separate black neighbourhoods — especially where
Asian communities are concerned. These need not become 'ghettoes'
in the American sense, partly because there is a considerable element
of voluntary separation involved, but also because the social and
economic pathologies of the American ghetto owe much to
peculiarly American circumstances. This should not, however, lead to
complacency, for, assuming that there are no changes in existing urban
policies, increased racial concentration in Britain's cities will lead to
further inequalities and will aggravate the disadvantaged position of
Britain's already badly off black population. If anything, the
prospects in the United States are even gloomier, for in that country
generally poor black communities face more affluent white
communities from the perspective of near total spatial, social and
political separation.

   In spite of the enormous problems involved in finding any
'solution', it is important to discuss the feasibility of those policies
which have already been suggested or tried.

(a) *Dispersal*

In the United States, the dispersal of low and moderate income housing
to white areas has come to dominate policy debate in the race and
housing area. It has hardly been a deliberately planned and organised
policy. Rather, the stark facts of racial segregation, together with the
availability of low income housing funds, have inspired community
organisations to challenge the racial and class exclusivity of near
autonomous suburbs. As, during the 1968-76 period, the federal
government was not willing to increase investment in the inner city
(indeed, Nixon's moratorium halted all federal housing programmes,
whatever their locale), the dispersal solution was a logical alternative.
Generally, these attempts did not involve dispersing individual *families*
but simply low income housing. In this sense, no element of compulsion
was involved — although given housing shortage and the general
conditions in the ghetto, there was no shortage of families willing to
move to almost any non-ghetto area. More draconian dispersal
policies, involving large population movements, are impossible in the

United States. Government's role in housing and urban society is too limited, and in any case, such policies would be fiercely resisted by just about all parties involved.

Siting low income housing in the suburbs is often portrayed in class rather than race terms.[13] The central issue is, so it is claimed, giving poor people access to middle-class neighbourhoods, rather than wanting to achieve racial integration. Up to a point this is true, and the problems of poor inner city whites are considerable. However, to most middle-class whites, federal low income housing is a synonym for black housing, and while acknowledging that the needs of poor whites should be recognised, the fact remains that the greatest demand for suburban low income housing comes from blacks and other minorities.

We have already discussed the near impregnable barriers to the achievement even of limited voluntary dispersal in the United States. One further problem which has not been discussed is that most of the occupants of 235 and 236 housing in the suburbs are generally not drawn from among the very poor, but from the 'moderate' income group.[14] If, therefore, future attempts to break down the racial and economic exclusivity of the suburbs are successful, this may have the effect of siphoning off the more economically productive blacks from the ghetto. As has been noted, the successful operation of civil rights administrative and judicial complaint procedures also has this effect. The same cannot be said for scattered site public housing, but, if anything, this is resisted even more fiercely by white communities than is 235 and 236 housing.

In Britain, the dispersal of black families in council housing has been seen by some local authorities as a means of preventing the emergence of ghetto-like communities. It has not worked because the rationing system in council housing operates in such a way as to make anything but compulsory dispersal unworkable. However, given the highly intrusive role that government plays in urban affairs in the UK, it is remarkable that local authorities have even considered the need for dispersal policies. This is especially so when it is remembered that Britain's public housing legislation was in part designed to help those most in need. That it has failed to do this and has been particularly inadequate as far as blacks are concerned, is explained by indifferent and inflexible national and local bureaucracies, institutional racism, and, in spite of massive housing programmes, continuing housing shortage.

But dispersal is no solution. It carries with it unacceptable connotations of compulsion, and above all, it implies that cohesive ethnic and racial communities are in some sense undesirable influences in society.

(b) *Revitalising the Inner City*

The position of British and American racial minorities is inextricably entwined with the problem of inner city decline and decay, and until the unequal and deteriorating state of inner areas is corrected blacks will remain disadvantaged. So far, governments have been singularly ineffective in arresting decline. Indeed, until very recently, inner city decline was not recognised as a serious problem in Britain. In the United States, the problem has long been recognised, but the realities of political power have meant that little has been done about it.

Britain's institutional and ideological arrangements lend themselves more readily to redistributive policies, and the government has, in 1976, at least announced a redirection of policy towards the revival of the inner city. However, fiscal and political constraints must lead us to be pessimistic about the prospect of a totally transformed inner city social economy. Some constructive changes can be achieved by modifications in policy. Rehabilitation of individual houses and areas rather than the wholesale clearance of slum areas is now official policy, and if extended, could arrest the decline of some neighbourhoods. Modifications in public housing allocation policies could help not only blacks, but also disadvantaged white families — although meaningful changes in this area will only come with changes in the housing stock and increases in inner city housing investment. Above all, government should encourage manufacturing industry to reinvest in central city areas, even if the effect of this is only partly to arrest the present flight of capital from the city.

It is important to stress that however great are the economic and political constraints on inner city revival, the immediate racial situation in Britain's cities makes it an urgent priority. At the moment, urban poverty in many of Britain's cities is not seen in racial terms. After all, whites continue to outnumber blacks in the inner cities by a considerable margin. If present trends continue, however, the presence of blight, decay and unemployment will, at least in some cities or parts of cities, be immediately associated with the presence of blacks. Once this happens, it is but a short step to the emergence of ghetto-like conditions.

(c) *Power and the Black Community*

It is rare to come across an American text on race and the city which does not end on a hopeful note. Much of this optimism is based on the possibly vain belief that community control and participation are the only feasible means whereby racial inequalities will be reduced. Hence Greenstone and Peterson conclude their comprehensive study of community action in American cities with this comment:

> Although racial oppression and inequality often seems virtually intractable, the policy most likely to eradicate it must follow the path of collective self-development that other ethnic groups utilised to establish themselves in a society that was at once white Protestant in its dominant cultural orientation, capitalist in its economic values, and only partially egalitarian in its political aspirations. Community control, for all its faults, can facilitate the forward thrust of black power in the American regime.[15]

As these authors and Bachrach and Baratz have shown, effective community control requires above all a certain level of political organisation and consciousness within black communities.[16] It is arguable whether this level exists in many black communities in the United States, and as has been noted in the present study, British blacks are remarkably unorganised politically. The implementation of civil rights laws and other inner city directed urban policies has undoubtedly helped raise the political consciousness of American blacks, however, and they could do the same for Britain's racial minorities.

But what most of the liberal American sociologists and political scientists tend to ignore is the overriding importance of investment in industry, commerce and the social infrastructure as a determinant of the economic, political and social opportunities of the residents of depressed inner city areas. As has been shown, the prospects in either country of dramatic increases in such investment are slight. Some conurbations or parts of conurbations will continue to prosper and grow, but in neither country is there much overlap between these areas and the spatial distribution of minority populations. There is little evidence that increased political awareness and public participation in American black communities have influenced investment decisions in any meaningful way, and there is no reason to suppose that a newly aware British black population would be any more successful. We have little cause, therefore, to be optimistic about the future of our inner city minority populations.

Conclusions

Notes

1. T. David Greenstone and Paul E. Peterson, *Race and Authority in Urban Politics* (New York: Russell Sage Foundation, 1973), p. 312.
2. Duane Lockard, *Toward Equal Opportunity* (New York: Macmillan, 1968), Chapter 4; see also, Leon Mayhew, *Law and Equal Opportunity: A Study of the Massachusetts Commission Against Discrimination* (Cambridge, Mass.: Harvard University Press, 1968).
3. Greenstone and Peterson, op. cit.
4. For a good discussion of the effects of political fragmentation and of the general literature on the subject, see Kenneth Newton, 'Social Class, Political Structure, and Public Goods in American Urban Politics', *Urban Affairs Quarterly*, Vol. 11, No. 2 (Dec. 1975), pp. 242-64.
5. Peter Bachrach and Morton Baratz, *Power and Poverty* (New York: Oxford University Press, 1972), Chapter 4.
6. In marked contrast to the United States where until recently academics have traditionally played a minor role in influencing social policy. For a discussion of the role of social scientists in American social policy, see Thomas F. Pettigrew and Robert L. Green, 'The Legitimising of Racial Segregation', *New Society*, 29 January 1976, p. 216.
7. For a general discussion of the problem of analysing the intentions of policy makers, see Anthony King, 'On studying the Impacts of Public Policies: The Role of the Political Scientist', in Matthew Holden Jr. and Dennis L. Dresang (eds), *What Government Does, Vol. 1, Sage Yearbooks in Politics and Public Policy* (Beverly Hills: Sage, 1975), pp. 298-316.
8. Hugh Heclo, *Modern Social Politics in Britain and Sweden* (New Haven: Yale University Press, 1974), p. 305.
9. Ceri Peach, Stuart Winchester, Robert Woods, 'The Distribution of Coloured Immigrants in Britain', in Gary Gappert and Harold M. Rose, *The Social Economy of Cities, Vol. 9, Sage Urban Affairs Annual Reviews* (Beverly Hills: Sage, 1975), p. 414.
10. Kenneth Newton, op. cit., pp. 253-4.
11. A burgeoning Marxist literature on 'fiscal crisis' claims that it is the central contradiction in contemporary capitalism. See particularly James O'Connor, *The Fiscal Crisis of the State* (New York: St Martin's Press, 1973).
12. This is a major reason why conservatives are so appalled by judicial activism. For a discussion of the role of the courts as social engineers, see Archibald Cox,*The Role of the Supreme Court in American Government* (London: Oxford University Press, 1976), Chapters IV and V.
13. See Charles M. Haar and Demetrius S. Iatridis, *Housing the Poor in Suburbia* (Cambridge, Mass.: Ballinger 1974).
14. See C. Berger, 'Homeownership for Lower Income Families: The 1968 Housing Act's Cruel Hoax', *Connecticut Law Review*, Vol. 30, No. 2 (1969).
15. Greenstone and Peterson, op. cit., p. 315.
16. Ibid., Chapter 10.; Bachrach and Baratz, op. cit., Chapter 7. There is burgeoning literature on the subject of community and neighbourhood control, for example see the collection of essays edited by George Frederickson, *Neighbourhood Control in the 1970s* (New York: Chandler, 1973).

INDEX

Aaron, Henry J. 76n, 116, 142n
Abbot, Simon 43n
Aberbach, Joel D. and Walker, Jack
L. 45
Ackerman, Bruce I. 77n
Africans, British 23-4, 81, 100-1
American Civil Liberties Union
130,133
anti-solicitation ordinances, 71-2
Ashford, Douglas 22
Asians, British 23-7, 33, 80-4,
89, 93, 101, 152, 154, 158-61
Attorney General: UK 38;
US 38, 63
Austin, Judge 130-2

Bachrach, Peter and Baratz, Morton
20n, 142n, 188
Banton, Michael 29, 108n
Bauer, Catherine 142n
Baum, Daniel J. 143n
Bellush, Jewell and Hausknecht,
Murray 142n
Berger, C. 189n
Berry, Brian J.L. 74n
Bindman, Geoffrey 111n
Birmingham (UK): inner city
housing 84-5, 92, 94; dispersal
policies 162, 164
Birmingham Community Relations
Commission 157
Black Jack, Missouri 137-8
Bradley v. Milliken 132
Brier, Alan and Axford, Barrie 14,
110n
Brooke, Edward 62
Brown v. Town and Country Sales
77n
Buchanan v. Warley 63
Burney, Elizabeth 43n, 92, 96, 109n,
153
Butler, David and Stokes, Donald
43n

Campbell, Angus 61
Chicago, Illinois: public
housing 129-33; racial
discrimination 49-51, 56-7, 65-6,
68-9, 129-33; Section 236 housing
122; HUD regulations 139-40
Chicago Daily News 143-4n
Chicago Heights, Illinois 127-9
Chicago Housing Authority 130-3
Citizens' Housing Corporation 126

Civil Rights Act: of 1866 63-4;
of 1964 12, 37, 60, 114, 126;
of 1965 37, 114; of 1968
12, 37-8, 62-72, 114, 123-5, 126,
176
Civil Rights Laws: study of 12-15;
consequences of 174-80
Claiborne, Louis 98
Clark, Terry 144n
Cleveland, Ohio 135
Collard, David 84, 109n
Commission for Racial Equality
39, 105, 106
Community Relations Commission
98-9, 110n, 171n
Congress, US 61, 62, 143n, 144n
Congressional Quarterly 61, 76n, 143n,
146n
Connolly, Harold X. 54
Conservative Party 27, 95
Cook County Housing Authority
128-9
Cook County Legal Aid 128-9
courts, the role of: in UK 38-9,
101-2, 105, 165-6, 184;
in US 38, 68-72, 126, 129-36,
184
Cox, Archibald 189n
Cox, Kevin 43n
Cullingworth, J.B. 110n, 111n
Cullingworth Report 150, 156-7,
162

Dahya, B. 108n
Dailey v. City of Lawson 134
Daniel, W.W. 20n, 109n, 110n, 153
Danielson, Michael 140
Davies, J. 108n
Deakin, Nicholas 43n, 111n
Democratic administration 61, 62,
139, 183-4
Denton, John 53, 76n
Derwinski, Edward T. 129
Detroit Free Press 144n
Dirksen, Everett 61-2
disadvantage, racial 29-30, 84-94,
152-62, 180
discrimination, economic 134-7
discrimination, racial 29-30;
and quotas 56, 72; in UK
84-94, 152-4, 174-7; in US
49-59, 123-42
dispersal of racial minorities: in US
129-36, 138-40, 185-7; in UK

thèqu